I0104926

Rebuilding Your Relationship After Sexual Betrayal

A Couples Guide to Healing and Recovery

Dr. Kevin Skinner, LMFT, CSAT-S

Copyright © 2023 Kevin B. Skinner, Ph.D.

All Rights Reserved

No part of this book may be reprinted, reproduced, or utilized in any form or by any electronic, mechanical, or other means, now known or hereafter invented, including photocopying and recording, or in any information storage or retrieval system, without permission in writing from the publisher. Printed in the United States.

Contents

Dedication

It takes a lot of support from others to write a book. This book is dedicated to my wife and children, who have encouraged and supported me throughout my long days and nights of writing. It would not have been possible for me to write this without their support.

I would also like to thank the many therapists who have read chapters from the manuscript and provided me with valuable feedback. I honor you and the work you are doing.

Over the past twenty-five years, I have witnessed so many couples struggle to make sense of their lives after sexual betrayal. So many have felt overwhelmed by the daunting task of rebuilding their relationship.

I have had the opportunity to meet with couples from all over the world who have trusted me to help them heal their relationship. They are my heroes. They have faced the storms of their lives and said, "We don't know how, but we can make it through this." The courage they have demonstrated has increased my desire to be better in my relationships. I know their challenges have not been easy to overcome, but I respect them for never giving up.

This book is dedicated to all the couples who have faced insurmountable challenges and found a way to heal. You have taught me to think outside of the box.

Author's Note

Throughout this book, most of the stories come from individuals and couples that the author has met with over the past twenty-five years. Additional support content comes from online assessments taken by thousands of individuals over this time. This work would not have happened if these courageous people had not been willing to seek help and support.

I honor the couples who have trusted my guidance throughout the most difficult times of their lives.

In order to protect the confidentiality of all clients and research participants, names and personal identifying information have been changed. In some cases, the author has also taken the liberty to combine cases to illustrate specific points.

This book should not replace medical or professional advice.

Introduction

I know you want the pain and the conflict in your relationship to end. You want to find answers, but they seem elusive. Over the past twenty-five years, I have seen hundreds of couples try to rebuild trust after sexual betrayal, and I know there is nothing easy about rebuilding your relationship after betrayal. I have observed, counseled, and studied individuals and couples who have forgotten the purpose of their relationship and feel overwhelmed by the daunting task of putting it back together. Both partners feel exhausted and worn out when they come to my office. Frequently, they have spent hours and hours fighting and arguing like never before. When they finally seek professional support, they often feel hopeless and helpless because nothing they have tried has worked.

Throughout my career as a marriage and family therapist, I have listened to many couples share the challenges they face when trying to rebuild trust; I have observed that many have no idea where to start. When I ask, "What brought the two of you together in the beginning?" I find that many have forgotten why they fell in love with each other. As we review their past, we inevitably discover the cracks that have crept into their relationship—the secrets, the unresolved frustrations, the wounds, and the pain. What started as seemingly small issues—a little argument, a feeling of rejection—has somehow become justification for hidden sexual behaviors. Faced with betrayal, they now confront a major obstacle in their relationship, one they are ill-equipped to address on their own.

The betraying partner has justified and hidden their behaviors for months or even years. Often, they say to themselves, "It's not that big of a deal," or "What they don't know won't hurt them," or "I deserve this because they don't give me the attention I deserve." But then they get discovered. A text message gives away an ongoing affair, or a random phone call in the middle of the night raises suspicions. Or perhaps pornography is found on a computer, or a credit card statement reveals a hidden rendezvous at a hotel. However, discovery happens, and it always shocks the relationship.

In many instances, the betraying partner has become lost in their secret world.

They have been in a sexual trance, exhilarated and excited but simultaneously full of shame and self-loathing. When their hidden sexual behaviors are discovered, many struggle. They don't know how to respond or what to say or do. Often, they revert to old patterns. They attempt to lie, discount, cover-up, minimize, or justify their actions. Or their shame leads them to deny their behavior, "I didn't do that," or to blame their partner, "It's your fault because…" I have asked many betraying partners about their initial response to being discovered, and most tell me that they were scared. They feared that their world would fall apart and that they would lose everything, so they attempted to keep their behaviors hidden.

But some betraying partners choose to reveal everything once their hidden sexual behaviors are discovered. They are relieved that they were caught and share everything in detail. Others get much more selective and choose to share only bits and pieces of what they have done. This often leads to a staggered disclosure, with more details being gradually revealed over time.

Some individuals continue to deny what they have done. They insist on covering up their behaviors and do everything they can to shift responsibility: "You're just insecure," You're just imagining things." In other words, they engage in gaslighting, which creates deep wounds that are difficult to heal and must be addressed for healing to occur.

On the other hand, the betrayed partner experiences a wide range of overwhelming emotions, including anger, hatred, rage, fear, disgust, and sorrow, all normal and understandable in such a situation. They often become a would-be interrogator, asking dozens of questions in a desperate need to know the truth. In many cases, they may have felt that something was off in the relationship, but they didn't know exactly what, and they feel foolish for not recognizing what was happening sooner. They often internalize their partner's betrayal and feel ashamed that something is wrong with them.

Once they discover their partner's hidden sexual behaviors, seventy percent of betrayed partners experience symptoms associated with post-traumatic stress disorder (PTSD). (1,2) Unfortunately, many feel like they are going crazy while both their betraying partner and society at large struggle to know how to respond effectively to their suffering.

Three Different Approaches After Discovery of Sexual Betrayal

After discovering sexual betrayal, couples tend to approach their relationship in three main ways.

In the first case, one or both partners recognize that their love has died. One partner has moved on and no longer desires to be in the relationship. This group includes couples who once shared similar values but have found that they no longer share common beliefs. These couples usually decide to divorce.

Other couples choose to stay together for the children's sake or out of financial necessity, but neither partner is happy. They often punish each other, or they ignore each other. These couples are the most difficult to help because they genuinely dislike each other, treat each other poorly, and avoid difficult discussions about their relationship. They put their heads in the sand, hoping that something will eventually change on its own. They are perpetually stuck in neutral. They aren't moving toward divorce or attempting to heal their relationship. This response to the discovery of betrayal is especially painful to watch.

After discovering betrayal, more resilient couples somehow channel the strength to fight through adversity in spite of many ups and downs. Even though one or both often want to give up, they continue through the storms. They endure many difficult and painful discussions. They yell, scream, and hurt each other with their words, yet they find a way to stay together and work through the painful healing process. Throughout their journey, they often fight, argue, struggle to feel like they are making progress, and repeatedly question their commitment. But in the end, they find a way to decrease their fights and increase their commitment to the healing process. Eventually, they find that this was the hardest thing they had ever done, but also the most important thing.

Couples who succeed in rebuilding their relationship after sexual betrayal also find that much of the personal work involves determining whether or not they want to stay in the relationship. For many, the effort to heal individually and rebuild their relationship means learning a lot about themselves. And they find that their increased self-awareness helps them to make an informed decision about their relationship. In the end, they intentionally choose their relationship again. They choose their partner again. And they don't feel like they stayed out of necessity or by default.

I have observed that sexual betrayal often ignites deep learning for both partners. Instead of turning to unhealthy sexual behaviors, the betraying partner learns to turn toward their partner and do everything they can to rebuild trust and to help them heal. The betrayed partner also goes through a transformation, finding the strength and the courage to face their fears and to learn to see their partner differently. They both discover more about themselves and gain a greater awareness of their strengths and weaknesses. These individual insights change their perspective about themselves and their relationship.

If you and your partner are committed to becoming a resilient couple, then his book is for you. Even if you aren't ready yet to fully commit to continuing your relationship, this book will guide you and help you to take the steps that lead to healing and recovery. If you choose, you can decide to take these steps together.

Where to Start?

Stopping unwanted sexual behaviors and healing from the trauma of sexual betrayal are both difficult, each in its own way. Sadly, many couples attempt this arduous journey alone, without the information and support they need to succeed. After watching many couples struggle to rebuild trust after sexual betrayal, I have learned that those who succeed implement similar strategies. This book traces the healing and recovery process I have observed in these successful couples. It provides the information you need to heal and rebuild your relationship after sexual betrayal if that is what you both want.

Most of the couples I have observed do want to rebuild their relationship and restore trust, but they feel overwhelmed. Many feel anxious because they don't know how to respond to each other. They feel lost and frightened. With years of experience, I have come to recognize that some relationships can't rebound from sexual betrayal. Often the pain is too great for the betrayed partner, or the betraying partner never returns mentally and emotionally to the relationship.

Fortunately, most couples want to try, and when they implement real solutions, they begin to succeed. It starts with healthy behaviors—empathy, compassion, honesty, trust, vulnerability, and openness, skills that are not inherited but learned. Throughout my career, I have asked thousands of people worldwide if their parents were good examples of healthy relationships. On a scale between zero for a bad role model for a healthy relationship and ten for a great model, more than half give their primary caregivers a score below five. How can we expect to succeed if we don't have a good model? Fortunately, we can develop healthy skills, even if we didn't learn them earlier. This book provides you and your partner ways to understand each other on a deeper level, including the tools that can help you heal and recover from sexual betrayal.

Successful couples not only have the right information, but they also have realistic expectations, and they actually apply what they learn. If you implement the principles outlined in this book, you will be able to form a new relationship that will be built on trust and accountability. You will see each other through a new lens as you will create a better relationship. You will develop the type of connection you both want but have yet to experience. Or you can keep doing what you have been doing. If you choose this route, you and your partner will continue to feel alone, empty, and frustrated. You will keep fighting. You will hurt others and will hurt yourself. This repetitive cycle will wear you out and wear you down. And you will continue arguing and fighting, eventually leading to bad physical and emotional health.

If you choose to work on your relationship, don't assume that your journey will be easy. In fact, I know it will be hard. But you need to understand that what you have been doing has not been working for you. I invite you to read this book with an open mind. I am confident that if you apply the principles outlined in this book, you and your partner will begin to see the benefits and the possibilities for your relationship. Before you dive into the first chapter, please know that I had someone like you in my mind as I wrote this book.

Over the past twenty-five years, I have worked with hundreds of couples dealing with sexual betrayal. These experiences have enabled me to gain deep insight into the pain of being betrayed and the burden of being the betraying partner. I hope that these insights will give you hope that relationships can heal, unwanted sexual behaviors can be overcome, and wounded hearts can be comforted. I believe that what we value most should demand our most extraordinary energy and attention. If you truly value your relationship, then I invite you to devote your most extraordinary energy and attention to practicing what you learn from reading this book.

What You Can Expect

In Chapter One, you will be asked to consider essential questions you both will need to address later. The primary questions are: 1) How did this happen? 2) What information do I need to decide how to move forward? 3) Do we both share a common desire to rebuild the relationship? When couples ignore these critical questions, they often find themselves repeating the same fights over and over again, or their relationship ends. It will take time and patience to answer these questions authentically. You may think you know your answer to these questions right after discovery. Still, thoroughly evaluating oneself and the relationship is essential before re-committing.

In Chapter Two, I will help you get to the root of the problem. Far too often, we look at sexual behavior as the problem. It has been my experience over the years that unwanted sexual activity isn't the root problem. Instead, it is a combination of unresolved relationship issues, resentments, childhood abuse, family of origin issues, a history of out-of-control sexual behaviors, and other challenges. In this chapter, we will focus on getting to the root of the problem. What you learn in this chapter will enable you and your partner to understand the real issues that you must address.

Chapter Three will focus on helping you create the right environment so healing can happen. Couples get stuck because they cannot escape their natural fight, flight or freeze response. Consequently, recovery is not possible. The critical steps outlined in this chapter will help you see why you have been stuck and what needs to happen if you are going to rebuild your relationship. You will feel empowered as you learn to create the right environment for healing.

Chapter Four addresses shame, one of the most significant barriers to individual healing and couple recovery. Historically, shame has been associated with the person who has been acting out. In this chapter, I will highlight how both partners experience shame. This chapter will highlight why shame needs to be resolved to rebuild your relationship. I will conclude this chapter by sharing a couple's story of how they addressed shame in their journey to healing.

The chapters in Section Two explain the mindset of both partners before, during, and after discovery. This section begins by establishing the importance of applying empathy and compassion to yourself and your partner.

In Chapter Five, I will explain how empathy and compassion can be implemented in your daily interactions. In this chapter, I will explain the difference between empathy and compassion. I will discuss the importance of developing these two relationship skills as you go through the healing process. If compassion and empathy are missing from your relationship, it will be very challenging to create a safe environment for healing.

In Chapter Six, I will utilize years of research to help both partners understand the mind of the betrayed. In this chapter, you will learn about the most common symptoms people experience after betrayal. I will also introduce some of the solutions I have found effective at reducing these symptoms.

In Chapter Seven, I will offer solutions to heal the broken heart of the betrayed partner. In this chapter, I will discuss four core components for healing: 1) finding a safe environment for healing; 2) resolving difficult emotions and beliefs; 3) developing a reliable support network; and 4) strengthening your inner self. During the past twenty years, I have found these components lay a foundation for long-term healing. In this chapter, I will also invite you to learn to listen to your body for cues on how to heal.

In Chapter Eight, I will offer insight into the mind of the betraying partner. I will explain that sexual behavior is the tip of the iceberg, and in order to create lasting change, we need to look beneath the iceberg to see what is driving the behavior. Some familiar drivers of unwanted sexual behaviors include ADHD, depression, anxiety, and loneliness. In this chapter, we will also explore the role that early sexual experiences have on current sexual behaviors. Finally, there is a discussion on arousal templates.

In Chapter Nine, I will discuss some of the critical steps betraying partners can take in their journey to recovery. The focus of this chapter is to provide a model for changing behavior. The chapter will begin with a discussion of what you want to change in your behavior and why. Then you will be asked to walk through a series of exercises to help you prepare for success. The chapter will conclude with a discussion on how you can model your recovery after others who have been successful.

Section Three is the "how to" part of the book for your relationship. Each chapter in this section is designed to help you understand the essential steps for rebuilding trust in your relationship.

Throughout my career, I have observed that many couples want to try rebuilding their relationship but struggle because they don't know what to do or how to do it.

In Chapter Ten, you will learn about five principles that can guide your healing process. A principle is a fundamental truth that doesn't change. If you and your partner apply these five principles to your lives, you will witness a significant change in your relationship. You will learn how to use the principles of 1) commitment to integrity; 2) commitment to affirming worth and showing genuine compassion; 3) commitment to growth; 4) commitment to the agency; and 5) commitment to trusting your instincts and own intuitive responses. Examples are given so you can practice implementing these principles in your relationship.

In Chapter Eleven, I will help you understand how healthy boundaries will become the guidepost to your new relationship. Many couples stay stuck without boundaries because they disagree about what steps to take as they move forward. In this chapter, you will be asked to create the new boundaries you want for your relationship as you move forward.

In Chapter Twelve, you will learn why "I'm sorry" doesn't work. I often hear betraying partners say, "I have said I am sorry, but it doesn't matter how many times I say it; my partner won't ever forgive me." In this chapter, you will learn why saying sorry isn't working. Then I will introduce a step-by-step process that will help you be more effective in your effort to make amends. If you want to earn forgiveness, you will want to apply the concepts introduced in this chapter.

Based on my research, Chapter Thirteen may be one of the most important chapters in this book. According to my research findings, gaslighting is one of the most damaging elements that come from betrayal. Gaslighting intensifies the PTSD symptoms in betrayed partners and simultaneously prevents the betraying partner from recovery. In this chapter, I will walk you through the steps that you can use to address the damage that gaslighting has had on your relationship. Applying the principles discussed in this chapter will significantly increase the chances of rebuilding trust in your relationship.

Chapter Fourteen is written to help you create moments that can change your relationship for good. As couples rebuild trust in their relationship, some moments accelerate the healing process. In this chapter, you will learn how to increase these bonding moments by developing skills so you can intentionally create these crucial moments.

In Chapter Fifteen, you will learn about seven types of intimacy. For far too long, intimacy has been primarily linked with sex. In this chapter, you will learn about seven kinds of intimacy and how to apply these types of intimacy in your relationship. As you and your partner practice the types of intimacy described in this chapter, you will discover a whole new way of being together. We long for human connection and true intimacy in life, yet we struggle to create it. In this chapter, I will provide a new way to create intimacy in your relationship. The kind of connection people worldwide have told me they didn't see growing up.

Finally, in each chapter, I have created support content. You can access that content, including assessments, additional support materials, and the appendix, at the following link: https://bit.ly/RYR

Are you ready to get started?

Chapter One

How Did Betrayal Happen in Our Relationship?

When Kurt and Allison first came to my office, they had been fighting nearly every evening for many months. After Allison discovered Kurt's affair, he admitted that he had an affair that had lasted just two months and that he had met up with his affair partner only a few times. But over the next few weeks, Allison began to put the pieces together as she tried to understand what had happened. She gathered information from credit card and bank statements and calendars and learned that Kurt had actually been having an affair for nearly eighteen months and that he had been involved in multiple sexual encounters with his affair partner.

Before she discovered his affair, Allison and Kurt had argued about his porn use—until Allison eventually gave up asking about it because she was busy working and dealing with their children at home. Now that the affair was out, Allison reported that most of their fights were about Kurt minimizing his behaviors and lying to her. Since she had to discover the extent of Kurt's affair through her own investigations, and because he had deceived her repeatedly, Allison was convinced that there must be more that Kurt still wasn't telling her. Allison felt angry and kept accusing Kurt of hiding information from her.

On the other hand, Kurt was getting tired of being told he was a liar and a cheat. He had repeatedly apologized to Allison and promised her that his affair was over. "I have told her everything," he said, "and she still doesn't believe me. I don't know what else to do." He also reported that he was tired of fighting, of being continually attacked for something he was sorry for, and he was beginning to lose hope that they could ever repair their relationship. He said that when Allison first discovered his affair, he was willing to take responsibility for his actions. But now he admitted that he had started talking back to Allison when she called him names or criticized him.

As I listened to Allison and Kurt each share their side of the story, and as I watched their fraught exchanges with one another, it wasn't hard to imagine how exhausting fighting must be for both of them. When couples get stuck in these fighting patterns, they need help finding a way out. Fortunately, this wasn't the first time I had worked through this type of conflict with clients struggling with sexual betrayal. I recognized that they both felt stuck in a painful rut, and neither knew what to do or say to get out.

Kurt and Allison needed direction. If their marriage was going to last, they had to change their destructive behavior patterns. I understood that if something didn't change, their relationship would likely be damaged beyond repair by unhealthy coping mechanisms, other affairs, domestic violence, or end in divorce. I recognized that they needed to learn how to change the negative interactions that had consumed their relationship.

At this early phase of therapy, I try to help couples assess their desire to heal and repair their relationship. Next, I teach them the importance of orienting themselves because what we orient to influences both what we do and how we think. And then, I seek a deeper understanding of the history of their relationship, their unique story of how they became a couple, and their early years together.

Your Desire to Heal and Restore Your Relationship

I invite you to read this section and rate your current desire to repair your relationship on a scale of zero for not at all committed to ten for totally committed. Then after you have read the entire book, completed all the exercises, and watched the supplemental videos, I will invite you to rate your desire to rebuild your relationship again to see where you stand at that point compared to where you stand now.

When I asked Kurt how committed he was to improving his relationship with Allison, he said that he was committed, but he didn't know if Allison wanted to. When I pushed him to rate his level of commitment, he said he was at an eight. Allison, on the other hand, was much more hesitant. She said, "I don't know because I don't know if he has told me everything. How can I commit without knowing the whole truth?"

She certainly had a valid point. I appreciated that she needed more information to make a decision, and at this stage, her specific rating didn't matter as long as she was willing to participate in therapy. But I asked her again anyway because I wanted to get a sense of her current level of desire for their relationship to be repaired before we forged ahead, and she said, "Maybe two or three."

While many couples seek marital counseling after sexual betrayal, individual counseling is also essential before effective marital counseling can even begin. Why? Imagine, for example, that after a few months of extensive marital therapy, Allison discovers that Kurt didn't have just this one affair during their marriage but that he already had two other affairs she didn't know about. All those months of marital therapy would now feel like a waste of time. For this reason, a full evaluation of Kurt's sexual history must be completed early on in individual counseling.

After only one session with Kurt and Allison, I still didn't know the extent of Kurt's sexual behaviors. I didn't know if he was telling the entire truth or if he was still keeping secrets. I didn't know the extent of his pornography use and how that influenced him. In addition, I didn't know how his sexual behaviors influenced his interactions with Allison. These issues need to be explored in-depth with Kurt and should be well understood before undertaking extensive marital counseling.

It would also be valuable to learn more about Allison. What is the extent of her trauma from sexual betrayal? How is she coping with her pain? Does she have the emotional support she needs? Has she told anyone about Kurt's affair, or is she keeping it secret? Did she have a history of trauma before she married Kurt? If so, how does her previous trauma affect her current suffering?

Ideally, Kurt and Allison would discuss these kinds of questions during individual sessions with their personal therapist. For more on why I suggest separate counselors, please watch my video "Why Having Your Own Therapist After Sexual Betrayal Can Save You a Lot of Heartache and Pain." See: https://bit.ly/RYR

Orienting

The discovery of sexual betrayal often brings chaos into the relationshipas both partners scramble to understand what is happening. Everything from denial and blame to criticism and rage is standard as couples interact after discovery. Sexual betrayal is a lot like a car accident. Imagine that the driver of the car is the partner who acted out, and the betrayed is a passenger in the vehicle. As the driver, the betraying partner has been driving recklessly with and without their partner in the car. They may think that nothing wrong will happen or that there won't be consequences for their dangerous driving behaviors.So,they are surprised when they get into an accident (are caught).

The shock of the accident puts both partners into a natural fight, flight or freeze response.Often,they walk around in a daze trying to figure out what happened. As they come out of shock, the betrayed partner feels the need to protect themselves and their family (fight mode). "Why were you driving that way? Don't you respect me and my life?" To this, the betraying partner may want to avoid the conversation (flee) by either minimizing or dismissing their behavior, "It's not that big of a deal; we made it out alive." Or "Why are you so upset? Accidents happen." They may also make promises like, "I'm sorry; I will never drive like that again."

Eventually, the betrayed partner will attempt to make sense of their partner's driving behaviors. They will start gathering information and will ask questions like, "How long have you been driving that way? Why were you so careless? Why did you run the stop sign? How can I trust you again? Can I ever get into a car with you again? Are you going to keep driving that way? Can I ever be safe with you again?" These are just a few of the questions betrayed partners ask.

One of the side effects of being in a car accident is you becomejumpier and more fearful. You may begin anticipating that something will go wrong every time you get into a car. As a result, you start monitoring your partner's driving to ensure you won't be in another accident. Similarly, the betrayed partner begins watching their betrayer with an eagle eye. They look for any movement or shift that suggests something is wrong (i.e., hiding one's phone, turning to another screen when the betrayed enters a room, or coming home fifteen minutes late). When a betrayed partner feels like something has changed in their partner, they often get upset and angry and make accusations (i.e., who were you talking to—your mistress?).

On the other hand, the betraying spouse may feel embarrassed because of the accident. If they feel attacked, they may become defensive because their partner asked so many questions. If this happens, they may say, "Fine. I know I am a bad driver. Maybe you should just ride with someone else." (Interpretation: If I'm so bad, why don't you divorce me and find someone who will treat you better). This type of response shifts the responsibility to the partner to decide while avoiding taking responsibility for the hurt and pain the passenger (betrayed partner) feels.

This type of response usually stems from shame. Often, betraying partners struggle with their own identity. They may be thinking, "What's wrong with me? Why can't I stop driving (acting) this way?" Internally, they often feel bad because they have been hiding their behaviors for so long. They often feel ashamed because they have hurt the people who are closest to them. However, being vulnerable and sharing their mistakes with their partner and others is hard. As a result, they may shift the responsibility by saying, "If you hadn't distracted me, we wouldn't have been in an accident." This is their effort to deflect the shame they feel.

These self-defense responses are frequently used to cover their internalized shame for the accident. If their shame is high and they are defensive, they could become aggressive (i.e., I wouldn't have acted out if we had been more sexual, or you didn't show that you cared about me until I had an affair). Unfortunately, these interactions leave the betrayed feeling blamed and the betrayer feeling attacked. Frequently, neither partner knows how to effectively respond to the other. As a result, they feel like there is no solution.

In order to change these endless patterns, it is valuable to pause and reflect. Researchers have discovered that one of the best ways to respond after an accident is to orient ourselves. While the natural response may be to fight or flee, orienting is an alternative response. It is the process of gathering information pertaining to significant stimuli. (1) In this case, the significant stimulus is betrayal. When couples orient themselves after sexual betrayal, they begin looking inside and outside themselves. They start asking essential questions and gathering relevant information so that they can make an informed decision about their relationship.

In contrast, when couples don't orient to the new information, they often make quick and rash decisions or say things that they don't mean (i.e., I hate you, I'm filing for divorce, I'm going to tell everyone what you did, or I had an affair because you are a terrible lover, etc.). While these responses are common, they are based on our basic instinctive fight-or-flight nature. When we slow down and gather information, we can make better decisions.

Over the past few years, I have become fascinated with the process of orienting as it relates to deer. Since I live in an area with many deer, I have been able to watch them closely and observe how they interact with me. In the picture below, you will see these deer orienting to me (an intruder). Their ears are up, and they stare at me, trying to use their senses to determine whether I am a threat. Looking closely, you will also see something interesting in this picture. Two of the deer are not orienting to me. They are distracted, eating their morning breakfast.

In most of my run-ins with deer, they are keenly attuned to my every movement. They are using their senses to gather information to determine their safety. They are orienting to me as a potential threat to decide if they should fight or flee. In most cases, they end up running from me.

Much like the deer watching me, I invite you to stop and orient yourselves to you (your thoughts, emotions, and body sensations) and your relationship. While the deer orient themselves to me quickly, sexual betrayal may take you and your partner weeks, months, or years to fully orient yourselves.

In the section below, I will help each of you with the orienting process by walking you through a series of questions that can help you prepare to make an informed decision about your relationship.

A critical difference between the deer and your relationship is thatin order foryou to orient, you need to be in a place where you can pause and evaluate. Orienting is most effective in environments where you feel safe and can reflect without interruption.

Before introducing the orienting questions, I need to mention something about the two deer still eating. They were not concerned about my presence. Perhaps they felt safe because the other deer were not sending a warning signal. Or, they may have become so engrossed in eating their breakfast that they didn't realize that I might be a threat (this might be analogous to ignoring an affair or other sexual behaviors by not talking about it or addressing what happened). Or perhaps the deer were so desensitized to humans that they didn't consider me a threat (the comparison to this might be saying that sexual betrayal outside of a committed relationship should be expected since cheating is so common).

These deer placed themselves at a much greater risk for harm by ignoring me—a potential threat. The same is true of your relationship; if you avoid or ignore the orienting process, you will likely experience many more challenges. By doing a deep self-evaluation and an inventory of your relationship, you will orient yourself in a way that will prepare you to make an informed decision regarding your relationship. Our best decisions are made when we take the time to gather important information and then determine the best course of action (in your situation, to work to improve the relationship or choose to move on).

When we orient well, "the orienting reflex assists us in remaining appropriately open and responsive to information-carrying events in the environment." (2)

The critical point here is that orienting will help you remain open to asking difficult personal questions, i.e., "How did I get to the point that I betrayed my partner," or "Do I have the desire to try and work through my partner betraying me?"

Below I will explain what the orienting process might look like for you and your partner. For now, it is essential to remember that orienting will help you gather important information (about yourself and your relationship), and it will help you be better in the decision-making process.

After the discovery of betrayal, orienting is the process of slowing down to give a serious evaluation of your relationship. Both partners learn to orient by searching within to determine what happened and if they want to move forward in their relationship. They also prepare to talk openly and honestly about the betrayal and what it means to their relationship now. Couples can make informed decisions based on their new information when properly orienting.

Strategies to Help You Orient Effectively

It is one thing to talk about orienting, and it is an entirely different thing to effectively orient in the moments you need it the most.

As explained above, after discovering sexual betrayal, it is easy to get emotionally hijacked and get stuck in a fight or flight response.

Dr. Daniel Siegel wrote regarding getting unstuck, "The fundamental issue in resolving traumatic stress is to restore the proper balance between the rational and emotional brains so that you can feel in charge of how you respond and conduct your life. When we're triggered into states of hyper-or-hypo arousal, we are pushed outside our 'window of tolerance'"—the range of optimal functioning. (3)

In Chapters Three, Five, and Fourteen, I will provide tools to help you develop the skillsnecessaryto find balance, as Dr. Siegel suggests.

The neuroscientist "Joseph LeDoux and his colleagues have shown that the only way we can consciously access the emotional brain is through self-awareness, i.e., by activating the medial prefrontal cortex, the part of the brain that notices what is going on inside us and thus allows us to feel what we're feeling." (4)

As you increase your self-awareness, you develop better orienting skills. This, in turn, can lead to working through trauma and stopping unwanted sexual behaviors.

Here are some research-based strategies commonly used to improve your orienting skills.

- Journaling—writing down thoughts and feelings you have about specific guided questions (see examples of questions below).

- Mindful breathing and relaxation—when we pay attention to our breathing, our heart rate generally decreases, and our body feels more relaxed. In this state, we can gather important information and communicate more effectively.

- Guided meditations—one way to increase your self-awareness is by listening to an expert who can guide you through a mindful exercise. For example, a mindfulness expert, Jon Kabat-Zinn, does a full mind-body meditation where you learn to listen to your entire body through a guided exercise. A full body scan is a very effective way to orient yourself. (5)

- Learning from your body (e.g., tightness, tension, sensations)—the somatic experience is designed to help you listen carefully to your body. This awareness can act as an alarm that you must pay close attention to your internal feelings and physical surroundings. By attuning to bodily sensations, you will learn how to naturally pay more attention to feelings of anxiety, sadness, depression, loneliness, and more.

You will notice that most items on this list are designed to help you slow down and see what is happening to your mind and body. Below you will find questions that can help you orient.

Orienting—For the Betraying Partner

I will begin by describing the orienting process of the betraying partner. When you betrayed your partner, you probably didn't consider the full impact your actions would have on your relationship.

In my experience, betraying partners rarely consider how their actions could influence their partners before they choose to act out sexually, and all of that changes once the betrayal is discovered and the truth of what happened has been revealed.

Betraying partners become painfully aware that their decisions have triggered significant anger and hurt in their partner. After the discovery of betrayal, most relationships change out of necessity.

When I work with betraying partners, I spend a lot of time at the beginning of our work helping them orient themselves. For example, in working with Kurt, I asked him to think about these questions:

Orienting Questions for the Betraying Partner

Personal Questions

- What drove me to engage in sexual behaviors outside my relationship? (e.g., a need for acceptance)

- Are my sexual behaviors out of control? If yes, how long have I felt they have been out of control? What happens inside me when I feel the most out of control (i.e., I feel stressed at work and upset at my partner)?

- Do I turn to sexual behaviors to escape from difficult experiences?

- When am I most prone to act out sexually?

- What thoughts did I have that permitted me to act out sexually? (i.e., what they don't know won't hurt them?)

- Are there unresolved issues from my past that make me seek comfort in others besides my partner?

- Do I need to be more open with others about my hidden sexual behaviors to heal?

- Do I have sexual behaviors from my past that I have told myself I will never share with anyone? If yes, how is this secret influencing me now?

- Do I genuinely desire to stop my sexual behaviors, or would I prefer to keep doing what I have been doing?

- Do I believe that it is possible to change my behavior, or do I feel hopeless because I don't think I will ever be able to stop?

- How have my sexual behaviors influenced me in the following areas: 1) my marriage; 2) parenting—if you have children; 3) how you interact with family and friends; 4) how you see and interact with other people (i.e., do you see people as sexual opportunities?)

Relationship Questions

- How important is my relationship with my partner? How committed am I to doing everything I can to rebuild my partners' trust in me?

- How have my actions hurt my partner?

- What can I do to help my partner heal?

- Why do I turn to others or pornography instead of my partner?

- Do I have a history of acting out sexually and hurting people close to me?

- Do I struggle with maintaining sexual boundaries in relationships? If so, why do I think I am struggling with this?

- Do I resent my spouse/partner for something that we have not been able to resolve?

- Do I make it easy for my partner to love me or do I complicate it? Please explain your answer.

- Is it hard to form a close relationship with others?

- What is my best strength in my relationships?

If there is one relationship skill that I could improve, what would it be?

Orienting (For the Betrayed Partner)

When I talk with betrayed partners, I hear about their racing minds, indescribable fear, and intense outbursts of anger. Many partners tell me that they don't feel like themselves.

The hurt and pain betrayed partners often feel manifest in two dominant emotions: anger and fear. In my research with over 20,000 betrayed partners, most describe feeling enraged at their partner.

Over 73% of betrayed partners reported being angry at least half the time while talking to their partners. At the same time, 74% reported feelings of indescribable fear. (6)

It is easy to get angry and anxious when you feel your partner does not understand your pain. Unfortunately, most betrayed partners feel misunderstood when they express emotions to their partner, making them even angrier. Their partner and others have told many that they need to calm down. In Chapter Six, I will discuss why being able to express fears and anger is an essential part of the healing process.

When others judge betrayed partners when they express fear and anger, they commonly feel alone and blamed. This makes it more difficult for them to heal and move on. For this reason, getting stuck in fear and anger are common. However, these emotions make it difficult to pause and reflect on deeper feelings (i.e., hurt, anguish, grief, and sadness).

When anger and fear become the two dominant emotions in betrayed partner's life, they become barriers to orienting. Fortunately, by learning how to orient, you can gain deeper insights into your thoughts and emotions. This, in turn, can help you process feelings like anger and fear, which will ultimately help you feel more in control of your emotions. (Chapter Six will encompass a detailed section on this topic).

One crucial part of your healing is learning to orient yourself to you. Ultimately, you will want to become an expert on your thoughts, emotions, and body sensations. Paying closer attention to your body will give you a deeper appreciation for your suffering. Since our bodies store trauma, you will likely feel muscle tightness and tension after betrayal. This can cause other physical health issues like headaches, irritable bowel syndrome, and chronic fatigue.

Some questions you will want to reflect on include: What have you come to believe about yourself due to your partner's betrayal? How has your partner's betrayal influenced how you see others? For example, are you holding back from others? Have you lost trust in people in general? How do you see people you used to trust (i.e., family and friends)?

These types of questions will help you begin the orienting process. Please take the time to consider the questions listed above and the ones below. It's time to pause and orient yourself to you and your relationship.

Orienting Questions for the BetrayedPartner

Personal Questions

- How has discovery made me see and value myself?
- How have I changed since my discovery?
- What are my biggest fears after discovery?
- What has discovery done to my physical health?
- What has discovery done to my mental health (e.g., depression, anxiety)?
- Since the discovery, what areas of my life have I changed most?
- Am I still able to find peace even in my pain? If yes, how? If not, what is preventing me from finding some peace?
- What is the hardest part of betrayal for me?
- Do previous life experiences remind me of how I feel now? If yes, what are the similarities?

- What do I need others to know about the betrayal that would help me feel understood and heard?

Relationship Questions

- What must I know about my partner in order to make a decision about our relationship?

- Do I have the desire to reconnect with my partner if they give their all to this relationship? If yes, why? If not, what is preventing me from moving on?

- What do I need my partner to know about how their actions have hurt me?

- Am I avoiding people that used to be close to me? If so, why?

- What do I need from others as I go through my healing process?

- Who can support me the most during this difficult time?

- What advice would I give to someone going through what I am?

- What is the most important thing my partner needs to know about my pain?

- Has betrayal changed how I see other people? If so, how?

- Do I believe that there are still people I can trust?

Please take time to answer the questions above. The more time and effort you put into responding to these questions, the more effective you will be at orienting yourself to you and your relationship. One way to get the most out of these questions is to write your thoughts and feelings in a journal and spend about twenty minutes every day answering them until you have responded to all of them. Write your answers by hand rather than typing them on a computer, tablet, or phone. Our best decisions are made when we understand ourselves on a deeper level.

Understanding Your Relationship Story—Your (Un) Love Map

Every couple has a story about their relationship. Their report includes memories and experiences from their dating and courtship, the early years of their relationship, and present events. I have found that as couples share their story with me, we begin unraveling what has brought them to this point in their relationship. This is what I refer to as understanding your story. One of my primary goals in this chapter is to help you understand the story of your relationship in a new way.

Throughout my career as a marriage and family therapist, I have observed that couples create stories about their relationship. Often in these stories, some events or experiences significantly influence the quality of their relationship. Positive experiences usually include having a child, buying a first home, and trips taken together. On the other hand, negative experiences include unresolved conflicts, discovered secrets, infidelity, dealing with in-laws, and a host of other issues.

Interestingly, a positive experience for one partner may be a neutral or negative experience for the other partner. I have observed that when couples are aligned in their interpretation of an experience, regardless of whether it was a positive or negative event, they are more open to resolving problems. They share more excitement for the positive elements of their story.

In contrast, the further apart couples perceive events in their relationship, the more likely they are to fight and stay disconnected. For example, when one partner views having a child as a positive experience, and the other is neutral or even regrets having a child, this couple will struggle to connect. As one partner bonds with their child, the other will develop feelings of jealousy and resentment. They will create a personal story about being replaced by their child. In this case, both partners became a parent. Still, their interpretation and its meaning to their relationship will create a significant barrier between the couple and weigh heavily on their relationship.

We cannot not create meaning in what we experience in our relationships. When working with couples, I highlight key events and experiences that have brought the couple closer together or pulled them apart. As a part of the therapy process, I have couples create a time line of critical events (positive and negative) in their relationship. As they explore their experiences,they often discover how various experiences influenced their relationship (for better or worse).

Once we have completed the relationship history time line (See Appendix A), we explore more intimate details of their relationship; I have made both partners complete a sexual history time line (See Appendix B). The sexual history time line explores each individual's sexual activity throughout their life. It is always extensive as it includes every sexual activity (i.e., first masturbation, all sexual encounters before marriage, experience with pornography, and all sexual activity since marriage). This in-depth self-analysis often illuminates the different expectations and experiences couples bring into their marriage.

One of the benefits of completing the sexual history time line is that it will bring to light the extent of sexual behaviors each partner has experienced throughout their life. Often, this helps both partners understand each other better.

In situations where there has been sexual betrayal, the time line highlights the potential extent of the problem. I have had betraying partners realize that their problem was much more extensive than they had previously thought. I also have had betrayed partners tell me that as they learned about the history of their partner's behaviors, it helped them feel less responsible. One client said, "While it was hard to hear about my partner's sexual history, it helped me understand the challenge he was facing. I realized his sexual behaviors began long before he met me. For some reason, this helped me take his recent behaviors less personally."

For couples who choose to work through sexual betrayal, the relationship history time line and sexual history time line provide a foundation for understanding each other. When couples succeed in rebuilding their relationship, these two exercises often help them begin their journey to creating a new story together.

As couples explore the story of their relationship and their sexual time line, they are more likely to understand their challenges differently. In most cases, essential differences and unresolved issues are brought to light. As couples learn to have difficult conversations about these topics, they discover whether they are heading in the same direction. At this point, most of the couples I work with feel uncomfortable since they have avoided discussing important issues for years that are now being brought to the forefront. This process requires two people willing to look at complex issues they may have ignored throughout their relationship.

I have observed that when couples begin the healing and recovery process, it is because they are both willing to engage in hard conversations about painful topics. In addition, on an individual level, both partners have experienced deep personal introspection so that they can engage in honest and truthful discussions. (If you have answered the orienting questions above, you have started the orienting process).

In Chapter Two, you will be asked to continue self-exploration. Often, the person who has sexually acted out evaluates their sexual development and has more insight into their behaviors.

Many have identified how their first sexual experiences are related to their current sexual behaviors. By examining how their behaviors have escalated, outlining their sexual activities, and exploring how they justified their sexual behaviors, they are now better prepared to move forward. This in-depth self-reflection is then shared with their betrayed partner in a formal disclosure process.

The disclosure process will be discussed in Chapters Ten and Thirteen. Also, a video explaining the steps of doing a disclosure can be found in the support material for this chapter at https://bit.ly/RYR.

Why Exploring the Past Matters

Sometimes, couples seek my help, but when I ask them about their relationship history, they want to focus on what's happening now and not the past. I have heard clients say, "Can't we just move on?" Or "Why do we have to bring up the past?" My response is usually something like this, "We can do that if you want, but we won't be as effective at improving your marriage as we could be." At this point, I introduce them to the Zeigarnik effect and how understanding this simple principle may be one of the essential components to healing their relationship.

If you are like most people, you have yet to hear of the Zeigarnik effect. So here is a short explanation as found in the book "The Science of Trust by John Gottman." In 1922, a petite 21-year-old newlywed Jewish woman named Bluma Zeigarnik sat in a café in Vienna as professional waiters listened carefully to huge orders from large gatherings without writing anything down. (7) Then she watched as the servers flawlessly filled their orders. Always the astute observer, Zeigarnik later interviewed these waiters. As they moved rapidly from table to kitchen to table, she found that they remembered everything the customers asked for. However, when she interviewed the waiters after they had filled the orders, they had forgotten everything.

In other words, when the orders remained unfilled, they remembered them, but after the orders were processed entirely, they were forgotten. Zeigarnik found that, on average, there is 90% better recall for "unfinished events" than for events we have somehow completed. (8)

It may take time to fully understand the significance of the Zeigarnik effect on you and your relationship. Let me explain why and offer a short example. Have you been in an argument with your partner and felt like it just wasn't going anywhere? Or do you ever feel like you've been stuck in a seemingly never-ending cycle of unresolved issues without any actual resolution or progress? If this sounds familiar to you, the Zeigarnik effect could influence your relationship.

In our relationships, it sticks in our minds when we can't resolve our disagreements (food order). If left unresolved, many of our relationship disputes never go away. The next disagreement will likely be more intense because the previous issue still needs to be resolved. Much like Bluma Zeigarnik discovered the servers, it is remembered perfectly if a food order still needs to be filled.

One other important finding that Zeigarnik discovered was that unresolved issues take up to 90% of our mental energy. (9) This is why unresolved personal matters (i.e., childhood trauma, abuse, negative self-beliefs, addictions, etc.) and unresolved relationship issues (i.e., arguments, fights, blaming, avoidance, etc.)

trigger many problems. If we spend 90% of our time thinking about unresolved issues, it will benefit us to find solutions to our challenges to complete the personal and relationship food order.

In the next chapter, we will explore strategies to understand the unresolved issues better and help you explore possible solutions.

One of the best ways to deal with today's challenges is to get to the root of the problem. That's what we will do in the next chapter as we help you look deeper into how betrayal came into your life and your relationship.

Key Takeaways from This Chapter

- Every individual and couple have a story. This chapter was designed to help you pause and evaluate yourself and your relationship.

- The process of orienting can help you slow down to evaluate yourself and your relationship. Through orienting, you were encouraged to reflect on questions that deal with your healing and recovery. After that, you were asked to consider questions regarding your relationship. If you didn't take the time to ponder and write your answers to these questions, I invite you to make it your priority this week.

- One way to increase your self-awareness and gain insight into your relationship is to complete the *Key Life Event Inventory* and the *Relationship History Inventory*.

- Unresolved issues occupy up to 90% of our mental energy. If you attempt to resolve past issues, you and your partner will have a better chance of healing your relationship.

Chapter Two

Getting to the Root of the Problem

"We cannot solve our problems with the same level of thinking that created them."
-Albert Einstein

A few years ago, my neighbor, an elderly widow, asked me to help her remove a rose bush from the front of her yard. I dug down a little over one foot and clipped the roots to the bush. I thought that was the end of that rose bush until the following spring when my neighbor teasingly asked me to come to look at the new rose she had in front of her house. The rose bush was back. In my second effort, I dug deeper until I was sure no more roots existed.

Much like my neighbor's rose bush, as individuals attempt to stop their unwanted sexual behaviors, deal with betrayal, and repair their relationship concerns, issues will inevitably come back if they don't get to the root problems. This chapter was designed to help both partners seek a deeper understanding of personal issues (addiction and trauma) and relationship challenges that need to be addressed if healing and recovery are going to occur.

In the previous chapter, you were asked to complete a relationship history time line and a sexual history time line. By completing these exercises, you should better understand how key events began eroding your relationship connection.

As you look at some critical events, you will likely see a direct relationship between the connection in your relationship (or lack thereof) and these key events.

Let's look at an example from Kurt and Allison's story.

Relationship Ruptures

At the beginning of their relationship, Kurt and Allison reported that they enjoyed each other and had a close connection. As we reviewed their relationship history time line, there was a specific time (about two years into their relationship) when they both reported a significant disconnect.

As we explored that time frame, the story began to unfold. At this time, Allison received a promotion at work and discovered that she was pregnant with their first child. She was busy at work and began feeling sick due to her pregnancy. Kurt reported that he was often stressed at work during that time frame and was hoping to spend time with Allison when he got home. He felt disappointed when she was unable or did not have the energy to connect.

He reported that this was when he returned to pornography to deal with his frustrations with Allison's schedule. He began resenting her and justified his behavior. While he had watched pornography as a teenager, he had tried to refrain from using it since their marriage. As I explored Kurt's feelings, it became apparent that he despised Allison's job because she was always so busy. By the time she got home from work, she had no time for him. His resentment grew when she announced that she was pregnant, and he acknowledged that even the pregnancy bothered him. He felt like everything took priority over him.

As we explored Kurt's thoughts from that time, it became evident that it was crucial for him. When I asked him if he attempted to talk with Allison about his frustrations, he said, "When I tried to talk with her, she told me I didn't understand how hard her job was and that she was doing her best." Her lack of acknowledgment made Kurt feel misunderstood, so he stopped trying to discuss his concerns with her. This was when he started justifying his porn use. In his mind, he told himself, "She cares more about her job than me."

Throughout my career, I have observed that when people sexually act out, they almost always mentally defend their behaviors. I explained to Kurt that it would be essential for him to identify the reasons he used to justify his behaviors. By increasing his insight into these thought patterns, he will be more prepared to respond effectively to them when they come up in the future. I talked with Kurt about his response when Allison was too busy for him; he was able to identify that during those times, he was more at risk for sexually acting out.

On the other hand, Allison reported feeling exhausted at the end of every day. She desperately tried to keep up with the new demands at work while simultaneously dealing with nausea from her pregnancy. It was hard maintaining her work pace while constantly feeling sick. By the time she got home, she only wanted to sleep. She was frustrated that Kurt couldn't understand all she was doing to contribute. It seemed like he did not understand the toll her pregnancy and job took on her. She noticed he was pulling away but figured it would work out over time.

Time Doesn't Heal All Wounds

A few months into her pregnancy, Allison discovered that Kurt was staying up late. One night she had a feeling to get up and check on him. When she entered the room, he quickly changed the screen. She asked him directly if he was watching pornography. Initially, he denied it, but after she gave him a look of disbelief, he confessed, "I was watching porn." Hurt by his admission, she got angry. She began yelling at him and telling him he needed to leave. Surprised by her intensity, Kurt said, "Why are you so angry? You don't have time for me anyway. Why do you care if I watch porn?"

This response made Allison even more upset. She responded, "I'm pregnant and am doing all I can to keep up at work and home. If you want those naked women, then you can have them. Kurt responded, "What are you even saying? I don't want to be with them."

To this, Allison responded, "Then why are you watching porn? It must be because I'm pregnant and not as attractive or as sexy as those women." At this point, Kurt raised his voice and yelled, "It's not because I'm not attracted to you; you don't take time for me anymore. All you do is work and sleep. You don't care about me or my needs."

Note: When Kurt said to Allison, "You don't care about me or my needs," he told her his belief—his core hurt. He had told Allison his true feelings. Unfortunately, his tone and body language drowned out his message. Ultimately, his approach felt accusatory to Allison; she felt like he was blaming her.

Allison found it challenging to respond to Kurt's explanation for turning to pornography because she interpreted it as him using pornography due to her lack of attention.

In other words, it felt like he was blaming her for his behavior. In addition to feeling blamed, she was feeling insecure in their relationship due to the changes she was experiencing with her pregnancy. Then to top things off, she had felt Kurt pulling away from her.

Allison and Kurt's Core Issues

It has been my experience that in difficult moments like discovering a partner's hidden sexual behaviors, couples rarely respond well. In Kurt and Allison's interaction, this was the case. Allison had at least three significant issues with Kurt's response:

His use of pornography hurt her.

When he accused her of working and sleeping all the time, it felt like he was blaming her for his use of porn.

He responded angrily by yelling at her when he mentioned he was turning to pornography because she didn't take time for him anymore.

Kurt's elevated voice was painful for Allison to hear because it reminded her of earlier life experiences she had while growing up with her dad. In essence, Kurt had yelled at her (reminding her of how her dad used to treat her) and then justified his behavior simultaneously. Allison struggled to respond between Kurt's gaslighting (blaming her) and her history with her dad. It felt like everything was her fault.

Speaking about the events of that night, Allison later told me that when Kurt blamed her, it triggered something inside of her. She told me that was when she felt her trauma settle in. Allison didn't know how to respond, so when she blew up and yelled at Kurt, even she felt surprised by her intensity. She didn't want to be angry and didn't want Kurt to move out, but in that critical moment, she did the only thing she could think of doing. She screamed at Kurt and told him to get out.

On the other hand, Kurt felt like a low priority on Allison's list of things to do. In his mind, he had tried to discuss his concerns with her before turning to pornography. Since that conversation did not go well, he justified his behavior. What Kurt failed to realize at the time was that Allison's busy schedule triggered early memories his parents, who were not available when he needed help.

By turning to porn to deal with his frustrations, Kurt shifted the issue from not feeling important to Allison to his use of pornography. Instead of his original concern being openly discussed and addressed, now the focus of their problems was turned to his use of porn. However, if the root issue had been explored previously, Kurt would have recognized that his main concern was not Allison's busy schedule but the unresolved traumas from his past that needed to be discussed.

Instead, when Kurt got frustrated and raised his voice at Allison, this turned the attention away from his genuine concern (not feeling close to Allison) and made his accusation and tone of voice the problem (which added to his shame). To add to their issues, how could Allison understand Kurt's genuine concern when he triggered her insecurities associated with changes in her body, and how could Allison hear Kurt when he raised his voice and reminded her of her father's behaviors when she was younger? After all, in her mind, he was acting like her dad.

Here are a few common responses we might hear from Allison at times like this:

- So, you are blaming me and saying it is my fault that you are watching pornography.
- If you want other people who look like porn stars, you have the wrong woman. I am pregnant and will never look like they do.
- Get out! I don't want to see you. Could you leave me alone?

Here are a few common responses we might hear from Kurt at times like this:

- You don't care about me anymore.
- All you do is work and sleep; you never make time for me.
- Your job is more important than I am.

Each of the responses mentioned above is normal and natural when we feel hurt by our partner, especially when they don't solve their problem. When couples escalate to this level of conflict, they will rarely solve their differences at that time. Instead, one of the partners will usually pull away and avoid the other for hours, days, months, and sometimes years.

In Allison and Kurt's case, she told him to sleep somewhere else. Kurt tried apologizing the next day, but Allison wasn't ready to hear him out. She told him she didn't want pornography in their home and would not tolerate it. Kurt could not understand why she was so angry that she asked him to leave. Over the next few days, they attempted to talk things out, but nothing was resolved between them. When Kurt asked if he could come home, Allison conceded, but on the condition that Kurt apologize. He told her he would never look at pornography again.

Unfortunately, this was just the first significant episode for Kurt and Allison. While he said he was sorry, they didn't discuss his core concerns and never addressed how overwhelmed Allison felt with her pregnancy and job. By glossing over these core issues, their disconnect only grew over time. This is a perfect example of the Zeigarnik effect from Chapter One. When couples don't know how to deal with their problems, they often bury them, hoping they will disappear. Unfortunately, unresolved issues come back to rear their ugly head.

Over the next few years, their original conflict surrounding Kurt not feeling like a priority and Allison's work-life balance, combined with having children, significantly contributed to their problems. Kurt's resentment towards Allison grew as she continued to stay busy with work, and then when their first child was born, he felt like she gave all her attention to the baby. On the other hand, Allison felt that Kurt wasn't even trying to understand her. She was overwhelmed being a new mom and felt pressure to return to work after maternity leave.

Eventually, she gave up resolving issues with Kurt because he would become defensive whenever they started discussing their problems. After their first fight about his pornography use, they both hesitated to discuss hard things.

The next big challenge for their relationship happened when Kurt started working with a new employee his company had hired. Feeling disconnected from Allison, Kurt found the new employee to be engaging and started enjoying talking with her. Over the next few months, with nothing changing at home, he started spending more time talking to his co-worker after work. Kurt reported feeling understood for the first time in a long-time. He began thinking more about his co-worker and less about Allison and their child. Eventually, the interaction at work transitioned from talking to going to lunch together and eventually escalated into an affair.

When I asked Kurt about his thoughts, he said, "I knew if Allison found out about this, then our relationship would be over, but in the middle of the affair, I didn't care. I was lost and didn't know anything better." The affair partner, however, became a problem for him. His other co-workers discovered their affair, which was reported to their boss and HR department. His employer warned him and said they would be forced to terminate his employment if he didn't stop. Meanwhile, the husband of his affair partner discovered what was happening and threatened to beat Kurt and tell his wife. Kurt was starting to experience some of the consequences of his affair, while Allison still didn't know.

It has been my experience that unresolved relationship ruptures often trigger many individuals to justify their sexual behaviors outside of their relationship. As couples work toward relationship repair, the betraying partner's story of why they did what they did is a story within the betrayal story that has to be understood and worked through as a couple.

The Stories We Tell Ourselves (Kurt)

When I work with betraying partners like Kurt, one of the core things we discuss is the thoughts that allowed (permitted) them to betray their partners. I have always explained to people that they must understand their thought sequences to justify their behaviors. These thoughts, if left unchecked, will likely lead to continued relapses.

I often ask, "What are some of the thoughts you had before acting out. There are two common responses, "I just acted without thinking" and "I don't know. I haven't thought about it." My follow-up statement to both responses is, "It is time to slow down and think about your thought process and how you felt at that time. I explain that it is important to gain personal insight into "your why." Understanding these thoughts will provide us with much-needed information.

Your *whys* are the thoughts that justified your behaviors. They include your thoughts, feelings, and beliefs before acting out. As you identify "your why," you will begin to understand yourself and your behaviors.

Here are a few of the benefits of going through this exercise.

The first reason is related to the Zeigarnik effect discussed in Chapter One. When we often justify our behaviors, it is because of some unmet need (in our minds). For example, how many times have you chosen to act out because you felt like your partner wasn't meeting your needs? Or have you justified your behaviors because you felt like your partner didn't care about you? Unresolved beliefs like these often help explain how you justified your behaviors.

The second essential reason is to understand the thoughts, feelings, and beliefs that lead to your acting out. You will likely feel and think something similar in the future. If you aren't prepared when you feel like your partner doesn't care about you, or you think to yourself, "I don't matter to them," you are at high risk of acting out again. The risk increases because, in the past, these thoughts and feelings triggered you to act out.

Third, your partner will likely ask, "Why did you do…?" As you work to make amends, it will not be enough to say, "I don't know." If you have given serious thought to what led you to act out, you will have a much better understanding of yourself which will help you better explain your behaviors to your partner (i.e., unmet needs, past wounds, and hurts).

To help you identify how you justified your behaviors, I have created a short exercise to help you think through some of your reasons for acting out. Here are some of the more common statements I have heard from my clients.

How many of the following thoughts did you have to justify your behaviors?

Justifying Thoughts	Yes	No
1. My partner doesn't really care about me. He/she is too busy.		
2. My sex drive is just higher than my partner's.		
3. If my partner really loved me, they would initiate sex more often.		
4. My partner doesn't show me the love that I need.		
5. What my partner doesn't know won't hurt them.		
6. I deserve this (sexual activity) because I have been working so hard.		
7. This is just who I am.		
8. I am just different than others. People don't understand my sex drive.		
9. My partner doesn't need me.		
10. I will just do it (sexual behavior) just this one time.		
11. My affair partner cares more about me and my needs.		
12. My sexual behaviors are my business, and nobody else needs to know.		

How many 'yes' statements did you check?

Higher scores offer insight into how you justified your sexual behaviors. You may also discover that these thoughts often accompany unaddressed frustrations with your partner (i.e., my partner doesn't show me the love I need). Over time, these resentments build up, making you vulnerable to acting out again. By unpacking these thoughts, clients often begin to understand the story they told themselves to justify their behaviors.

Over the years, it has been my experience that unwanted sexual activity is rarely the root problem when individuals seek my help. Instead, when people sexually act out, there is a combination of unresolved relationship issues, resentments, childhood neglect, abuse, family-of-origin issues, loneliness, a history of addictive behaviors, and various other challenges.

Now, let's look at one more part of Kurt's story.

Usually, when individuals come clean or get caught acting out, they often have a long personal history of stories they have told themselves over the years. To help Kurt gain a deeper self-understanding of his sexual history and how these experiences have influenced his life, I gave him this exercise.

Excercise: Take a few minutes and identify a sexual experience you have had that you are not proud of. Then place the thoughts, feelings, behaviors, and beliefs you formed about yourself due to your identified sexual behavior.

Experience	Influence on Thoughts	Influence on Feelings	Influence on Behaviors	Influence on Beliefs
My parents caught me viewing pornography on the family computer. My mom told me it would ruin my relationships.	I was confused. I felt like I had done something wrong. I thought that there must be something wrong with me. At the time, I also felt curious and wanted to see more of it. My conflicting thoughts made me think that I was different than everyone else.	I was embarrassed. My whole family knew what I had done. I was ashamed. I felt like a liar when I got older and began hiding my porn.	I didn't want to keep looking, but I was a curious teenage boy, so I learned how to cover my tracks. I hid my behavior and learned to lie.	I'm a fraud. If others knew what I was doing, they wouldn't want to be with me.

Getting caught viewing pornography by Allison	I have let another person down.	I was scared, especially when she asked me to leave. I felt like a failure.	I wanted to stop and never do it again. That's what I told her, but I kept returning to it when we weren't getting along or when I felt stressed at work.	There is something wrong with me. I can't control myself.
Having an affair	I was so lost and confused. I knew I had ruined my marriage. I didn't like myself.	I felt worthless. I was angry at myself. I was angry at Allison. I was angry at where I was in my life.	I threw caution to the wind. It was like I didn't care. Then when I realized how stupid I was being, I wanted to make things better, but I didn't know how to. I still don't know what to do or say.	I am a failure. I am worthless. I can't control myself.

Note: You will find a blank worksheet like the one Kurt completed in Appendix D.

The Stories We Tell Ourselves (Allison)

In my work with betrayed partners, I often listen carefully to words my clients use to describe their partner's behaviors. Deceived, lied to, rejected, and not enough are some common statements betrayed partners use to describe how they feel about their partner's behaviors. In Allison's case, we explored how Kurt's porn use and affair influenced her thoughts and beliefs about herself.

As she described his use of porn, she reported it as feeling inadequate. If I had asked her the question, how did his porn use influence you right after her discovery, she likely wouldn't have had a good answer. She wouldn't have had enough time to give meaning to the experience. It usually takes us time to make sense of our experiences. What was natural was the anger she felt. His behavior had triggered a fighting response inside of her. She found herself yelling and telling him to get out.

That initial experience was now in the past, and since then, she and Kurt had been through many other challenging experiences, including his affair. While sitting in my office, we had the opportunity to explore the stories running through her mind. As we explored her responses to Kurt's behaviors, new understandings emerged.

One day I asked Allison about her feelings of inadequacy. This single question and the following conversation helped Allison gain significant personal insight. For years before meeting Kurt, she had felt inadequate. Allison thought she needed to be more intelligent, prettier, and skinnier. When I asked where the idea that she wasn't good enough came from, she quickly replied, "Oh, that's easy; I never felt like I was enough for my dad. While growing up, her father made it clear that she had to work hard to prove her worth. He would find fault in her actions even when she gave her all. She worked and worked to establish that she was enough for her dad and others, but no matter how hard she worked, she never felt like she was good enough.

As Allison pondered on her new awareness, she wondered if her need to be good enough had made her seek validation at work. After thinking about it, she answered her question, saying, "I can't believe it. I am still pushing myself so hard at work, looking for validation. How stupid is that?"

As we continued to explore the impact of her father's attitude on her life, she gained another insight. I asked her how feeling inadequate had influenced her marriage. She pondered the question and replied, "I thought that if I worked hard enough at work and came home and worked hard, Kurt would appreciate all I was doing. I just wanted his acceptance. I honestly thought that is what Kurt wanted." This was a hard thing for her to realize.

I asked her what she thought Kurt wanted from her. She thought about it and said, "My attention. Before I caught him viewing pornography and his affair, we fought because I was so busy at work and was sick dealing with my first pregnancy." Then Allison, being vulnerable, asked me, "Do you think I made him turn to porn and have an affair?" I have been asked this question many times and have thought through how to best respond to this question. Here's what I said, "Absolutely not!"

I explained to her that we can't make anybody do anything. They have agency and choices. For example, Kurt could have continued to express his desire to connect with you. He could have said, "What is happening at home concerns me because I feel like we aren't spending time together, and I want a closer relationship."

I asked her, "If he had done that, how would you have responded?"

"Honestly," she said, "I would have loved to have heard that. Although, I must admit that Kurt did try a few times. I was so focused on getting things done at work and home that I didn't hear what he was trying to say."

I continued answering her question by saying, "In Kurt's mind, he may have justified his action by saying you were unavailable, but in reality, he turned to those coping mechanisms because he didn't know how to reach you. Even then, he was still responsible for finding another way to respond."

I then said, "It isn't hard to find blame. You can blame him; he can blame you; you can blame yourself; he can blame himself. But, ultimately, blame won't help you solve your issues. Think about it; you were doing what you had been taught your whole life. You genuinely thought that if you worked hard enough, you might eventually be enough." Then jokingly, I said, "That was up until ten minutes ago; now you know you are enough, right?" She laughed, and I knew something significant had changed inside her. She wasn't upset at herself, and she seemed less angry at Kurt. She had begun to understand their story and the roots of their problems.

I explained that we all live with unresolved issues from our pasts. When we enter a new relationship, our past thoughts, feelings, experiences, and beliefs do not simply disappear. Instead, they show up as we interact with each other. I said, "Think about your need to be enough. You thought you would eventually feel like you were enough if you worked hard." We all have these blind spots in our lives. As a result, most of us can't see how our past influences our approach to adult relationships. We must seek to understand the past to recreate the same scenarios hoping for a different outcome.

Allison asked me, "How many other blind spots do Kurt and I have?" I replied, "I don't know, "but I do know that you are asking the right questions. Over the subsequent few sessions, we focused not only on the hurt she felt from Kurt's betrayal but some of the beliefs she had formed about herself while growing up.

From our work together, here are a few of the stories that Allison had told herself based on early life experiences and her relationship with Kurt:

Experience	Influence on Thoughts	Influence on Feelings	Influence on Behaviors	Influence on Beliefs
Dad told me I had to work hard to amount to anything	I always thought I had to work harder than everyone else to be noticed or liked.	I was sad and discouraged. I worked so hard for acceptance.	I worked so hard that everywhere I was noticed for my hard work, but even then, I didn't feel like I was good enough.	I believed I was inadequate.
Mom, I forgot to pick up my younger sibling one day on the way home from school. Mom yelled at me and told me I was letting everyone down.	There is something wrong with me. I can't even do small things right.	I was miserable. I felt like I was letting everyone down. I wanted to curl up in a ball and die.	I worked harder. I made sure I never forgot anything again. This helped me get things done in some ways, but it was too late. I am hyper-focused on getting tasks done to a fault.	I am a failure, and I am not enough.
Kurt's use of porn and his affair	So many... main thoughts. I knew this would happen. There is something wrong with me.	I have been so angry and hurt. The person I trusted the most let me down. This just validates that I am not enough.	I have been angrier than I have ever been. I can't sleep well. I don't let him get close to me.	I am inadequate, and I am not enough.

After working through the exercise above, Allison came prepared to deal with the negative thoughts and beliefs plaguing her since she was a little girl. She acknowledged that she and Kurt still had a long way to go, but this exercise helped her shift her beliefs and how she interacted with Kurt. The Zeigarnik effect was now working in their favor. Kurt was more aware of how he had justified his behaviors and began owning his misbehavior. Allison shared with Kurt her past and how his betrayal had triggered wounds from her past.

You will gain important insights as you and your partner take the time to get to the root of your personal and relationship challenges. A few strategies to help you get to the root of your issues include: a) working through an exercise like the one above, b) evaluating your past, c) talking with a therapist, and d) journaling about your past. It has been my experience that individuals and couples who explore the stories they have told themselves develop a better understanding of themselves and their relationships. If you want to improve your awareness, you should take the time to evaluate how your past experiences have influenced you and your approach to your most important relationships.

Before we end this chapter, let's explore another strategy to help you get to the root of the problems in your relationship.

Where Do We Learn Unhealthy Patterns?

In my work with couples, I have observed them often getting stuck in the same patterns. When I ask them how they deal with their disagreements and fights, it takes little time for us to identify their patterns. One partner says or does something hurtful, and the other reacts defensively. They then begin fighting—sometimes with words and sometimes through giving their partner the silent treatment.

In other couples, one partner pulls away, and the other pursues until they get their partner to react. Usually, this results in a raised voice or accusation (i.e., will you ever stop asking about this?).

Another typical pattern I have observed is when both partners pull away (emotionally and physically) for a few days or weeks as they ignore the issue. Eventually, one of them will try to make things right, but the core issues are rarely discussed, and on the surface, it feels as if the problem is resolved.

So, there are two key points here: 1) When couples fight, they often do so in predictable and unhealthy ways, and 2) They rarely talk things through to the point where both feel satisfied with the solution.

When we disagree or fight in our relationship, we all must choose how to respond. While fight patterns are predictable, what needs to be more understood (and rarely discussed) is why each partner responds or deals with conflict the way they do. Why do some people yell while others shut down, and why do some people do everything to make the arguing and fighting stop?

Have you ever considered how you deal with conflict and why you approach it the way you do? To help you better understand your patterns, consider answering these questions:

1. Where did you learn how to deal with conflict?

2. What model for conflict resolution did you experience growing up?

3. How do you deal with conflict similar to or different from your primary caregiver's relationship?

Usually, when I ask these questions in couples' therapy, I find that my clients approach conflict as their parents did. Or, in other cases, they try to do something different than what they learned from their parents. Unfortunately, most people do not have a good model for conflict resolution. As a result, we flounder when faced with relationship difficulties because we don't know what to say or do. As a result, we say and do hurtful things to our partner (e.g., I hate you) or ourselves (e.g., we avoid bringing up the hurt or pain because we don't want to fight, so instead, we end up suffering in silence).

If you and your partner are going to succeed in healing and recovery, it is going to be essential that you learn to deal with conflict more effectively. There has been betrayal and hurt and pain, but how you deal with each other and work to resolve your problems moving forward will be critical to your relationship recovery. Breaking the old patterns and establishing new ones is essential. This will require you to understand your relationship problems in a deeper sense. Some of the issues you will need to deal with on a personal level are relationship issues that need to be resolved between you and your partner.

To help you identify unhealthy patterns you have established in your relationship, here is a short exercise.

Exercise: Think about the last conflict you had with your partner and answer these questions:

1. What was the primary issue to which you fought?

2. What role do I usually take during a conflict?

3. What role does your partner usually take during the conflict?

As you start considering how you and your partner deal with fights, you should also consider looking into the work of Dr. Stephen Karpman. He found that when we argue, we take one of three roles. The three roles are:

Victim: This person believes that other people are out to get them. They often feel like they are not good enough or something is wrong with them.

Persecutor: This person is usually in attack mode. They are critical and often put their partner down through their words or their body language (e.g., gestures, facial expressions, etc.)

Rescuer: The role of the rescuer is to make things better. They attempt to make things better in a variety of ways (e.g., I bought a book for you, maybe it will help you, or they may say, "I'm sorry, please forgive me," but in reality, they say, I'm sorry just to stop the conflict. In most cases, in their attempt to improve the situation, they push their will onto the other person.

Below is an image of what the three roles look like:

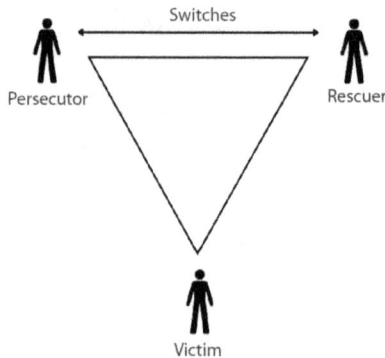

Dr. Karpman observed couples and found that individuals take one or more of these roles in almost all conflicts between two or more people. He also observed that during the conflict, individuals switch roles. For example, one person might initially feel like a victim (e.g., I'm not enough for you), but when their partner does something to push their buttons, they choose to retaliate (e.g., I am so tired of you telling me that I'm not enough. I can't believe I had stayed with you this long. You have wasted my time). In this case, they have shifted from feeling like a victim to lashing out and becoming the persecutor with their words.

Below is an example of both partners who are caught in the Karpman Triangle (aka the Drama Triangle).

3 Roles We Take on During Conflict Betraying Partner	Things I Have Done
Victim	I'm not good enough for you; you should leave me.
Persecutor	You are never going to forgive me.
Rescuer	I will do anything; just tell me what you want me to do.
3 Roles We Take on During Conflict Betrayed Partner	Things I Have Said or Done
Victim	You don't want me.
Persecutor	You are an idiot. Why don't you go screw your mistress?
Rescuer	I bought this book. Would you read it? I think it can help you with your problem.

Note: You can find a copy of this exercise in Appendix D.

According to Dr. Stephen Karpman, couples usually take on one of these three roles when they fight. However, he has found that it is common for couples to switch roles, shifting from the victim role to the persecutor role or the persecutor role to the rescuer role. He believes the more switches couples make as they interact, the more intense their fighting will be. Over the past few years, I have used an experiential exercise with couples using the Karpman Triangle to show them how these patterns appear in their relationship. When couples understand these roles and how they have influenced their relationship, they ask me, "How do we get out of the triangle to break these habits?"

Below is a list of six steps I have used to help couples address these unhealthy fighting patterns.

- We fight based on unmet needs or expectations. We must address the unmet need and expectations.

- When couples fight, they usually trigger unresolved issues from their past together and personal life problems that haven't been resolved earlier.

- Couples need to discover how their personal beliefs (i.e., I am unlovable, I don't matter) manifest in their relationship and address the belief).

- If change is going to occur, both partners must take personal responsibility for themselves and choose not to engage in the conflictual behaviors described in the triangle.

- Both partners must explore different options when problems arise in their relationship (e.g., take a short break so the fighting does not escalate, choose to listen to seek understanding, etc.).

- Both partners must work together to solve their relationship problems and identify ways to negotiate, even when disagreeing.

Based on what you know of Kurt and Allison's story, here's what that would look like for them in their relationship:

We fight based on unmet needs or expectations. We want to discuss the unmet needs and expectations.

Kurt: I expected you always to be there, and I didn't express my need to connect effectively.

Kurt's Solution: Instead of getting upset when you are tired or worn out, I can support you and ask if we can relax and hold each other for a few minutes.

Allison: I expected you to support me in my work and pregnancy. I thought that if I worked hard enough, you would love me.

Allison's Solution: I will be aware of when I get caught up in proving myself and slow down so I can genuinely be with you.

When couples fight, they usually trigger unresolved issues from their past together and personal life problems that haven't been resolved.

Kurt: I had struggled earlier in my life with porn and wasn't honest with you when we married. That was a mistake.

Kurt's Solution: While I wasn't honest with you about my past porn use, I can be frank with you moving forward. I am committed to being accountable.

Allison: I had unresolved issues with my dad from childhood that made me feel inadequate. I have been trying to prove that I am enough.

Allison's Solutions: I will address the belief that I'm inadequate and not enough that was formed in my childhood. When I do this, I want to feel adequate and that I am enough.

Couples need to discover how their personal beliefs (i.e., I am unlovable, I don't matter) manifest in their relationship and address the belief).

Kurt: I am a failure; I am not enough.

Kurt's Solution: I need to resolve these shame-based beliefs. Over time he would come to believe he is enough and not a failure. I am committed to resolving these beliefs.

Allison: I am inadequate; I am not enough.

Allison's Solutions: Address her experiences with her dad and other experiences that contributed to her negative beliefs. She would eventually come to know that she is enough and not inadequate.

If change is going to occur, both partners must take personal responsibility for themselves and choose not to engage in the conflictual behaviors described in the triangle.

Kurt: I was playing the victim role. I felt like Allison didn't love me because she was busy.

Kurt's Solution: I can stop acting out. I will seek professional help. I need to understand Allison better and be more supportive. Instead of withholding love and affection, I need to be more loving.

Allison: I felt angry at Kurt and withheld love. I have been the persecutor because I felt hurt and angry.

Allison's Solution: I don't have to be angry to express my hurt. I can communicate openly and honestly about my pain.

Both partners must explore different options when problems arise in their relationship (e.g., take a short break so the fighting doesn't escalate, choose to listen to seek understanding, etc.).

Kurt: I shut down when Allison wasn't responsive. I became resentful because she was busy, and I believed she didn't have time for me.

Kurt's Solution: Instead of shutting down and ignoring Allison when I am frustrated, I can approach her and let her know I want to talk and connect with her. I can practice my deep listening skills (See Chapter Five).

Allison: I used to feel like Kurt was acting like my dad. I needed to meet his expectations if he disagreed with me on something. In truth, that made me feel angry with him, and I focused more on our child and my work.

Allison's Solution: When Kurt reminds me of my dad, I must remember he is NOT my dad. I need to stay present with him and understand his request.

Both partners must work together to solve their relationship problems and identify ways to negotiate, even when disagreeing.

Kurt: In the past, we couldn't negotiate. I would feel like Allison shut down my attempt to communicate and would be the victim. I also felt angry and attempted to rescue myself by acting out.

Kurt's Solution: When I feel frustrated with Allison, I will take a step back and remember that she felt like she was not adequate or enough. If I remember that, I will see the real her instead of feeling like she is hurting me.

Allison: I have been angry at Kurt and haven't wanted to connect with him. I have yet to see the value in discussing our issues.

Allison's Solution: I will listen to Kurt's concerns or desires instead of showing my anger. I will practice seeing him, not how he has hurt me. I will remember that he does feel shame for what he did. He felt like he was not enough. I need to remember this when we are in conflict.

The Karpman Triangle exercise was designed to help couples understand how they deal with conflict. While it does help identify these patterns, it also allows couples to recognize how their personal beliefs influence their relationship, how taking personal responsibility can help them stay out of unhealthy conflict patterns, and how to more effectively solve the problem by exploring options together and learning to negotiate differences when they arise.

As a quick review, in this chapter, the focus has been on getting to the root of the problem in your relationship. It is important to note that Kurt and Allison's story, as shared, took place over a couple of years and included many difficult challenges.

The personal awareness and insights shared in the later part of this chapter took them months and months of hard work. Please don't be discouraged if you and your partner aren't at this place in your healing and recovery journey.

I have shared Kurt and Allison's journey and responses so that you can see what is possible. Their story inspires me because it gives me hope for your relationship and countless other couples. Their story can be yours. You can heal and recover.

As you continue reading this book and practicing the exercises outlined, you will gain new insights and ideas on rebuilding your relationship. You will have the same information and tools that they were given. You and your partner can do this, but remember that lasting change takes time and effort; it is a process.

Key Takeaways from This Chapter

- Relationship ruptures from the past need to be understood and addressed. One way to address relationship ruptures is to identify the stories we tell ourselves in our relationships.

- Another way to get to the root of our problems is to identify the patterns we have created in our relationships, especially around conflict.

- An effective way to understand our patterns is to look at how we take on one of three roles in conflict (Victim, Persecutor, Rescuer)

- If we are going to break out of old patterns of conflict, we need to: 1) Identify and discuss our unmet needs and expectations; 2) Recognize that our fights usually trigger unresolved issues from our past; 3) Identify how personal beliefs are influencing the way we approach relationships; 4) Take personal responsibility for yourself and choose not to engage in the con-flictual behaviors outlined in the triangle; 5) Couples need to brainstorm together as many options as possible so when they are in conflict they have a plan; 6) Couples need to work to solve issues together by learning to negotiate, especially when they disagree with each other.

Chapter Three

Create the Right Environment for Healing and Recovery

"Our capacity to destroy one another is matched by our capacity to heal one another. Restoring relationships and community is central to restoring well-being."
-Bessel van der Kolk—The Body Keeps the Score

The Role of Safety in Healing and Recovery

Five therapists had told the client sitting in front of me that she had a personality disorder. In my profession, individuals dealing with personality disorders are some of the most difficult to treat, and usually, they do not stay in therapy long enough to make significant progress. Fortunately, I am no longer concerned about labels or what someone's diagnosis may be.

When she told me about other therapists' diagnoses, I said, "I don't want to offend you, but I don't care what others have said. I am most concerned about helping you find more peace and happiness. So, for now, I just want to get to know you and learn more about what you are going through." She looked surprised and said, "Ok." She was visiting my office from another state and was hoping I could help her and her husband work through issues related to his sexual betrayal.

Over the next three days, I listened and learned about a woman who had suffered deeply in her childhood. She discussed abandonment early in her life by her father, an emotionally unavailable mother, and abuse from random people who came in and out of her life. After listening to her story, I concluded that I would probably have every diagnosis in the DSM-V (Diagnostic and Statistical Manual for Mental Disorders) if I were her. She didn't have any reason to trust me or anyone else.

What do you say to someone who has suffered so much from neglectful and abusive parents? How do you help someone who can't trust others because almost everyone in their life has let them down? Sadly, her trauma was not just from her childhood issues. The one person she thought she could trust cheated on her.

Throughout my career, I have asked myself over and over how I could be of help to such individuals. I conclude that I can be attentive and listen, so they feel heard and understood. Then, when I have earned their trust, I can provide guidance and support. I have also learned not to push for change; instead, I have discovered a need for my clients to feel safe and pace themselves with my support.

She and her husband were sitting in my office. They had flown in from out of state to meet with me and see if I could help them salvage their marriage. They were both worn out. While they both desired to repair their relationship, they were skeptical that their patterns could change. She felt hopeless that she could risk trusting him again, and the emotional roller-coaster of their relationship wore him out. She was begging him to comfort her one moment, and she was yelling at him the next.

Over the three days that we met together; I spent hours listening to her story. As I asked questions, and she responded, her husband was surprised at how much she shared. She had never opened up like this to him. At one point, she looked up and said, "I don't know how to say this, but you are the first person who has ever listened to me like this. I feel heard and understood for the first time in my life." At this point, I knew that I had earned her trust. Simultaneously, her husband had learned to listen to her with a different set of ears. Our natural ears hear anger and yelling, and our compassionate ears hear suffering and sorrow.

I open this chapter with this story because true healing and real recovery will most likely occur when you feel safe enough to share your pain, hurt, secrets, and untold stories. The first principle of ALL human connections is safety. When we feel safe, we can let down our guard to create meaningful human relationships.

In contrast, we are protective, defensive, scared, and avoidant when we don't feel safe. At this time, due to betrayal, you and your partner are likely struggling to create a safe environment in your relationship. I hope to help you discover the principles that lead to safety and trust so you can reconnect in your relationship. This is essential to your healing because researchers have discovered that it is only in safe and trusting environments that our bodies overcome their most natural tendency to fight or flee. (1)

Safety in Relationships

When we are safe in our relationships, we relax in each other's presence. This safety allows us to openly share our thoughts and feelings, good and bad, with each other. Only when we feel safe can we let our guard down and connect on a deeper level.

Throughout this book, we will continually return to this principle—Human intimacy and connection are only possible in an environment where we can relax. If you want to rebuild your relationship, you and your partner must learn how to create this type of environment with each other. If you cannot create safety, the depth of your relationship connection may be limited.

Many of you reading this book do not yet feel safe enough to be vulnerable with your partner. That is expected at this point in your journey. However, as you proceed through this book, I aim to provide you with ideas to increase the safety and connection in your relationship. I assume you are reading this book because you want a better relationship. If that is accurate, let's help you do what you can to build upon the first principle of human connection: SAFETY.

I can hear you asking, "Is that possible in our relationship after sexual betrayal and years of lying and deception?" My answer to this question is, "Yes, even in relationships where significant betrayal has occurred, safety can be re-established. It won't be easy, but it is possible." In this chapter, I will walk you through the core principles that build safety in relationships, and then I will help you understand how to implement them in your relationship.

How, you ask? In your relationship, the healing process begins when you trust yourself. It is difficult to connect in relationships until you have established safety with yourself. If you have been working on the steps outlined in the first two chapters, you have already started the healing process. Those chapters included a significant amount of personal work and orienting yourself. You are increasing your awareness by gaining insight into yourself and your hurts and pains. The change process improves as our insight grows. As you work through personal issues, your mind will begin to re-establish your place of safety. Let me explain more about how you can be safe with yourself.

Being Safe with Yourself

Throughout my career, I have sat with men and women whose lives have been turned upside down because of sexual behaviors. I have seen grown men cry and women who have been irreconcilable. In each case, the pain and anguish has been palpable. My heart hurts for each of these individuals. As I have sat with them, there is one common theme I hear, they say, "Something is wrong with me." Ultimately, the guilt of hurting one's family triggers feelings of being a failure, not good enough, and powerless. At the same time, sexual betrayal opens one up to feeling like they are not enough, or they are unlovable. In my experience, both the betrayed and the betrayer have thoughts and accompanying emotions that lead them to conclude that they are flawed in some way.

I have often asked myself, how do incredible people come to believe that they are unlovable, not enough, or a failure? The easy answer is that my partner cheated on me; what else am I supposed to believe? Or, I have ruined my family. How could I not feel like a failure? However, such thoughts are limiting and prevent us from feeling other emotions or thinking differently. After all, what are any of us supposed to do with the thought, "I am a failure" or "I am unlovable." These limiting beliefs are often felt and thought but are not true. I learned long ago that just because we have a thought doesn't mean it is true.

Let me give you a few alternatives:

- You are a person of infinite worth and value.

- You matter.

- You are important.

- You can heal.

- You can recover.

If you are like most of my clients, you need help with this list. You have become accustomed to the other thoughts and emotions (i.e., I am a failure, not good enough, etc.). Regarding our thoughts and emotions and how they influence us, Dr. Joe Dispenza wrote, "You know that when you repeatedly recreate the same emotions until you cannot think any greater than how you feel, your feelings are now the means of your thinking. And since your feelings are a record of previous experiences, you're thinking in the past. And by quantum law, you create more of the past." (2) He continued by writing, "Most of us live in the past and resist living in a new future. Why? The body is so habituated to memorizing the chemical records of our past experiences that it grows attached to these emotions. In a very real sense, we become addicted to those familiar feelings. So, when we want to look to the future and dream of new vistas and bold landscapes in our not-too-distant reality, the body, whose currency is feelings, resists the sudden change in direction." (3)

In essence, we become stuck in thought patterns and emotional states. If I could be in your head 24/7, what thoughts would I hear, and what emotions would I feel?

If I could track every thought you had for twenty-four hours, how many of them would be positive, and how many would be negative? Naturally, we humans tend to be more biased toward negative thinking, so much so that some researchers believe that up to 80% of our thoughts are negative. (4)

To make matters worse, according to the research of Dr. Fred Luskin of Stanford University, a human being has approximately 60,000 thoughts per day—and 90% of these are repetitive. (5) It is not easy to change our thoughts and feelings without developing a plan.

If you create lasting change in your life, you will have to think of new thoughts, experience new emotions, act in different ways, and alter the negative beliefs you have formed about yourself. I cannot emphasize the importance of this enough in the healing and recovery process. You may wonder how you can change these core areas, thoughts, emotions, behavior, and beliefs.

Let me begin my answer with a short story. A few years ago, my 4-year-old daughter put on a cute dress as we prepared to attend a meeting. She looked beautiful with her dress and wonderful smile. I looked at her and said, "You are beautiful." She looked up at me and said, "I know."

I wish she kept that attitude through her junior high and high school years, but like most teenagers, she had other life experiences that made her question her original belief. I have concluded that we are all born with high self-worth and that only life's experiences make us question that worth. At some point in our lives, we are confronted with life events that make us question our identity, worth, and value. However, I am convinced that we wouldn't question our worth or value if we could see the pure and innocent baby (us). We would inherently know that we are good.

So, what happened? Life. Trauma. Abuse. Neglect. Addiction. Abandonment. Being bullied. Being rejected and being told we are not enough. These and many other life events make us question our core identity. So how do we decide who we really are? Are we the sum of our life experiences? Does our value or worth depend on others' validation? Can imperfect human beings determine your worth and mine? I think not!

> *We are all of infinite worth and value, and no one or no life experience can alter this fundamental truth.*

If our most natural state is one like my 4-year-old daughter's (you are beautiful—I know), then the alternative negative thoughts such as I am stupid, not enough, unlovable, or a failure will create internal stress for us because these thoughts are not congruent with our true self. If you can accept this idea, then your healing from trauma and recovery from unwanted sexual behaviors will be accelerated by simply coming back to your true identity. You will be safe(r) being with yourself.

Three Barriers to Establishing Personal Safety

#1: Avoiding your own emotions

Unfortunately, when we are in emotional pain and distress, we want to escape and escape from ourselves. Instead of learning to be with ourselves in emotional pain, we seek to avoid our thoughts and emotions by numbing ourselves out. As a result, we often turn to other things to soothe ourselves (e.g., spending, drinking, working, gambling, etc.) to avoid being with ourselves. It is common for us to attempt to get away from emotional pain; that may be why 34% of individuals report that they engage in some form of self-harm after discovering their partner's betrayal (6) and why 68% of individuals who turn to porn report feeling hopeless after viewing it, and 78% feeling bad about themselves after consuming it. (7)

One of the solutions to avoiding or ignoring our inner pain and hurt is to have the courage to turn and face difficult emotions. To illustrate how we often avoid our painful thoughts and feelings, I would like to share a short story about cows and buffaloes, as shared by Rory Vaden. Rory grew up on the plains of Colorado, where he observed that cows and buffaloes share the same land. He noted that seeing how these two animals responded when storms came over the mountains was always interesting.

He wrote, "When storms come, they almost always brew from the west and roll out toward the east. What cows do is very natural. Cows sense the storm coming from the west, so they try to run toward the east. The only problem is that if you know anything about cows, you know they aren't very fast. So, the storm catches up with the cows rather quickly. And without knowing any better, the cows continue to try to outrun the storm. But, instead of out running the storm, they actually run right along with the storm. Maximizing the amount of pain, time, and frustration they experience from that storm!" (8)

In contrast, he observed that the buffaloes respond quite differently when the storm comes. Regarding the buffaloes' response, he wrote, "What buffaloes do, on the other hand, is unique for the animal kingdom. Buffaloes wait for the storm to cross right over the crest of the peak of the mountaintop, and as the storm rolls over the ridge, the buffaloes turn and charge directly into the storm. Instead of running east away from the storm, they run west directly at the storm. By running at the storm, they run straight through it. Minimizing the amount of pain and time and frustration they experience from that storm." (9)

As I have reflected on the importance of learning to be with ourselves when experiencing difficult emotions, the story of the cows and the buffaloes often comes into my mind. It is hard to find peace when our inner core is not at ease. We need to learn how to deal with difficult emotions. Colorado's cows and buffaloes demonstrate two different approaches to dealing with the weather, much like we do with emotional pain. While running away may seem more attractive in the short term, facing our emotions head-on will benefit us more in the long run. While it may not be easy in the beginning, by facing challenges in your life, both personal and relational, you are more likely to increase your feeling of safety.

#2: Unresolved Shame

In my work, shame is one of the biggest barriers to feeling safe with oneself. When we feel shame, how we see ourselves and others becomes a barrier to creating safety in our relationships. Researchers have discovered that shame often leads us to shift the blame or responsibility of our actions towards others. Regarding this, Tangney and Dearing wrote, "Individuals of all ages in states of shame are likely to 'shift the blame elsewhere,' externalizing the problem and directing rage at the supposed source of the problem." (10) Shame has also been found to influence our ability to feel empathy for others. According to Tangney and Dearing's research, individuals feeling guilt are more likely to have empathy, whereas those who are caught up in shame are less empathic. (11)

Shame often manifests itself in thoughts such as, "I am not enough," "I am unlovable," and "I am a failure." Shame also shows up in emotional expressions like anger and rage. When these thoughts and feelings run through our minds and behaviors with others, we cannot feel internal peace or safety.

Shame is also a tremendous barrier to creating safety in relationships. When you feel like a failure or that you can never be enough, and in worse case scenarios that it would be better if you were never born, it is hard to be safe with yourself, let alone with your partner. Shame influences how we see ourselves and others. Usually, when shame is high, we avoid connecting with others. (12) Later in this book, I will spend more time discussing the essential role of shame reduction in healing for both partners. I now bring shame into the spotlight because it is one of the most significant barriers to creating a safe environment.

#3: No Boundaries

One of the difficulties of being a therapist is hearing the most painful stories our clients have been through. It is hard to understand how humans choose to treat other humans. Some of the most challenging stories I have heard deal with individuals whose personal boundaries have been violated. While describing his life, one man said, "I feel like I am walking around with a shirt on that says, "Abuse me, everyone else has." Many individuals who come to therapy report having never felt safe with others. Sadly, when there are no boundaries, there is chaos and pain—the opposite of safety.

One of the most important ways to find inner peace and peace in our interaction with others is by establishing and creating boundaries in our lives. In the book, *Setting Psychological Boundaries*, the authors describe the importance of creating boundaries in our lives this way, "As we draw invisible boundary lines, we are not building walls to keep the enemy out. On the contrary, we keep our lines intact to preserve our relationships. Once we clearly define our boundaries, we begin to communicate openly and directly. And we establish guidelines for what we expect of others—and what we should give them in return. But suppose we grow up in homes that don't function well in terms of communication or understanding or enter into destructive marriages. In that case, boundaries are not respected, and we become confused, vulnerable, and insecure. We don't attempt to defend our rights because we don't realize we have any!" (13)

Later, in Chapter Eleven, I will discuss boundaries and their role in the healing and recovery process. For now, however, it is vital to understand that your ability to establish personal boundaries will significantly influence your safety. If you have acted out, your boundaries will protect you from further harming yourself and your partner. Your boundaries will help you feel more secure if you have been betrayed.

Introduction to the Polyvagal Theory

A few years ago, as I reviewed the results of more than 10,000 individuals who had been betrayed, I discovered that nearly 98% of the respondents reported being angry when talking with their partner after discovery. I thought to myself, 98% report that they are angry. The same percentage of people also indicated they were more critical of their partner after discovery. (14) Rarely in research do we find such elevated numbers.

For years, I have been trying to understand what sexual betrayal does to the mind and body. When the results revealed that 98% of betrayed partners reported being angry and critical of their partner, I naturally wanted to understand why anger was the most common response.

Upon further reflection, I didn't want to settle with the idea that people just get angry after betrayal. I tried to understand why anger was one of the most common emotions after sexual betrayal. I wanted to understand what drove the anger. It was at this time, while searching for answers, that I discovered the Polyvagal Theory and the work of Dr. Stephen Porges. Below you will find a few of his quotes that have significantly increased my understanding of why betrayed partners frequently respond angrily.

Dr. Stephen Porges: "As long as people (and animals) feel threatened, they cannot meaningfully engage with members of their tribe and will resort to more primitive and solipsistic fight-or-flight behaviors (mobilization mediated by the sympathetic nervous system) to ensure survival." (15)

My Thoughts: Sexual betrayal triggered many responses (i.e., anger with a spouse and isolation from others. As I reviewed research data and asked my clients about their reactions to sexual betrayal, most reported that the stability of their relationship felt threatened. As a result, most of them felt unsafe connecting with their partner on a deeper level. Unfortunately, it wasn't just their partner that they struggled to feel safe with; as many as 73% of my research participants reported that they struggled to trust anyone after discovery, and 68% said that they felt like they didn't belong in social settings anymore. (16)

Dr. Stephen Porges: "When the environment is appraised as being safe, the defensive limbic structures are inhibited. This makes it possible to be socially engaged with calm visceral states. (17)

My Thoughts: When I realized that only when we appraise our environment to be safe do we let down our natural desire to protect ourselves, I realized that betrayed partners struggle to appraise (or make sense of) their partner's betrayal. What they initially thought was safe no longer feels safe and predictable. This understanding helped me comprehend the physiological response of betrayed partners. When we don't feel safe, we naturally turn to a fight or flight response. This information made it much easier for me to understand why betrayed partners were angry and why they were struggling to reconnect with their partners and others in society.

Here are a few other concepts that came from the polyvagal theory that helped me better understand the critical role that feeling safe plays in relationship connections:

Neuroception is the process through which the nervous system evaluates risk without requiring awareness. (18) Our bodies have a built-in mechanism designed to assess safety and danger.

What allows engagement behaviors to occur while disabling the mechanisms of defense? To switch effectively from defensive to social engagement strategies, the nervous system must do two things: (1) assess risk, and (2) if the environment looks safe, inhibit the primitive defensive reactions to fight, flee, or freeze. (19)

The collective work continues to emphasize that our mental and physical health can thrive only when our autonomic nervous system is in a state of safety. (20)

The idea of neuroception can seem overwhelming, but it is pretty simple. The key concept is this; our bodies have a built-in safety mechanism that helps us determine if we are safe or not. If we feel safe with others, our bodies relax, and we can bond with our partners and others socially. Conversely, when we don't feel safe, we put up our defenses and shift into a protective mode, which is to fight or flee. In worst-case scenarios, we completely shut down to the point we don't fight or flee; we freeze.

Finally, after years of study and research, the work of Dr. Porges helped me better understand why betrayed partners frequently responded with anger after discovering their partner's sexual betrayal. I had spent hundreds of hours listening to betrayed partners share their stories of how their partners' unwanted sexual behaviors had made them so angry.

I had also met with hundreds of betraying partners, who were fighting back due to the intensity of criticism they received from their partners. It is natural to fight back when we are feeling attacked. As a result, both partners are prone to escalate anger. The betrayed are fighting because they feel deceived and scared. The betraying partner, at times, would fight anger with anger (by shifting the blame elsewhere—I wouldn't have done this if you hadn't… or they would flee—leave the room/house when their partner was upset or angry). The Polyvagal Theory helped me understand both partners' responses after the discovery of sexual betrayal.

Furthermore, I realized that both of their responses are common. The human body has a predictable reaction during tension or conflict. The autonomic nervous system (ANS) kicks into action and takes over, which triggers a natural response to fight, flight, or freeze.

What happens when couples get stuck in the ANS fight, flight, or freeze response? Usually, the outcome is a lot of late nights arguing about the details or avoiding each other because nothing good happens when you try to talk about what happened. Throughout my career, I have noticed couples feeling helpless and hopeless, as if they are stuck because they don't know how to resolve their problem. The consequence is that they develop many unhealthy behaviors in their relationships. For many, safety feels like it is nearly impossible. Many clients report that their medical doctors told them they had to reduce stress. Telling a person to reduce stress is entirely different from explaining how to do it. Here's a short list of some of the most common challenges individuals and couples face when they can't resolve their issues: a) elevated stress—blood pressure; b) health problems—IBS, chronic fatigue, weakened immune system; c) loneliness; d) lack of productivity at work and home; e) depression; and f) anxiety.

What Safety in Relationships Looks Like

Hopefully, by now, it is clear that finding and creating safety in your personal and relationship life is key to your healing and recovery. Dr. Bessel van der Kolk emphasized this idea when he wrote, "Being able to feel safe with other people is probably the single most important aspect of mental health; safe connections are fundamental to meaningful and satisfying lives." (21)

This chapter will conclude by focusing on the basic tenets of creating safety in your life and your relationship.

I want to reiterate what safety is and what safety is not. When we are safe in relationships, we never fear for our physical safety. When we are safe, we can let our guard down and share our more profound thoughts and emotions (i.e., fears, worries, anxieties, hopes, and dreams). We can share our thoughts and ideas without fear of being judged or criticized. In safe relationships, we feel valued and understood. As one client said, "I feel like I am at home."

However, safety is not just about the thoughts we have and the emotions we feel. When we are safe, our body responds and relaxes in the other's presence. In other words, our bodies are telling us that we are safe.

Recently, while working with a couple during a three-day intensive, I observed a couple shift from being rigid and cold towards each other to being cuddly and connected. During the first two days, they refused to sit close to one another. They could hardly look at each other. Then after our second afternoon together, they left my office with a better understanding of their unhealthy patterns. They had discovered how their actions were harming their relationship. That evening they reported slipping back into their old fighting pattern. However, instead, they both choose to pause and listen to each other. They validated the other person's pain and hurt.

The next day, the husband asked if he could address the group. He began by apologizing for his behaviors and openly expressed to his wife that he was sorry for gaslighting her and being distant and cold. He also acknowledged that he wanted a better relationship with her. By the end of the third day, they were holding hands, looking into each other's eyes, and being playful.

I share stories like this because I want you to have an end goal in mind. Even though most of you reading may not be close to this type of safety in your relationship, I hope that you will realize that as you apply the concepts discussed in this book, you will choose to create safety in your relationship. If you succeed in rebuilding your relationship, creating a safe relationship will be a natural outcome.

The Polyvagal Model for Creating Safety

To heal your relationship, you must engage with each other in new ways socially. The old patterns will not work. Therefore, activating your social engagement system so connections can occur will require you to think new thoughts, feel new emotions, act better, and change unhealthy beliefs. Below is a model that will explain the end goal. It was developed by Deb Dana, who has helped therapists understand how to implement the Polyvagal Theory with their clients.

Safety	Outcome
Ventral Vagus	Calm, relaxed, comfortable, creating, connection, fun
Autonomic Nervous System (ANS)	Fight = conflict and tension
	Flee = avoidance, ignore, escape.
Freeze (Dorsal Vagal)	Stuck, Hopeless, Helpless

Deb Dana has identified a great way to describe how we move from one emotional state toward another. Her model is called the Autonomic Ladder. In her ladder, there are three rungs. On the lowest level is the freeze response. When we freeze, we feel stuck and hopeless.

Regarding this place, Dana wrote, "Our oldest pathway of response, the dorsal vagal pathway of the parasympathetic branch, is the path of last resort. When all else fails, when we are trapped, and action-taking doesn't work, the 'primitive vagus' takes us into shutdown, collapse, and dissociation. Here at the very bottom of the autonomic ladder, I am alone with my despair and escape into not knowing, not feeling, almost a sense of not being. I might describe myself as hopeless, abandoned, foggy, too tired to think or act, and the world as empty, dead, and dark." (22)

In a frozen state, our mind struggles to make sense of information. While in the frozen state, connecting with self and others is difficult. Betrayed partners often report feeling numb. I have also had betraying partners describe moments after discovery where they felt hopeless and in despair as they realized how their behaviors harmed their partner and children.

Next is the middle rung on the ladder. This is where the autonomic nervous system (ANS) resides. Dana described the middle of the ladder, "The sympathetic branch of the autonomic nervous system activates when we feel a stirring of unease—when something triggers a neuroception of danger. We go into action; fight or flight happens here. In this state, our heart rate speeds up, and our breath is short and shallow; we scan our environment looking for danger—we are "on the move." I might describe myself as anxious or angry and feel the rush of adrenaline that makes it hard for me to be still. I may only listen to the sounds of danger and wouldn't hear the sounds of friendly voices. The world may feel dangerous, chaotic, and unfriendly. From this place of sympathetic mobilization—a step down the autonomic ladder and backward on the evolutionary time line, I may believe the world is a dangerous place, and I need to protect myself from harm." (23)

When I first heard this description from Deb Dana, she perfectly described my clients. Clients would often monitor their partner's every move to determine whether they were honest or lying. Ultimately, after betrayal, many betrayed partners seek confirmation by asking this question of their partner, "Am I safe with you?" Because they cannot tell, they often turn to self-preservation (fight or flight).

Simultaneously, the betraying partners are dealing with their frustrations. They often feel ashamed of their own behaviors and report that they don't know how to respond to their partner. They have explained it to me this way, "At times, my partner wants me to comfort them, and at other times, I am being screamed at." This emotional roller coaster often makes them put up their guard for protection. As a result, they are also in self-preservation mode. Here are the options when both partners are in fight or flight mode:

Both Partners in ANS	Outcome
Fight-Fight	A big battle
Fight-Flee	One person is on the attack while the other leaves. The person on attack often feels abandoned because their partner won't stay and work things through. The one leaving feels emotionally overwhelmed and, as a result, flees the conflict.
Flee-Flee	Both partners avoid each other. They give each other the silent treatment. Eventually, one partner attempts to reconnect. This is what is called a bid attempt. Sometimes the effort to reconnect is met with resistance or continued avoidance of the issue.

Think about what that means for your relationship. You cannot heal if you or your partner are stuck in the autonomic nervous system (Fight or flight) or dorsal vagal

(Freeze) response. If you find yourself or your partner in fight, flight, or freeze mode, you already know that connection is impossible in these emotional states.

What Is the Solution?

The answer lies in our ventral vagal pathway. This is how Dana described this essential part of our ANS, "Safety and connection are guided by the evolutionarily newest part of the autonomic nervous system. Our social engagement system is active in the ventral vagal pathway of the parasympathetic branch. In this state, our heart rate is regulated, our breath is full, we take in the faces of friends, and we can tune in to conversations and tune out the distracting noises. We see the "big picture" and connect to the world and its people. I might describe myself as happy, active, and interested and the world as safe, fun, and peaceful. From this ventral vagal place at the top of the autonomic ladder, I am connected to my experiences and can reach out to others.

Some of the daily living experiences of this state include being organized, following through with plans, taking care of myself, taking time to play, doing things with others, feeling productive at work, and having a general feeling of regulation and a sense of management. Health benefits include a healthy heart, regulated blood pressure, a healthy immune system decreasing my vulnerability to illness, good digestion, quality sleep, and an overall sense of well-being." (24)

Given your current situation, the idea of safety does not sound reasonable. Our goal should be to find ways to be "firmly grounded in our ventral vagal pathway." (25) Doing so will make you feel safe and connected to yourself and others. We can be calm and engage in socially bonding activities. When I introduce this concept to couples at the beginning of their healing and recovery journey, they look at me like I am speaking a foreign language.

In the rest of this chapter and subsequent ones, I will share some principles that can shift your relationship from one based on fight, flight, or freeze to one where budding elements of safety and connection can begin.

Beginning Steps to Create Safety and Connection After Sexual Betrayal

Throughout my career, many clients have asked me if they can ever feel safe again in their relationship after sexual betrayal. My answer is never simply a yes or a no. Instead, I offer the strategies I have found to be effective with clients who have successfully rebuilt trust. For example, couples have a better chance of creating safety when each of the following elements is a part of their healing journey together.

Safety with Self

Early in this chapter, the importance of being safe with yourself was discussed. I want to re-emphasize that being kind to yourself is essential to creating safety in your relationship. If you are mentally beating yourself up, it is hard to stay present with others when they share good or difficult things with you.

Therefore, the first step to creating safety in your relationship is to be kind to yourself. If you hurt your partner through your actions, you may think I need to make things better with them first. By moving towards personal healing and recovery, you are setting the foundation for personal and relationship healing.

Regarding the importance of self-kindness, Dr. Kristin Neff wrote, "When we soothe our agitated minds with self-compassion, we're better able to notice what's right as well as what's wrong, so that we can orient ourselves toward that which gives us joy." (26)

In order to be kind to yourself, you need to resolve internalized shame and deal with negative thoughts that run through your mind. Strategies to deal with shame are addressed in Chapter Four.

Emotional Regulation

When I work with clients with infidelity and betrayal, I hear stories from both partners that they have felt out of control. Betraying partners say things like, "My behaviors were out of control,' and betrayed partners have said, "I have never been this angry." After discovery, emotions tend to be all over the place. Yelling, screaming, criticizing, and intense exchanges are the norm. I have found that in some cases, the intense interactions between couples increase instead of decrease (not decreasing) over time. I believe this is due to the Zeigarnik effect, which suggests that we spend up to 90% of our energy dealing with unresolved issues. When couples cannot resolve their conflict, they naturally feel tension when they are together. As a result, couples' unresolved issues continue to play a significant role in their future conflicts. I have had many couples tell me that they repeat the same fight over and over. Constant fighting creates helplessness and hopelessness as the conflict reduces their hopes of finding a solution.

While there are many components of the healing process, emotional regulation is one of the more effective solutions for resolving conflict and reducing tension in relationships. Researchers have discovered that emotional regulation helps us respond effectively in difficult relationship situations. If you haven't heard the term emotional regulation, you may be familiar with the term affect regulation. The general idea is that we increase our capacity to interact with others in difficult situations by learning to respond to our emotions effectively.

Daniel Hill, the author of *Affect Regulation Theory*, wrote about emotional regulation, "When affect is regulated, the organism is integrated and able to respond flexibly to the internal and external environments. We experience a sense of self-mastery, and indeed, when regulated, we are optimally functional. When affect is dysregulated, we become dissociated (disintegrated) and reduced to automated processes and isolated portions of our memory. In other words, the organization of the self is affect state dependent. We organize and disorganize depending on whether or not we are regulated." (27)

Hill's explanation helps make sense of why so many people feel "out of sorts" after betrayal. They have a hard time organizing their thoughts and emotions because they can't regulate them. This may be especially true for individuals who have experienced other life traumas. Dr. Bessel van der Kolk, in his book *The Body, Keeps the Score*, added, "Since emotional regulation is the critical issue in managing the effects of trauma and neglect, it would make an enormous difference if teachers, army sergeants, foster parents, and mental health professionals were thoroughly schooled in emotional-regulation techniques." (28) I want to add couples and parents to his list.

As we learn to regulate our emotions, we naturally feel more in control of ourselves. By developing our skills in affect regulation, we gain deeper insights into ourselves and others. Below are the top method researchers have found to be effective in developing our emotional regulation skills.

The neuroscientist Joseph LeDoux and his colleagues have shown that the only way we can consciously access the emotional brain is through *self-awareness* (i.e., by activating the medial prefrontal cortex, the part of the brain that notices what is going on inside us and thus allows us to feel what we're feeling). (29)

Neuroscience research shows that the only way we can change the way we feel is by becoming aware of our inner experience and learning to befriend what is going on inside ourselves. Simply noticing what you feel fosters emotional regulation and helps you stop trying to ignore what is happening inside you. (30)

Some of the best research-based approaches to help you gain more self-awareness include:

- Mindfulness
- Yoga

- Neurofeedback
- Guided meditations

While self-awareness is key to increasing your emotional regulation, it is also essential to develop relationship awareness. By raising your personal awareness, you can become curious about your partner. Clients who have betrayed and been betrayed see their partners through the lens of fear. Their partner is no longer predictable or someone they feel they know. In an effort to help couples improve their relationship awareness, I encourage them to go through this five-step process outlined below:

#1. Pay close attention to your thoughts, feelings, and beliefs about your relationship. Identify, without judgment, how your thoughts, feelings, and beliefs are influencing your interactions with your partner.

#2. Inquire how your partner is feeling and thinking about your relationship. Pay close attention to see if you can identify their fears and worries. Notice if they share a personal belief (i.e., I am unlovable, I don't matter to you, etc.).

#3. Ask yourself how your partner's thoughts, feelings, and beliefs may influence their interactions with you. Initially, asking yourself these questions may be difficult since your partner might have a lot of negative things to say about you. However, by asking your partner how they feel, you learn more about them and the potential barriers to healing your relationship.

#4. Identify how you would like your partner to think or feel about you. Please make a list of things that you hope they will see in you. Then write down things you can do to increase their chances of seeing you that way.

#5. Now that you have identified how you hope your partner will see you, be vulnerable and let them know how you hope they can view you. If you have betrayed your partner, make sure to express that you know it will take time, but your desire is for them to see you that way in the future. You may say something like, "I hope someday you can see me as a trustworthy person. I know it will take time, but that is my hope." If you have been betrayed, you may express to your partner your desires (i.e., I want you to see how hurt I am and not just my anger; I want you to see my patience instead of my insecurities).

Learning to regulate our emotions is a lifelong skill that takes time and effort to develop. If you want to increase the level of safety in your relationship, developing your skill at emotional regulation will be a great place to start.

Note: I have just touched the surface of the importance of emotional regulation. For this purpose, I have created a short video, *The Power of Emotional Regulation in Couple Healing and Recovery*, to accompany this book. In the video, I discuss some best ways to develop your emotional regulation skills in your relationship. You will find this resource in the support material that accompanies this chapter.

Curiosity

Have you ever wondered why we act the way we do in relationships? Why do we get angry at each other? Why do we say critical things to one another? Why does one person cheat on their spouse? Why does one person feel the need to avoid conflict while the other feels the need to pursue their partner? And why do humans treat other humans poorly? I could go on and on with these questions, but I would like you to contemplate each question. It would be best to write down your answer to each question.

When we ask the right questions, we are more likely to get better answers. Unfortunately, one of the many problems in our society is that we stopped asking questions long before entering junior high school. Researchers have discovered that most children stop asking questions by the age of 11. (31) This doesn't mean that we can't resume asking questions; it simply suggests that our curiosity skills went down before we left high school. Now it is time to wake up those early life questions to discover more about yourself and your partner.

Paul Wilkes wrote, "Self-examination cannot exist when we continue to act on impulses and have so much going on that we don't have a moment to really think, think deeply." (32)

When we are curious, we are less likely to jump to conclusions and judge our partner and others. In my work, when couples begin to be curious, they ask different questions about the betrayal. It is these questions that help them create more safety in their relationship. Here's how their questions change:

Old Question (Betrayed)	New Question (Betrayed)
Why did you cheat?	I wonder what drove you to hide your behaviors and not come to me when you were feeling vulnerable.
Why was I not enough for you?	I am curious about what was happening in our lives that you felt the need to step out on me.
Old Question (Betraying)	**New Question (Betraying)**
Why can't you forgive me and move on?	I am wondering what I can do to earn back your trust.
Why are you so upset and angry all the time?	I realize that I hurt you, and I am wondering if there is anything I can do to help you feel safe with me again.

Honesty

While reviewing the research of other therapists who have studied couples that survived infidelity, I was very interested in some of their key discoveries related to honesty and the disclosure process.

The first finding came from the work of Dr. Peggy Vaughn, who discovered in her research with more than 1000 couples where infidelity had occurred, that couples who discussed the details of the affair were much more likely to stay together than couples who did not talk about the details. In her study, 86% of couples who discussed the details were still together after an affair. In contrast, only 59% of the couples who didn't discuss the details of the affair were still together. (33)

Vaughn also reported that when couples thoroughly discussed the whole situation, they were more likely to heal:

- 35% of those who discussed the situation very little felt somewhat or mostly healed.

- 51% of those who discussed the situation a good bit felt somewhat or mostly healed.

- 54% of those who discussed the situation a lot felt somewhat or mostly healed.

Source (34)

Other researchers, Drs. Corley and Schneider found that "most couples did not split up after a disclosure," which led them to think that the couples who had acknowledged the secrets had a better chance of saving the relationship than those who had not. (35) As I reflect, I have seen the betrayed and betraying partner relax after the truth has been revealed. Initially, being honest may seem like the wrong decision. However, over time, the evidence suggests that it may be one of the best ways to save your relationship and, in the process, help your partner heal.

Dr. Anna Lembke described the power of honesty in relationships when she wrote, "Telling the truth draws people in, especially when we're willing to expose our own vulnerabilities. This is counterintuitive because we assume that unmasking the less desirable aspects of ourselves will drive people away. It logically makes sense that people would distance themselves when they learn about our character flaws and transgressions.

In fact, the opposite happens; people come closer. They see in our brokenness their own vulnerability and humanity. They are reassured that they are not alone in their doubts, fears, and weaknesses." (36) To emphasize her point about being honest in our relationships, Dr. Lembke wrote, "Radical honesty promotes awareness of our actions. Second, it fosters intimate human connections. Third, it leads to a truthful autobiography, which holds us accountable to our present and future selves. Further, telling the truth is contagious and might even prevent the development of future addiction. (37)

Throughout my career, many people have said to me, "I can never tell my spouse…" It may be true that they feel that they can't tell their partner. Their fear of their partner's response holds them back from being honest. Sadly, in many cases, their partner knows something is wrong, but they can't put their finger on the problem.

According to Vaughn's research, over 60% of betrayed partners suspected that their partner was cheating on them. (38) There is power in being honest in your relationship. While the initial pain may be challenging, there is ample evidence that, over time, honesty significantly increases your chances of creating an environment for healing and safety.

> *Here are two examples of honesty after infidelity that I have observed:*
>
> Betrayed Partner's Honesty: *I am having a hard time reconnecting. I don't trust you, and I don't like you right now. I know you would like me to forgive and move on, but I am struggling. So, I am asking you not to push me for a connection right now.*
>
> Betraying Partner's Honesty: *I know that my behaviors have hurt you. I still have times when I am tempted and feel vulnerable. I wish I could say that I don't have cravings or temptations, but I do.*

Additional Steps to Create Safety in Your Relationship

Below I have identified specific steps you and your partner can take to increase the level of safety in your relationship. I have included specific chapters in this book so that you can learn more about each of these steps.

Steps to Create Safety for the Betraying Partner

- Increased self-awareness (orienting) (Chapter 1)
- Create safety with self (Chapter 2–this chapter)
- Put down your defenses (Chapter 11)
- Core-Values exercise (Chapter 11)
- Commitment evaluation (Chapter 1)
- Emotional regulation (Chapter 3–this chapter)
- Develop a better understanding of your partner's pain (Chapters 6 and 7)
- Deepen your understanding of betrayal by reading chapters for betrayed (Chapters 6, 7)
- Steps to make amends (Chapter 12)
- Avoid unhealthy interactions (Chapter 11)
- Practice deep listening (Chapter 13)
- Practice relationship skills – Increase in empathy and compassion (Chapter 5)

Steps to Create Safety for the Betrayed Partner

- Increased self-awareness (orienting) (Chapter 1)
- Identify the hurt and pain (Chapter 4)

- Practice emotional regulation (This chapter)

- Self-compassion (Chapter 6)

- Avoid focusing on forgiveness; instead, focus on healing the pain (Chapters 6 and 7)

- Letting the anger go (Chapter 6)

- Allowing yourself to feel inner peace (This chapter)

- Self-care (Chapter 6)

- Finding your support (Chapter 7)

- Avoid unhealthy interactions (Chapter 10)

- Practice deep listening (Chapter 5)

- Practice relationship skills (Increase in empathy and compassion (Chapter 5)

Accompanying Video: *Steps Couples Can Take to Create Safety in Their Relationship (See support Material)*

Key Takeaways from This Chapter

- Healing after sexual betrayal begins with establishing a safe environment in your relationship.

- Safety begins with yourself (listen to your own internal dialogue).

- Three common barriers to establishing safety include: 1) avoiding or ignoring your own emotions; 2) unresolved shame; and 3) not having boundaries.

- The Polyvagal Theory helps explain how our bodies respond when we feel safe and when we feel threatened. When we access the vagus nerve, we can connect in our relationships. When we do not feel safe, we will naturally be in fight, flight, or freeze mode.

- Four steps to creating a safe connection after sexual betrayal include: 1) start with being safe with yourself; 2) learn how to regulate your emotions—respond to stress; 3) be curious and interested in yourself and your partner; and 4) be honest.

Chapter Four

Shame: Remove One of the Biggest Barriers to Your Healing and Recovery

"Shame is an affective experience that violates both interpersonal trust and internal security. Intense shame is a sickness within the self, a disease of the spirit."
-Gershan Kaufman

Matt's body language in my office made it clear that he felt embarrassed and ashamed. He could hardly look at me. His shoulders were hunched inward, and he was slumping over. When he did speak, I could barely hear him. He was shutting down, and we had just begun our session.

His wife, Amy, had joined us for our first session. Her pain was on the surface as she cried every time she spoke. Between her tears, she made sure to tell me that I was their last hope. The story of their relationship was filled with many ups and downs. Their courtship was fun and exciting as they planned their future together. The first couple of years went well. However, in the background, Matt had a sexual history that was unresolved. He had been exposed to pornography at the age of nine and was heavily into it during his junior high and high school years. In college, Matt often used pornography as a stress reliever. When he met Amy during his third year of college, he felt hopeful about their future together. He believed his porn use was over.

Sadly, a couple of years into their marriage, Amy had a complicated pregnancy, significantly influencing her energy and desire to be sexual. Feeling lonely, Matt began dabbling in internet pornography. Initially, he only watched it a few times each week. Amy noticed something was off and started asking questions because she felt disconnected from Matt. Matt, not one to hide his behaviors, disclosed to her that he had been watching pornography. His confession triggered tremendous fear in Amy. She had experienced many difficult sexual experiences while growing up and had developed an intense hatred for pornography. Matt knew about some of Amy's early life experiences, but he had no idea that Amy would respond with such intensity. While Amy expressed her expectations and Matt told her he would avoid pornography in the future, this initial experience was not entirely resolved.

Some of the interactions that changed in their relationship included how they played with each other. Early in the courtship and throughout the first couple of years, they flirted and were playful with each other. Amy reported trying to keep the same mindset after Matt's disclosure but couldn't. Matt noticed Amy's shift and felt he had to be more careful around her. Things also changed in the bedroom. Amy was more hesitant to relax and allow herself to enjoy their sexual interaction. Matt became frustrated because their sex life wasn't relaxing and playful like it once was.

As often happens, time passed while Matt and Amy were busy with children, work, paying bills, taking care of the house, and other responsibilities. Matt, in particular, became engrossed in his work. After being married for about ten years, his job demanded working with many women. While he had never really thought about having an affair, he found himself ruminating about one of the women at work. It didn't help that she was flirtatious with him. Soon, they were having lunch together and enjoying each other's company. After a few months, they began having an affair.

Amy had noticed a change in Matt's attitude and began feeling more insecure. She raised her concerns about his work and some of the women, but Matt downplayed the interaction. However, Matt's attitude and desire to do family activities were waning. He spent more time at work and less at home and said he was busy with projects. One night Matt took his affair to another level by leaving home in the middle of the night to be with his affair partner.

When he got home, Amy was waiting for him. She knew he had been lying to her and confronted him. He didn't deny his actions; instead, he was quite defiant. He began by asking for a divorce. Startled, Amy asked for the reason. He said he wanted a divorce because the other woman was kind and caring. Upon hearing that, Amy felt devastated.

If Matt's affair were alcohol, he would have come home drunk that night. The chemical high of the affair blinded him as he expressed unkind words. Throughout my career, many clients have reported moments like these. In most cases, when the person acting out comes down from their high, reality settles in, and then they deal with the details of their actions. They ask themselves questions like: Do I want a divorce? Am I willing to give up what I have for this other person and lifestyle? Do I want to do this to the children? Do I want to walk away from this life?

In Matt's case, even though he had told Amy he would file for divorce, he realized he had said those hurtful things in the heat of discovery. Embarrassed but still reeling from his risky behavior, he asked Amy to give him a few days to think through things. Amy was not ready for him to come home, so she readily agreed to have him stay elsewhere. While staying at a friend's home, Matt began thinking about his relationship with Amy. He didn't want to ruin his family but thought he was falling in love with his affair partner. He was confused. They both needed a break to figure things out.

As often happens in cases like this, once an affair is discovered, the excitement and intensity of cheating dissipate, and reality settles in. In Matt's case, his affair partner began pushing him to leave his wife. When he was hesitant, the affair partner became angry. He hadn't seen this side of her before, and he began wondering what he had gotten himself into and why he had cheated on Amy.

At this point, I met Matt and Amy for the first time. Matt was starting to see and feel the consequences of his actions. Amy was suffering deeply. She had not been sleeping well, and she was having a hard time keeping her food down. Her body was shutting down. They were both lost and confused about how to proceed.

I have heard stories like Matt and Amy's and countless others throughout my career and found common themes. One of the most consistent outcomes is the shame that comes with betrayal. Usually, when we think of shame, we associate it with the person whose behaviors have been out of control (i.e., drinking too much, getting caught in an affair, or struggling with an addiction). However, I have observed that both partners experience tremendous amounts of shame when it comes to betrayal. While each partner experiences shame in their own unique way, the betrayal triggers a cascade of negative emotions. In this chapter, I hope to help you understand shame's role in preventing personal and relationship healing and why working to resolve shame is essential for couples who want to rebuild their relationship. I will conclude the chapter by sharing some of the most effective strategies I have found to help my clients reduce their shame.

Both Partners Experience Shame

In our first session, by observing Matt's body language and tone of voice, it was easy to see his shame was high. Amy was also experiencing tremendous shame.

However, most people might not identify what she was experiencing as shame. Before I explain how Amy was experiencing shame, let me define shame and describe how it shows up in our lives.

One of the best explanations of shame is described by Gershen Kaufman, the author of *Shame: The Power of Caring*. In his book, he describes shame this way, "Shame itself is an entrance to the self. It is the effect of indignity, defeat, transgression, inferiority, and alienation. No other affect is closer to the experienced self. None is more central for the sense of identity." (1)

For more than twenty years, I have observed and assessed individuals engaging in unwanted sexual behaviors and their partners. To better understand sexual betrayal, I co-authored an assessment exploring how infidelity and other sexual activities outside a committed relationship influenced partners. Based on my clinical experience and research by Barbara Stefans and Robyn Rennie, my colleagues and I hypothesized that sexual betrayal would increase betrayed individuals' symptoms of post-traumatic stress disorder (PTSD). After many years of research and study, in 2019, in partnership with Heidi Vogeler and her colleagues, we published an article that validated our assessment. Our findings reaffirmed Stefan's and Rennie's findings that sexual betrayal triggers PTSD symptoms in at least 70% of betrayed partners. (2)

For over a decade, well over 20,000 participants have shared with me how sexual betrayal has influenced their lives. Thanks to these courageous individuals, I better understand how infidelity and other unwanted sexual activity outside of a committed relationship impact partners. One of the most profound findings is how one's self-identity changes after discovery. Feelings of not being enough, unlovable, and embarrassed were a few ways that betrayed partners' self-perception had changed.

As the research data began coming in, I was shocked at how many betrayed partners were experiencing PTSD symptoms. I had witnessed betrayed clients' anger, reliving the events, and social isolation behaviors, but I wasn't fully aware of how the betrayed internalized their partners' external sexual activities.

Here are a few of the key research findings that helped me better understand how shame manifests in betrayed partners:

Early in my career, I would not have seen these statements as someone experiencing shame. However, as my awareness has grown, I understand the following statements, "I am not good enough, it's my fault, I feel ashamed of what my partner did, I am a terrible person, I'm different than everyone else, and I am unlovable are all internalized shame-based thoughts.

If we review Kaufman's definition of shame from above again, it is clear that betrayed partners are experiencing indignity, defeat, inferiority, and alienation. This awareness has significantly changed how I interact with betrayed partners because I now understand that internalized shame is a crucial barrier to healing. It is hard to connect with others when you feel like you are not enough or unlovable. I have found that as long as shame is untreated, betrayed partners' desire and ability to reconnect in their relationship is limited. Before I offer strategies for reducing shame, explaining how shame influences our approach to relationships is important.

How Shame Influences Individuals and Their Relationships

In her book, *Understanding and Treating Chronic Shame,* Patricia DeYoung wrote, "Shame feels like solitary pain, and chronic shame seems like a personal failure due to one's own negative thinking and low self-esteem. But in fact, shame in all its forms is first of all relational." (3) Traditionally, we have considered how shame influences one person. Yet, when we explore shame and its influence on how people approach their relationships, we see the truth of DeYoung's comments.

In this next section, I will discuss six ways shame influences how individuals approach relationships, and then I will share an example from my work with Amy on how we addressed her shame.

#1 Shame and Isolation

One of the first ways that shame influences individuals is that they begin isolating themselves. When individuals feel unworthy, unlovable, or not as good as others, they will naturally pull back from others. The betraying partner often holds back from a deeper connection because they do not feel worthy of love. They think others would reject them if they knew about their sexual behaviors. On the other hand, the betrayed partner often feels unwanted, unloved, and like others are judging them. Therefore, when shame levels are high, "to survive, a self disconnects from the source of pain and learns how to live in emotional isolation. Thus, the pain of a broken relationship morphs into lifelong patterns of disconnection from self and from others. These patterns are stressful and debilitating; they hold identities of unworthiness, expectations of failure, and demands for perfect performance…" (4)

#2. Shame and Shutting Down

Dr. David Hawkins discovered that shame produces the lowest energy level while studying human consciousness. Regarding the influence that shame has on individuals, Hawkins wrote, "Because it pulls down the whole level of one's personality, Shame results in a vulnerability to the other negative emotions, and, therefore, often produces false pride, anger, and guilt." (5) Shame usually triggers intense feelings of hopelessness and helplessness in those who internalize these feelings. Shame, according to Hawkins, produces an energy level of 20." After studying the energy levels that our emotions create, Hawkins wrote, "All levels below 200 are destructive of life in both the individual and society at large; in contrast, all levels above 200 are constructive expressions of power." (6) While shame is the lowest energy-producing emotion, the two highest energy producing emotions are peace and enlightenment.

When shut down, individuals cannot respond to others' emotional needs because their shame is using their energy. One of the significant consequences of elevated shame is that betraying clients struggle to stay connected with their partner's pain. Regarding this, author Daniel Hughes wrote, "Attachment relationships are fragmented, fragile, and unstable when a person's subjective experience is frequently restricted by shame. (7)

#3: Shame and Worthiness to Be Loved

A typical shame-based response after being discovered is to tell the person to leave you because you don't deserve their love. Throughout my career, many betraying partners tell me they aren't worthy of love. One of their fears is that they will be unable to stop and, therefore, will continue to hurt their spouse. They conclude that their partner would be better off without them. I have had many clients in such a place of despair who shared their hopelessness with me. Fortunately, I have learned to hear this statement in another way. Their shame is much like what Adam and Eve must have felt after partaking of the fruit. The holy writ says, "They hid because they did not want to be seen." In its most insidious way, shame harms us because we do not feel worthy of love, leading us to pull away or sabotage our relationships. Connection is no longer an option when you want to hide and not be seen.

Note: Unfortunately, while the betraying partner is being critical of themselves, the betrayed partner wants to know that the betraying partner will fight for their relationship. They want to hear about commitment and recovery. They are looking for something to comfort them, and instead, their partner tells them they should leave them because they will never overcome their problem. Many betrayed partners have explained that when their partner tells them they should leave, their partner's words come across like this, "I don't love you anymore," "I don't want to be with you," or "I am never going to overcome this problem." The shame-filled client often says, "I am feeling hopeless right now, and I want to stop hurting you. However, I don't have the confidence in myself right now to promise that I can stop my behaviors."

As a therapist, I would say, "Don't give up. Fight for your freedom by learning everything you can. Add more structure to your recovery. And be vulnerable with your partner and tell them that you are scared and worried about your behaviors, but you will do everything possible to be the best person you can be.

#4. Shame and Anger

After discovery, when clients' shame is usually the highest, we often see increased anger and fighting in the relationship. A good example would be what Matt said to Amy when he returned home after sneaking out during the night to be with his affair partner. He told her, "I'm going to divorce you because the other woman treats me better." He had been caught and responded with hurtful words.

I have also wondered whether some of my betrayed clients' anger is also a manifestation of their shame. Here's my reasoning for this theory. When your partner's behavior trigger feelings of not being enough or remind you of your other weaknesses, simply being around them can trigger shame-based feelings. If I was tracking the thought sequence, a betrayed partner might not say aloud, "You remind me of my insecurities; therefore, I hate you. Their partners trigger their negative beliefs (i.e., something is wrong with me).

Psychotherapist and author Dr. Daniel Hughes shared how we respond when our unhealthy behaviors are discovered. He wrote, "When, under the conditions of shame, one is not able to hide, but remains exposed to the other, one is likely to lash out in a state of rage." (8) Then, quoting researchers Tangney and Dearing, he wrote, "Individuals of all ages in states of shame are likely to 'shift the blame elsewhere,' externalizing the problem and directing rage at the supposed source of the problem. An added benefit of moving from shame toward rage at others is that by becoming angry, the person is 'reactivating and bolstering the self, which was previously so impaired by the shame experience'" (9,10)

#5: Shame and Gaslighting

Based on Tangney and Dearing's research, when individuals feel exposed, they naturally attempt to shift the blame elsewhere. This is referred to as gaslighting behavior. If you have never heard of gaslighting, here is a definition found in the dictionary. "Gaslighting is "psychological manipulation of a person usually over an extended period of time that causes the victim to question the validity of their thoughts, perception of reality, or memories and typically leads to confusion, loss of confidence and self-esteem, the uncertainty of one's emotional or mental stability, and a dependency on the perpetrator." (11)

In 2003-2004 when I began researching betrayal trauma and post-traumatic stress disorder (PTSD), I questioned if certain behaviors would increase betrayed clients' PTSD symptoms. As my clients shared their experiences, I heard stories of lying, deception, and minimizing behaviors.

Some of the statements I have heard that are associated with gaslighting include:

- We are just friends. It isn't that big of a deal.

- I would not have cheated if you had been more available.

- You never wanted sex, so why do you care.

- You are making this out to be worse than it is.

- You are responding this way because of your childhood issues.

I am often asked why people use gaslighting in their relationships. Over the past twenty years in my research, I have found that gaslighting is one of the most common behaviors that betraying partners use before and after discovery. Much like what Tangney and Dearing found, I believe that when our mistakes are exposed to others, our shame kicks in, and we naturally shift responsibility or blame onto others. In my research, I have discovered that gaslighting raises betrayed partners' PTSD symptoms more than any other behavior in relationships. (12)

Since gaslighting is an essential topic for couple healing and recovery, I have dedicated an entire chapter to it. In Chapter Twelve, I will discuss how to address specific gaslighting behaviors and then provide strategies you can use to address the pain it has created in your relationship.

#6 Shame and Empathy

As couples begin their journey towards healing and recovery, they often struggle when the betraying partner has difficulty empathizing with their betrayed partner's pain. Throughout my career, many betrayed partners have told me their spouse does not understand their pain. As a result, one of the primary barriers to couples' healing is the lack of empathy.

If betraying partners have difficulty showing empathy, the first question we should ask is why? What prevents individuals who have been sexually acting out from showing empathy to their partner who is suffering because of their actions? One possible answer to this question is that they experience empathy, but it over-whelms them. This theory was put forth by researcher Stephen Porges who wrote, "'Empathy is frequently operationally defined as feeling someone else's pain or negative emotion.' (13) If we deconstruct empathy from a neurobiological perspective,

84

empathy should be associated with the activation of the sympathetic nervous system." You will recall that the sympathetic nervous system is associated with a fight or flight response.

I have observed many clients who have betrayed their partners in my career. I conclude that they feel empathy, but as they genuinely try to feel their partner's hurt and suffering, they get emotionally overwhelmed. As a result, they feel the need to escape (flee) or argue (fight).

Another critical point in understanding shame and empathy is described by researchers Tangney and Dearing, who studied the differences between shame and guilt. They discovered that individuals who experience guilt are more likely to show empathy, while individuals who have shame are less likely to feel empathy. (14) This finding is critical to our understanding of why resolving shame is essential to the healing process for individuals and couples. I have found that couples do not heal without empathy after sexual betrayal.

Strategies for Reducing Amy and Matt's Shame

I began this chapter by sharing how Matt and Amy presented in our first session. Matt's energy was low as he sat on my couch. Being ashamed, his first words were, "I feel like a failure." He said, "I do not even know who I am anymore. I have let everyone down my wife, children, parents, employer, and even the religious leaders. When he first came to see me, he felt hopeless and helpless.

On the other hand, Amy was experiencing a wide range of emotions. For the most part, she was in shock (dorsal vagal shut-down) and fight or flight. When Amy did speak, her tears would flow, and then she would become silent. She, like Matt, did not know where to begin the healing process. I have discovered that, in this early phase, couples need as much direction and support as possible. I began by helping them understand what to expect (i.e., emotional ups and downs, lots of questions, fighting, and a lot of self-reflection). After discussing with them what to expect, they began doing individual sessions and couples therapy.*

Note: *If you want to learn more about the different phases of the healing and recovery journey, I have created a short video explaining some of the critical steps couples need to make to heal. To learn more, see the support material for this chapter. It is important to note that Matt and Amy would have their own therapist and a couple's therapist to help them in their healing journey.

Hopefully, the importance of addressing shame as couples go through the healing and recovery journey is evident. Let's now focus on each partner's shame and strategies for healing.

Amy's Shame

During our sessions, Amy explained that she would never be good enough for Matt. She was so embarrassed by Matt's behaviors that she avoided social activities and other gatherings. Attending church services, being with friends, and participating in social groups was stressful for her. As we continued our discussion, it was clear that we had to address her fear of being around others. She was isolating herself away from others. In my research, I have found that staying connected to others is one of the keys to healing.

I could tell that I was gaining Amy's trust by the amount of information she began sharing with me. In one session, she revealed more of her childhood trauma and how Matt's behaviors brought painful memories. His behaviors also validated a belief she had had since she was young—that she was unlovable.

Amy began by sharing some of her difficult childhood memories. She told me there were times when she would be alone for hours because her mom was hanging out with men all night. Her mom, a single parent, was trying to provide but rarely did she have new clothes. Her mom gave her a roof over her head, but she was alone with everything else. Kids at school bullied her and made her feel like she did not belong with them.

By the time she was in high school, she was raising herself. She was fortunate enough to find good jobs during the summer. These jobs provided enough money for her to provide for herself.

While in high school, she made some new friends. For a while, she thought her life was turning around. She had friends and financial stability. High school was one of the best times of her life. However, soon after graduating, she experienced another life-changing event. She had accepted a new job and enjoyed interacting with her co-workers. Then one day, the company's owner began making comments to Amy that made her uncomfortable. The other co-workers said nothing, so Amy just let it go. However, she started feeling uncomfortable around him.

One night, while closing the store, it was just Amy and her boss. He began hitting on her and invited her to come home with him. He then started touching her shoulder. She responded by telling him no and asking him to leave her alone, but he did not stop pursuing her. She again asked him to stop, but he persisted. Again, she told him that she was not interested. He still didn't stop. The owner violated her when she left the store that evening.

As Amy shared her story with me, I found myself getting angry at that man. I wanted to take revenge on her behalf. It genuinely hurts when I think of the pain that she went through. When I asked what had happened to the guy, she said she was too embarrassed to say anything because she felt it was partly her fault for not leaving. I asked if she still felt that what had happened was her fault. She said no, but her emotions betrayed her. I felt the hesitancy in her response. This poor woman had been carrying that painful memory for over twenty years and still felt like she had done something wrong.

As mentioned in previous chapters, our beliefs guide everything we do. Since beliefs are that important, I have learned to listen carefully as my clients share their experiences. Usually, their beliefs reveal how they interact with the people around them and their environment.

In Amy's case, her beliefs influenced how she saw herself (I am unlovable), her relationships (people will let me down), and the world around her (do not trust anyone). Amy had enough evidence that each of these beliefs made complete sense.

After hearing about her life experiences, I thought I would feel the same if I had been through what she had been through. Her parents had let her down in her childhood by not protecting her, then, as a teenager, she was taken advantage of by an older adult; why would she trust anyone? As if these early experiences were not challenging enough, Matt's behaviors compounded her pain and made her question everyone around her. She was having a hard time finding safety anywhere.

When we don't feel safe in the presence of others and feel like we are not worthy of love, the deepest levels of shame come forward. Life begins to feel like it has no purpose. I believe this is why 60% of betrayed partners report having suicidal thoughts after discovering their partners' betrayal. (15) Fortunately, most of those with suicidal thoughts do not want to die; instead, they want their pain to disappear. They want to feel safe and secure; they want comfort.

As Amy's trust in me grew, I introduced her to a treatment called Attachment-Focused Eye Movement Desensitization and Reprocessing (AF-EMDR). Laura Parnell created this approach, and since then, it has been used by therapists worldwide. I told Amy that we would focus on helping her address some of her negative core beliefs. By this time, she and Matt had been through full disclosure (*See Video—What to Expect in the Disclosure Process*), began attending group sessions, and worked diligently on their healing and recovery.

Amy was making good progress. She communicated purposefully and did a good job creating the boundaries she needed with Matt. However, one of her core shame-based beliefs, "I'm unlovable," had not diminished. As a result, when Matt or others were kind to her, she quickly dismissed their efforts and did not believe anyone who complimented her.

I began by outlining the steps we would take to do AF-EMDR. First, I asked her to identify a safe place in her mind. I told her this place could be in the mountains, by a beach, at a park, in her home, or anywhere she would feel safe and secure. After identifying her place of safety, I asked her to identify three people who would represent 1) a nurturer; 2) a protector; and 3) a wise person.

We began the exercise as outlined by Laura Parnell. She chose her grandmother as her nurturer, a college roommate as her protector, and an elderly lady from her support group as a wise person. I had her enhance the image of her nurturer as much as possible. I followed the established protocol using bilateral stimulation (BLS)** with Amy. Her body relaxed, and she deepened her connection with her grandmother. She began crying. During the EMDR process, therapists are asked to check in with their clients by asking questions like, "How was that for you?" and, "How do you feel?" or "What are you noticing now?" In this case with Amy, I asked her, "How was that for you?" Her response was precious. She said, "My grandma was with me in my safe place. She was holding me and telling me everything would be alright."

Amy began crying again, except this time it came from someone genuinely loving and nurturing her. She said, "My grandma continued by telling me what happened in my childhood was not my fault. She also told me that she loved me."

We continued this exercise by having her go through the same process with her protector, her college roommate. Again, we enhanced the presence of her roommate, and when Amy was ready, we began the BLS. When the process was completed, she seemed to have even more strength. I asked her again, "How was that for you?" She responded, "Kayla, my roommate was with me at my safe place; she looked me in the eye and said, 'I am here, and whatever has happened to you in your life… what these people did to you was wrong. I am here with you; you are not alone.'" This was a powerful moment of change for Amy. I could tell that her belief that she was unlovable was shifting.

We concluded this powerful exercise by having the wise person, the friend she met in her group, join her at her safe place. Again, we enhanced the connection with the wise person and began the BLS. When we finished, Amy looked at me and said, "She told me that all these things that happened to me were not my fault. I am enough, and I am loveable." We completed the exercise by having each person hug her as we did one more BLS. When we finished, Amy looked at me and said, "I am lovable. I am going to get through this."

As a therapist, it is an honor to witness clients as they reprocess memories and shame-based beliefs. This powerful experience helped Amy shift her negative core belief, which was evident from her body language. She appeared to have more confidence and trust in herself, and the shame-based belief had lifted.

While this was a powerful session, it did not completely bring back Amy's trust in Matt or others. What it did was remove the negative beliefs that Amy had about herself. She realized she had been holding herself back in friendships and other relationships. She resolved to become more friendly and outgoing. She was going to practice receiving compliments from Matt and others. And finally, she would have more self-compassion for the times when she was self-critical.

Note: **Bilateral stimulation (BLS) can be completed in different ways. One way is through tapping on the client's hands or knees. Another method is through eye movement that tracks my fingers as they move from right to left. There are new electronic devices that produce the same right-to-left movement through sounds or hand-held devices.

Not all clients have the same experience in their first session of AF-EMDR. However, there is power in having a nurturer, protector, and wise person guide them through challenging experiences and memories. All of us need a trusting person by our side during difficult times. We all need someone to be with us when things are hard. Unfortunately, many people suffer through difficult experiences all by themselves.

Not everyone has a nurturer, protector, and wise person. When this happens, I have had my clients think of people who they believe would be a nurturer (i.e., Mother Teresa, Mother Mary), a protector (Superheroes, the Hulk, Ironman), and a wise person (Jesus, Buddha). On more than one occasion, I have witnessed that these mental images can be as powerful as people my clients have known.

Matt's Shame

We reviewed a technique AF-EMDR that helped Amy address her shame; now, we will focus on Matt's shame. It didn't take us long to identify his shame-based beliefs. For years, Matt had felt like a failure. When I asked him why he felt like a failure, he began discussing a long history of porn use. As he discussed his sexual history and identified critical events, it became clear that he felt flawed. He had always thought that his sex drive was higher than others. While growing up, Matt's dad cautioned him about using pornography and told him he could come to him anytime if he had questions or concerns. This invitation prompted Matt to talk with his dad a few times. When he spoke with his dad, they discussed a few ways to avoid pornography, but that was the extent of their conversation.

While in his sophomore year of high school, Matt began looking at pornography daily. Given the embarrassment of how frequently he consumed it, he stopped talking with his dad. As we discussed that period of Matt's life, he realized that was when he started feeling like a failure. He wanted to stop but couldn't on his own, and his dad's ideas didn't help either. This was when he started feeling like something was wrong with him. As a result of his frequent use of pornography, he started holding back from participating in some social activities. He thought others would reject him if they knew what he was doing. Fortunately, his social life changed during his junior year of high school when he found a good group of friends. These friends made him feel accepted. Over the next couple of years, he reduced his use of porn and developed many social skills.

However, things changed again after high school when his friend group left, and everyone went to different colleges. He was in a new environment with a lot of pressure to perform. He was a hard worker and did well in school. His social life was hard because he didn't have any friends. This was when he began watching pornography more often.

It was during his third year of college that he met Amy. They hit it off quickly, and Matt thought his problems with pornography were over. This may sound like a typical story, but Matt never resolved the belief that he was flawed. He had done his best to overcome this belief but was insecure. He felt like he wasn't as good as others. When he met Amy, he thought she was better than him. When he told her he was interested in dating her, he was surprised she liked him back too.

Notice the power of Matt's unresolved negative beliefs. Throughout my career, I have been surprised at the power of our beliefs. Matt had come to believe that there was something seriously wrong with him. He felt like a failure. He wasn't able to recognize his good traits. He was a good student, and people liked him. His family was also positive and supportive, and yet, he felt like he was flawed.

If you wonder how Matt came to this conclusion, you think like me. As I listened to Matt's story, I wondered what experiences led him to believe he was a failure. This was when I introduced him to an activity created by Dr. David Burns, an expert in helping people evaluate their core beliefs.

An Exercise for Matt to Respond to Shame

Begin by identifying a typical situation where you feel down, or your thoughts are negative about yourself. Once you have identified your negative thought, ask yourself these questions:

1. If that thought were true, what would it mean to me?

2. Why would it be upsetting to me?

Matt: I have let my wife, children, and parents down.

Question: What would it mean to me if that thought were true?

Response: I am a failure

Question: Why would it be upsetting me?

Response: I don't want to disappoint people, but I do. I hurt people.

Dr. David Burns said regarding this process, "Asking this question will usually cause a new negative thought to pop into your head." (16) We continued following this line of questioning based on Dr. Burns' approach.

Question: Why would it be upsetting me?

Response: I don't want my actions to hurt other people. Something is wrong with me. I am flawed. No. I am bad.

This was the core belief that Matt had been carrying around for years. It was time to identify what experience or experiences had made him think he was bad. He was ready to do EMDR based on his belief.

We began by identifying specific times when he felt like he was bad. His initial response took him back to a time in high school when he hid his porn use from his parents. Then he thought for a minute and said, "There it is."

I replied, "There it is?"

Yeah, I got it. I was hanging out with other guys during my sophomore year as they discussed attending an upcoming dance. I was interested in going with one girl but didn't think she would want to go with me. When I told them who I wanted to go with, one of the guys replied. "Are you kidding me? She wouldn't go with someone like you." I didn't say anything after that and didn't ask her out. I went home, waited until my parents were in bed, and watched pornography. That night, I remember thinking, "I am bad; nobody would want to have me."

After years of carrying that hidden memory, Matt identified when the core belief entered his memory banks. This insight provided us with what we needed to begin the EMDR protocol. If you are unfamiliar with how EMDR works, it is a step-by-step process designed to help individuals desensitize and reprocess difficult memories. In one of the steps, clients are asked to identify what they have come to believe about themselves due to the experience. In another step, they are asked what they would prefer to believe about themselves instead.

Matt's Belief: I am bad.

What Matt Wanted to Believe Instead: I can be a good man. I am good!

We began the EMDR protocol by helping Matt find a safe, calm place. Then I asked him to recall the memory of being with those friends and what happened when he went home. When he had intensified that memory, I had him repeatedly track my fingers as I moved them from right to left for about 45- 60 seconds. When I stopped moving my fingers, I asked him, "What are you noticing now?" Here's his response:

"I saw myself with the guys. I felt out of place. When the one kid told me, 'She would never want to go with you.' I realized he was probably joking with me because he wanted to go with her. I have never thought of that."

I said, go with that, which is part of the EMDR protocol, and we continued. When I stopped the second time, Matt was visibly upset. Tears were coming down his cheeks. I asked, "What are you noticing now?"

Matt's Response: "I saw what happened when I went home. I was feeling reject-ed, but I didn't tell anyone. I don't understand why I didn't talk with my mom or dad." Then, he teared up and slowly continued telling me what he saw while doing the EMDR. He said, "My mom has died, but I know even if she were alive, she would have told me I was good enough for that girl. She would have told me to ask her anyway. Instead, I kept my hurt feelings inside and didn't tell her. I was so stubborn."

I said, go with that and continued following the EMDR protocol. After the next set, Matt's mind took him to the time he interacted with Amy. He recalled early in their marriage, when he felt down, instead of opening up to her, he turned to pornography.

As we prepared to finish the EMDR protocol, I asked Matt about his belief that he was bad. Then he said, "For years, I have been keeping people out because I thought I was bad. I now realize that I don't have to keep people out. I can learn to be open and stop hiding who I am. Matt's belief was shifting.

Matt's Response: I am not bad. I have done hurtful things, but I am not bad. Now I must learn to be open and stop hiding things from people I care about.

Key Takeaways for Addressing Shame-Based Beliefs

One of the things we know about beliefs is that when we believe something is valid, we will act consistently with that belief. If my clients think other people are unsafe, they will do whatever it takes to avoid others. They will stop hanging out with friends, attending social activities, shopping at a mall, or spending time with family. If they feel unlovable, they hold back and avoid connecting with others. Ultimately, their belief guides their behavior. Once a belief is accepted as a truth in our minds, we stop questioning whether we are right or wrong. This is how our beliefs influence our behaviors.

When my clients identify a negative self-belief (i.e., I'm a failure), there is always a story or incident that made them come to that conclusion. When training other therapists, I often say, "There is always a story; our job is to help clients understand their story so we can address the root of their problems and help them resolve the shame they feel. When a client tells me they are not enough, the next question I ask is, what experiences have you had that make you feel like you are a failure? With this simple prompting, my clients often make a mental list of experiences that validate their beliefs. The memories are often difficult for my clients to review; however, this is where clients begin freeing themselves from the burdens of their past.

Once again, I bring up the Zeigarnik effect. Difficult memories from the past do not just go away on their own. Using the therapeutic strategies outlined above to desensitize and reprocess such memories, I have watched clients healthily process hurtful experiences and resolve them as much as possible, given the difficulty of the events.

In conclusion, let me review the steps for addressing shame. Here are four steps that I have found helpful in reducing the toxic emotion of shame. In my book, *Treating Sexual Addiction: A Compassionate Approach to Recovery*, I discuss these steps more in-depth.

Step #1: Identify the Stories (Memories) Associated with the Shame

We are not born with shame. Our life experiences make us question ourselves and where we fit in society. My suggestion to work through these memories is first to identify the memories or experiences that made you feel ashamed of yourself.

Next, please make a list of each memory that comes to your mind (i.e., my teacher told me I was stupid in front of the whole class).

Step #2: Look for and Review the Language of Shame

"The voice of shame is sneaky. It creeps into our minds while we aren't looking, and suddenly we find ourselves saying things like "I'm so stupid" or "Who would ever want me?"

When this happens, I tell my clients that we must increase awareness; that the purpose of building self-awareness is to prevent thoughts from running wild.

As clients slow down and pay attention to their thoughts, they will gain a deeper understanding of their thought patterns.

Ironically, just sitting with our thoughts can help us alter them. (18)

Step #3: Observe and Work to Resolve the Emotions of the Shame

The third step to resolving shame is to discover the emotions associated with it. If we learn to pay attention, our emotions can teach us so much, but we must learn to listen to what they are trying to teach us. While shame is an emotion, other emotions are often associated with it. "Shame is an unpleasant self-conscious emotion often associated with negative self-evaluation; motivation to quit; and feelings of pain, exposure, distrust, powerlessness, and worthlessness." (19)

Step #4: Desensitize and Reprocess the Memories Associated with the Shame

The final step usually needs to be done with a professional therapist who can guide you. The general premise is similar to the Zeigarnik effect in that we often get stuck thinking about specific memories. When we cannot make sense of these disturbing memories, they will replay in our minds. The desensitization and reprocessing of shame-filled memories help individuals navigate through experiences they haven't made sense of in their minds.

Usually, these memories have created negative shame-based thinking (e.g., "I am unlovable," "I am a failure," etc.). When this happens, individuals internalize the shameful experience and begin believing they are unlovable or a failure. Professional therapists have been trained to help individuals deal with such painful memories. Some of the most effective treatment approaches include:

- Eye Movement, Desensitization, and Reprocessing (EMDR),
- Accelerated Resolution Therapy (ART), and
- Internal Family System (IFS)

Chapter Five

The Key to Healing and Recovery: Empathy and Compassion

"Hurting hearts and addicted minds change when empathy and compassion are combined in the healing journey."

Four men were sitting in my office. We were in the middle of a three-day intensive to help them accelerate their recovery. I designed this specifically to help them improve their relationship skills on the last day. I had sent them back to their hotels with an assignment the evening before. Their task was to think about a recent conflict that they had had with their wife. I asked them to write in detail what triggered the conflict, what they fought/argued about, what they did or said during the argument, and what their partner did or said. All four had completed their assignment and were anxious to get started.

I asked for a volunteer. James quickly raised his hand. I told them that we were going to practice by role-playing their situation. I told James his job was to be his wife, and I would be him. No problem, he said; I have been listening to her criticism and anger for months; this will be easy.

I had him begin.

He started with some real zingers.

Client: You are such a jerk; I can't believe you cheated on me. You are a liar. You have hurt me and our children. Do you realize what you have done?

My response as a client: I have lied to you. I have also hurt the children by my actions.

Client: See, you admit it. I don't know if I can ever forgive you. You are a cheater. Cheater, cheater, cheater, that's who you are. When will you understand the pain you have created?

My response as a client: I did cheat. I realize my behaviors have created a lot of pain for you. I did things I regret. I have hurt you deeply.

Client: You will never understand the pain you have created.

My response as a client: You are right. My actions were wrong. I can't fully understand the pain I have created for you.

My client stopped the role play and asked, "How are you doing this? I have a hard time staying angry at you." I told him that relationship skills, empathy, and compassion guided my response. Generally speaking, good things happen when these fundamental skills are applied in our communications with others.

In this chapter, I hope to help you and your partner discover the value of applying empathy and compassion in your relationship. If you feel like you need to improve these skills, the good news is that they can be learned. The short role play described above is filled with practical concepts that are discussed throughout this chapter, through which I will teach you the ways to change how you apply these skills in your relationship.

Unfortunately, many people have grown up in homes without these essential relationship skills. As a result, it is hard for them to show others empathy and compassion when they have not experienced them themselves. I hope you will see this chapter's vision for these relationship-changing skills.

I will begin this chapter by defining empathy and compassion, and I will include a short quiz you can take to evaluate your current level of empathy and compassion in your relationship. Then, I will discuss the difference between empathy and compassion.

While most people view empathy and compassion as the same thing, knowing their differences may help you individually and change how you see your partner's behaviors.

Next, I will provide more examples demonstrating how empathy and compassion can help you repair your relationship. The chapter will conclude with a few exercises that will help you practice developing your empathy and compassion skills.

Exploring Empathy in Relationships

To understand why empathy is so crucial in our relationships, we need to identify how it works and how it can help you heal and recover.

Empathy is a complex emotion that's beyond the understanding of someone else's feelings. It requires us to take on their perspective and connect with them emotionally. When we are empathic, we can accurately identify when someone else feels and responds with compassion rather than judgments or criticisms. As we develop our empathic skills, we also become more aware of our feelings.

Consider each of the statements below and give yourself a score on each item:

Empathy Questions	Not at All	Somewhat	About Half the Time	Often	Completely
When my partner is upset, I seek to understand their feelings without getting defensive.	1	2	3	4	5
It is easy to understand my partner's perspective.	1	2	3	4	5
I respond to what my partner is thinking or feeling without judgment or criticism.	1	2	3	4	5
I can accurately identify what my partner is thinking or feeling.	1	2	3	4	5

Assignment: Add the score from each statement. Then take a few minutes and write down your score from each item. In this assignment, there is no right or wrong answer. Instead, it is designed to increase your insight into how much empathy you have in your relationship.

Note for Betrayed Partners: This exercise can be very frustrating if you are like many of those I have worked with over the years. Betrayed partners often tell me that it is really hard to care about their partner's feelings. Why should they try to understand their partner when their partner has hurt them so deeply? Please know that I understand this feeling. I expect your scores to be low in the early healing and recovery phase. I only ask that you complete the assignment, and once you and your partner have finished reading this book, you retake it.

Note for Betraying Partners: I understand that it may be hard for you to empathize with your partner. When they are upset or angry, it may be challenging to hear them yell at you and put you down. Or perhaps it is difficult for you because you feel shame. After all, it is your behavior that has triggered their anger. I realize that empathy may be hard for you right now. However, I ask you to complete this exercise, and when you have finished reading this book, you retake the assessment.

Exploring Compassion in Relationships

The word compassion comes from the Latin roots com (with) and pati (suffer), or to "suffer with." When we learn to be with our suffering and the suffering of others, we develop a compassionate mindset. His Holiness, the Dali Lama, has said, "Compassion is being sensitive to the suffering of self and others with a deep commitment to try to prevent and relieve it." (1,2) Author of *The Mindful Path to Self-Compassion*, Christopher Germer wrote, "When we offer genuine compassion, we join a person in his or her suffering. Being compassionate means that we recognize when someone is in pain, we abandon our fear of or resistance to it, and a natural feeling of love and kindness flows toward the suffering individual." (3,4)

Germer's point regarding shutting out the pain is an interesting idea to consider. Why would we shut out our pain or the pain of others? While there are many possible answers, here are a couple of them that I have considered. First, we may not want to feel others' pain because we are suffering. It is hard to give to others when our pain is high and our energy is low. Second, when people are experiencing shame for their behaviors, it is hard to see beyond their negative thoughts. It is tough to see others' pain when you are dealing with your own pain. And third, when we feel hurt by or resentful of others, our desire to comfort or care for them is hampered.

Following is a short quiz regarding the compassion you feel for your partner:

Relationship Compassion Questions	That Is Not True at All	Some-what True	True About Half the Time	This Is Often True	Completely True
When I feel my partner is struggling, I want to be with and comfort them.	1	2	3	4	5
When my partner is suffering, I get overwhelmed and cannot help them.	5	4	3	2	1
I am so upset by my partner; I am glad when they are having a hard time.	5	4	3	2	1
I can feel when my partner is suffering, but when I try to help, I make matters worse.	1	2	3	4	5
When my partner is struggling, I want to be with them in their suffering.	1	2	3	4	5

Assignment: Add your score from each statement. Higher scores indicate that you are comfortable feeling your partner's pain and being with them as they go through difficult times. On the other hand, lower scores suggest that you are having a difficult time having compassion for your partner. Please take a few minutes and review your scores. Then write down any thoughts and impressions you have about your responses. Are you satisfied with your score? What would need to happen for your scores to improve?

Delayed Compassion

When it comes to healing in your relationship, compassion is essential, but timing matters too. In the beginning, right after discovery, showing kindness to each other is usually not an option for many couples. This may not be very reassuring for you, but most couples in the early discovery stage are too emotional. Usually, they feel tremendous shame and are not emotionally aware of the depth of their partner's pain. Instead, they experience their partner's emotional intensity. While the betrayed partner may want their partner to show compassion for the pain they have created, the betraying partner struggles to make sense of what they have done.

While one partner is dealing with the aftershock of discovery and the other shame, neither partner is in an emotional place to attune to the other's suffering. When betrayed partners learn of their partner's behaviors, anger and rage take over. In this emotional state, the betrayed partner will likely have zero desire to show compassion for their partner. Then facing their partner's emotional intensity, the betraying partner pulls away. In most cases, this is precisely the opposite of what the betrayed spouse wants or needs.

Often, the betraying partner has no idea what to say or do. As a result, they will struggle to offer authentic emotional support. A more likely scenario is that a betraying partner, consumed by their shame, will attempt to shift the blame elsewhere. I have also witnessed some betraying partners who want their partner to forgive them and move on. They are hoping for a quick resolution, and in some cases, they want to be comforted through words of affirmation (it will be okay) or physical contact (sex). However, in seeking comfort (compassion) from the betrayed, they do not understand the depth of trauma their partner feels. This lack of awareness will further trigger the betrayed partner because, while they are suffering, their partner is seeking comfort.

These patterns result in both partners likely being in fight, flight, or freeze mode after discovery. When I work with couples, I emphasize the importance of compassion increasing over time. Otherwise, without this awareness, individuals will be let down due to their expectations. Let me emphasize; I do not believe healing from betrayal is possible without compassion. However, understanding the timing of when it comes back into a relationship is also essential.

So, what can you expect? Compassion is more likely to increase when the following things are happening or have happened:

Safety returns to the relationship—this is the goal. Everything else listed below are strategies designed to increase safety:

Betraying Partner's Tasks:

- Self-exploration (personal orienting) (See Chapter 1)
- Address wounds old and new (See Chapters 2, 8, and 9)
- Personal disclosure (See Chapter 9)
- Address shame (See Chapter 4)
- Increase in self-discipline (see Chapters 8 and 9)
- Establishing personal boundaries (See Chapters 8 and 11)
- Increase in empathy and compassion
- Address gaslighting behaviors (See Chapter 12)
- Improved relationship skills (e.g., listening, sharing, relaxing) (See Chapters 14 and 15)

Betrayed Partner's Tasks:

- Self-exploration (personal orienting) (See Chapter 1)
- Address wounds old and new (See Chapters 2, 6, and 7)
- Limiting beliefs (See Chapter 6)
- Address Shame (See Chapter 4)
- Reduce PTSD symptoms (See Chapters 6 and 7)
- Incorporate Model for Healing into life (See Chapter 7)
- The decision to move forward
- Increase empathy and compassion
- Improved relationship skills (e.g., listening, sharing, relaxing) (See Chapters 14 and 15)

Note: These lists are not exhaustive but should be considered as a starting point for couples looking for safety and, ultimately, more compassion in their relationship.

In my work, when I teach couples the principle of delayed compassion, many look at me with discouragement. I know they need someone to feel their pain and be with them in their suffering; unfortunately, it is usually not their partner at the beginning of the healing journey. Now that you have the reality, let me share with you what gives me hope.

What I am going to share with you makes me excited. **Compassion is a learned skill.** We can develop our skills of being with others in their suffering at any time. It is best to think of compassion as being present with someone who needs us. We do not always feel compassion; that would wear us out. However, we learn to attune to others' emotions and needs and comfort them. Thus, compassion comes and goes in our lives. The more we practice being compassionate, the more skilled we will be. We can develop a compassionate heart and show it at any time.

According to Dr. Stephen Porges, our head and heart are in sync when we feel compassion for others. Dr. Porges wrote regarding this state of mind, "From a neurobiological perspective, compassion is not equivalent to empathy, given that compassion engages vagal pathways. If compassion is associated with a calm vagal state, it will promote a physiological state associated with the safety of self that projects calmness and acceptance toward the other." (5)

When we are experiencing a calm vagal state, we feel safe within ourselves, which in turn allows us to project calmness and acceptance toward the other.

Stephen Porges, Polyvagal Safety

If you have never felt compassion from others, showing care for others may be hard or scary. Giving others what you have yet to be given is often hard. However, you will have developed a lifelong skill by learning to be with others in their suffering while not being overwhelmed by their needs. You will be better in your relationships, and most likely, you will begin to see that others want to be with you when you are suffering.

Developing Compassion for Self and Others

Hopefully, I have piqued your interest in compassion, and by now, you will want to learn how to develop this skill. The answer may surprise you. The first step you can take is to increase compassion for yourself. Yes. That is right. We are more likely to feel others' pain when we discover how to be with ourselves.

In the book *Mindful Compassion*, Paul Gilbert and Choden wrote, "Developing our inner compassion is like becoming our doctors and healers. (6) Unfortunately, when people think about compassion, they look externally at others (e.g., I feel bad for that person, or those people are having a hard time). However, when these people suffer, they often become self-critical (e.g., I'm so stupid, why didn't I see that coming).

Beyond helping us develop compassion for others, increasing our self-compassion has many benefits. Researchers have discovered that self-compassion positively affects mental health and well-being. Self-compassion can make us more aware of our emotions, motivate us to change what we don't like in ourselves, and help us feel connected to others. (7)

Being compassionate towards yourself means understanding, kindness, and accepting your faults and challenges. Self-compassion involves knowing your weaknesses and consciously acknowledging your strengths and successes. Self-compassion is not about self-pity or self-indulgence; instead, it's about cultivating a sense of understanding and caring toward ourselves to create lasting and meaningful personal growth. (8)

Here are three additional benefits of self-compassion:

#1. Self-compassion can reduce shame and guilt by helping us accept our mistakes and shortcomings nonjudgmentally. As we develop this skill, we increase our capacity to recognize personal suffering and recognize when we're playing the blame game. Self-compassion ultimately allows us to forgive ourselves instead of feeling inadequate or not enough. (9)

#2. Self-compassion encourages personal growth by motivating us to identify what needs to change and where to take action. It allows us to recognize our potential and take steps toward achieving it. Finally, self-compassion can give us the courage to address our mistakes, change our lives, and become more confident. (10)

#3. Self-compassion can help improve our relationships with others by reminding us that none of us are perfect. Self-compassion can make it easier to accept that we all make mistakes and that our flaws don't define us. Self-compassion can also help us to be more understanding and compassionate towards others, which in turn helps create stronger relationships.(11)

Self-compassion is essential for developing healthy self-awareness, acceptance, and understanding. It allows us to look at our mistakes and shortcomings with kindness, forgive ourselves, and move forward. By cultivating self-compassion, we become self-aware of our emotions and increase our sense of connection to others.

When Empathy Overwhelms

Earlier in this chapter, I shared a quote from Dr. Porges regarding the difference between empathy and compassion. He described the differences this way, "From a neurobiological perspective, empathy should be associated with the activation of the sympathetic nervous system." Porges continued by suggesting that the autonomic response to pain is characterized by a withdrawal of vagal influences and activation of the sympathetic nervous system (fight or flight response). Thus, from a neurobiological perspective, compassion is not equivalent to empathy, given that compassion engages vagal pathways. (12)

As I work with betrayed partners, I often hear them telling me that their spouse does not experience empathy. Initially, when clients shared their concerns, I focused on helping betraying partners develop empathy. However, after reading Dr. Porges's research, I am not convinced that it is empathy that needs to be developed. Instead, it is compassion.

The key difference is that too much empathy can overwhelm the neurobiological system, especially soon after discovery. It is common to revert to a fight or flight response when this happens. In contrast, by increasing compassion, clients can utilize a calm vagal state to offer support, safety, and acceptance of their partner's suffering.

While working with couples, I emphasize the physiological difference between empathy and compassion. Here's an example of how I do this with couples.

In one of my sessions with Andrea and James, Andrea looked at me and said, "James, he does not feel empathy. Can he learn because I can't keep feeling like he doesn't care about what he did? James didn't say much. He just listened to Andrea. When I asked him how he felt about showing empathy to Andrea, he said, "I try to, but I don't do it right." He continued, "She has repeatedly expressed concern, but I don't know what to say or do. I have tried, but nothing has worked."

I turned to James and said, "It sounds like you want to understand Andrea but don't know how to show it. I asked him, "Were you able to express your emotions as a boy?" He responded with a chuckle, "Are you kidding me? My mom would not tolerate emotions. If I showed any emotion, she would tell me to stop it. I wasn't allowed to be sad or disappointed, and anger was not tolerated. I learned to hide my emotions from her."

> Note: *I ponder situations like Andrea and James. How can you do something that you have been told is wrong? Asking James to show empathy and be comfortable with emotions seems like a tall task since expressing emotions got him into trouble as a boy. Now as a married man, his wife wants to see him be comfortable showing empathy.*
>
> *While I understand James' inability to express empathy through expressing emotion, Andrea deserves more from him. His infidelity and sexual betrayal have hurt her. She should want him to feel remorse and feel her pain. When we've been hurt by someone who loves us, should we not expect they would like to make us feel better?*
>
> *This is where many couples get stuck. One partner needs empathy, while the other struggles to express their emotions. In this case, even though James struggled to express his feelings, he made it clear that he wanted to improve. The question I have asked is, "How can James improve?"*
>
> *Fortunately, by understanding the polyvagal theory, I have discovered how couples can better understand each other and respond more effectively. By exploring the polyvagal theory, individuals can better understand how to shift from feeling overwhelmed by empathy towards increased compassion. With this knowledge comes the potential for deeper connections with ourselves and others.*

The Polyvagal Theory in Action

As I reflected on my conversations with James and Andrea, I remembered that in an earlier conversation, Andrea had told me that James was good with their children. The example she shared with me was when she and James took their daughter Maggie for a routine medical check-up. The nurse had told them that Maggie needed a standard shot. As the nurse prepared to give their daughter the shot, James knew their daughter would be in pain, so he stood up to leave the room. When Andrea asked why he said, "I can't stand to watch her in pain."

After recalling this story, I asked James to remember that event. "What were you feeling and thinking?" James did not hesitate. I was upset; I have difficulty watching my children when I know they are in pain.

I replied, "So when you left the room, you were leaving because it was too hard to watch your daughter suffer?" I turned to him and said, "The problem is not that you do not have empathy; the problem is that you get emotionally overwhelmed when others are in pain." He agreed with that assessment.

At this point, Andrea's interest in our conversation increased. She asked, "Are you saying there isn't a problem with empathy? I replied, "I think the issue is that he feels empathy, but he doesn't know how to deal with others' emotions, and as a result, he flees."

I turned to James and said, "If my theory is right, the solution you are seeking is how to stay present when your wife or others are suffering. In the past, when emotions have been tense, you have not had a plan or strategy. As a result, your natural defenses have been to flee the situation. The consequence is that your wife has felt like you did not feel her pain or suffering. Then when she brought up your failure to comfort her, it escalated your feelings of letting her down. This triggered your shame, and you either moved yourself further away from her or argued with her because you were embarrassed." Does this sound right, or am I off?

He looked at me and said, "That feels completely true. It makes sense to me. I see why I have been shutting down. All along, I thought that there was something wrong with me, that I couldn't feel emotions. Now, I get it. I have been running from emotions because they overwhelm me. So, what's the next step?"

Note: I feel great joy when clients like James discover that they are not broken and realize they need to learn new skills like compassion. When clients gain this awareness, I know they are turning the corner toward healing and recovery.

The next step, as I explained to James and Andrea, is developing compassion. By increasing your compassion, you will be physically calm and be able to offer Andrea the emotional support she needs as she expresses her hurt and pain. I continued by saying that this will take practice and increased awareness.

Over the subsequent few sessions, we discussed strategies for staying present when Andrea or the children were having a hard time. I taught him how to stay present and share their pain by practicing a deep listening exercise. I explained to James that men have been taught to fix things in our culture. I told him that the best way he could help was to avoid trying to fix things. Instead, it would be enough if he could listen with an open mind and try to be with his loved ones while they were in pain.

This idea was best explained by author and mindfulness expert Thich Nhat Hahn when he wrote, "In Plum Village, our practice place, deep listening is a very important practice. Every week we get together once or twice to practice listening deeply to each other. As we listen, we do not say anything; we breathe deeply, and we open our hearts in order to really listen to one another. One hour of this kind of listening is very effective, and it is something very precious that can be offered to the person you love." (13) Hahn also included this sound guidance, "So if we love someone, we should train in being able to listen. By listening with calm and understanding, we can ease the suffering of another person." (14)

How Compassion Changes Everything

I began this chapter with the story of a group of men practicing compassion. Since developing compassion is a skill, I told them the more they practiced, the better they would be. In one case, I had the opportunity to see the fruits of practicing compassion. One of the men in the group wanted to bring his wife for one of our three-day intensives, so I had the chance to work with this couple. In our first meeting together, I asked her how she was doing. Her response was, "He is a different man. For the first time in our marriage, he genuinely listens and acknowledges the pain he created in our family."

- It had been a few months since her husband had been in our men's intensive, and he was still incorporating what he had learned. Here are some of the key takeaways that he shared:

- I realized I did not have to be right about everything. I had been selfish. I did things my way for so long and did not listen to my wife.

- I was so focused on my shame that I could not see her pain.

For so long, I would tune her out when she came to me with a concern or problem. She needed me to listen and not fix things. Now I am trying to listen and identify what she needs.

The exciting outcome of this client's change is that his wife began asking him questions. Together, they talked about his childhood and some of the challenges he faced while growing up. He opened up about using pornography in his childhood and college years. As they learned to listen deeply to one another, their understanding grew, and they felt less threatened by the other.

I am convinced that sexual betrayal makes us think and see the worst in others. The pain is so profound that both partners stop seeing, listening, and understanding each other. As couples go through the slow process of healing, both partners turn toward the other's suffering. Usually, the process is accelerated when the betraying partner can genuinely acknowledge the pain they have created. This is often a notable shift, as it is a good sign that unresolved shame from the past has been addressed. Clients' compassion for their partner increases as they lean into their partner's pain without becoming overwhelmed.

Note: If you would like to increase your level of compassion, at the end of this chapter, I have included links to Compassion Exercises that I have developed over the years. Often these practices evoke strong emotions, so it is vital that you are aware of when you are being triggered into shame or anger.

Final Thoughts on the Role Empathy and Compassion Play in Healing

I could easily have a tainted view of our society because I have listened to thousands of stories where others have failed to offer empathy and compassion to those in need. It would be easy to think we are failing these two critical relationship skills. However, I am optimistic. Here's why…

I know that empathy and compassion are learned skills that can be taught. I also know that most people want to have better relationships, but in most cases, they need to learn how to create them. With the correct information, most people can significantly improve their relationships. I have witnessed people who have been told they have no empathy cry and weep when they have learned how to listen without being overwhelmed. We can all be more compassionate and discover the power of being with others in their suffering. The gift we can give those closest to us is to be with them in their ups and downs; we can offer a compassionate heart to them.

Compassion Exercises

Compassion Exercise #1: Seeing Your Partner

This exercise aims to help you see your partner in a new way. Begin by taking a few deep breaths. You will want to continue your deep breathing throughout this exercise. Once you feel calm and relaxed, imagine that you are observing your partner as a child. See them in your mind. You are watching them play, laugh, smile, and enjoy life. They are running, jumping, climbing, and having a great time. Imagine being with them and playing together. What you are experiencing is their original goodness.

Now continue breathing and let your mind gently shift to another time.

Again, imagine your partner as a child. See them, their suffering, hardships, scraped knees, bruised elbows, and tears—the moments when they felt scared, alone, and afraid. See the challenges, the unspeakable times they alone have carried, and feel these burdens. See them as they are by themself, feeling alone. You may want to be there to comfort them. What you are now experiencing is the heart of compassion.

Now we are going to move to another part of seeing your partner. Let yourself see the happiest moments of your partner's life. See their best adventures as a young child and watch the creative force within them in awe. Imagine them taking risks, laughing, conspiring with you in adventure, seeing their success, and their joy of being alive. As you sense their happiest moments, their laughter and triumph, their deepest joy and gratitude for life, know that as you open to this, you are experiencing Mudita (Pāli and Sanskrit: मुदिता), which means joy, especially sympathetic or vicarious joy, or the pleasure that comes from delighting in other people's well-being. (15)

Take a breath or two, release the joy to be open in a new way, and let your awareness now drop deeply like a stone, sinking below where words can touch the deep consciousness.

Now we turn our attention to one more exercise. See your partner through an eternal lens. See them as being young and old… awake and asleep…. see them in different roles as a child, a friend, a teacher, a student. Now imagine them as your partner, teacher, or student. Now, together you are sharing this moment of time. Who are they really? And who is this person you have been thinking about?

As you close this exercise, take a few more deep breaths and let your mind relax and be clear. When you are ready, take a few minutes and write down the thoughts and impressions that came to mind as you went through this exercise.

Note: This exercise was adapted from an audio recording by Daniel Siegel and Jack Kornfield titled *"Mindfulness and the Brain."* (16)

Compassion Exercise #2: Providing Emotional Support for Your Partner

In this exercise, your task is to list the common emotions that your partner shows in your relationship. Take two minutes and write down the common feelings you see your partner expressing (e.g., sadness, anger, fear, anxiety, joy, happiness). You can write your list in the box below in the left column:

What Is My Partner Feeling?	Why Are They Feeling This Way?	How Can I Be with and Support My Partner?

Now, you should have a list of emotions written down. If you still need to write them down, please take two minutes and complete this exercise before moving on to the next stage of this exercise.

In the middle column is the question: Why are they feeling this way? Write down as many answers as possible for the next three minutes. Then write whatever comes to your mind. If nothing comes to your mind, allow yourself to keep thinking about their emotions and ask another way, "I wonder why they are feeling this way?"

In the final part of this exercise, in the right column of the box above is the question, "How can I be with and support when they are having a hard time?" Please take three minutes to brainstorm as many responses as possible about how you can be with your partner and support them with their emotions. Again, if nothing comes to your mind, ask yourself another way, "I wonder if there is a way I can be with and support my partner?"

Note: You may not be ready to provide emotional support for your partner. I am fully aware that this exercise requires individuals and couples to be further down the path to healing. However, it is often by going through these exercises that individuals gain a deeper understanding of their partner. You may want to go through this exercise on a regular basis, as it can help you become more aware of your partner's needs.

Key Takeaways from This Chapter

- Empathy and compassion are relationship skills we learn. Short quizzes were provided so you could see your current level of empathy and compassion.

- Delayed compassion is common for couples experiencing betrayal. As a result, it is essential to have realistic expectations of your partner in the early stage of healing and recovery.

- Developing self-compassion allows you to have more compassion for others. Specific suggestions were given to help you increase your compassion (See couples task list above).

- Empathy can overwhelm individuals and prevent them from being present when needed most. Learning how to shift to a more compassionate approach was discussed.

- Two exercises were provided to help you develop your compassion skills.

Additional Resources:

I have included additional activities and exercises to help you increase your level of compassion.

Additional Compassion Development Activities for the Betraying Partner:

- Watch "The Other Side of Infidelity"

- Read Chapters Six and Seven in this book

- Listen to "During the Discovery Exercise" (If you choose one, make sure you listen to this one.)

Additional Compassion Development Activities for the Betrayed Partner:

- The What Exercise—answer questions about how their behaviors started

- Read Chapters Eight and Nine in this book

- Listen to "Having Compassion Doesn't Mean You Ignore the Problem" https://bit.ly/RYR

Chapter 5: Video: How to respond when your attempt at compassion is met with anger.

Chapter Six

Understanding the Mind of the Betrayed Partner

"You may think you are going crazy, but you are not."

What is a normal response to the discovery of your partner's betrayal? I have asked this question to individuals who have been betrayed by their partners, religious leaders, and therapists worldwide. I usually ask this question because our society does not understand the significance of sexual betrayal in the lives of the betrayed. In an effort to understand the influence of betrayal in committed relationships, over the past twenty years I have gathered research from more than 20,000 betrayed partners. It is one of the world's most extensive sets of such research.

When I started this research project, I had no idea how much it would change my life and understanding. After years of gathering the data, I began sharing the results with others. In 2017, I was invited to give a TEDx talk and had eighteen minutes to share my findings. Since then, over one million people have viewed my address. I have received many messages from individuals who have been betrayed, telling me they had no idea what they were thinking and feeling was so common.

In this chapter, I hope to share the key results from my findings in a way that will help the betrayed, their partner, and anyone else trying to understand the impact that sexual betrayal has on individuals and our society. I will share stories and quotes from numerous betrayed partners so that their voices are heard. If you are the betraying partner, or you have difficulty understanding why someone who has been betrayed is so emotional, I invite you to pause and reflect on my initial question, "What is a normal response to the discovery of your partner's sexual betrayal?"

What Is Normal?

When 75% of people respond similarly to an event or events, we refer to their response as common or normal. When I tell betrayed partners that their racing minds, heightened anxiety, and anger are normal responses to sexual betrayal, many look at me with questioning eyes. Many of my clients tell me they have felt as if they are losing their minds. They report episodes of absolute rage, which validates their fear that they are losing their mind. "What's wrong with me? I have never been this angry before." This is a common question and statement I hear when betrayed partners seek my help. I often tell them that what they are experiencing is betrayal trauma, and what is making them feel "crazy" is their mind trying to find a way to protect them from further harm.

Yes, anger is a defense mechanism of protection. Yes, the racing mind simply tries to make sense of the new information that it does not understand. Avoiding people and places that remind you of your betrayal is also expected. I could go on and on with the symptoms.

After nearly twenty years of studying the effects of sexual betrayal on individuals in committed relationships, it is clear that a majority (at least 70%, but more likely, 75-80%) report post-traumatic stress (PTSD) symptoms. (1,2)

Unfortunately, for years betrayed partners have felt alone in their trauma. Their feelings have been minimized, overlooked, and shut down. Their sufferings increase when people share hurtful remarks regarding the betrayal. Here's a short list of common responses others have made to my clients over the years:

- Just move on.
- Cheating is normal.
- Get over it.
- Why are you so upset?
- Maybe you should spice things up in the bedroom.
- You know s/he still loves you, right?
- Wandering happens even in the best of relationships.

When these types of comments are made, they have an accumulative effect on the betrayed partner's mind. "Am I wrong to think and feel this way? Why can't I just get over this and move on?" When they try to move on, the images of what their partner did to them run through their mind, and their heart starts racing.

Now their body is upset and filled with anxiety and fear. "Why can't I stop thinking about this? What is wrong with me?" They question themselves.

I have yet to mention what happens when they go out in public and feel threatened by how people are dressed or how their partner looks at others. The betrayed partner feels threatened by anything that reminds them of what their partner did. They struggle to know who to trust and who not to trust. They have a hard time being with friends and family in social settings. Their sleep is disturbed by difficult dreams and nightmares. In essence, many betrayed partners have no mental peace day or night.

If I could shout from the mountain tops and be heard, I would beg everyone to understand that *sexual betrayal triggers PTSD symptoms in at least 70% of betrayed partners. What they are experiencing is a natural protective response.* While the betrayed person's intense response may seem over the top, it is self-maintenance. I also want everyone to know that there are solutions to help reduce their suffering. Fortunately, with proper support and treatment, PTSD symptoms can be resolved.

My goal in this chapter is twofold. First, I want to share my research findings so that you understand the PTSD symptoms that sexual betrayal triggers. I hope that this information will help betrayed partners have more insight into what they are experiencing and why. Next, I hope that betraying partners will better understand their partners. Finally, I hope those who support and treat betrayed partners will learn more effective strategies to help the betrayed.

What PTSD Looks Like in Betrayed Partners

When I met Lucas, he was emotionally exhausted. He had discovered his wife Emma's affair while she was in the shower. She had received a text message from her affair partner. Lucas read the words, "Can't wait to see you again. Yesterday was so much fun." He was shocked. Was she having an affair? If so, how long had it been going on? Was she going to leave him? Why was she doing this? How should he respond when she gets out of the shower? What was happening to his life? His heart was racing, and his mind was filled with questions.

When Emma was done showering, Lucas approached her and blurted out, "Are you having an affair?" Stunned by his question, she said, "How do you know?" He told her about the phone message he saw. Then he asked question after question. Emma did her best to answer his questions, but she minimized the extent of the affair, how long it had been going on, and how many times she had met with her affair partner.

Over the next few weeks, Lucas peppered Emma with more questions. Where did they meet? How often did they meet? Was this the first guy, or were there more guys? Was she in love with him? On and on, the questions kept popping into his mind. Initially, Emma did her best to respond, but eventually, she was worn out and told him she couldn't handle all of his questions. This made him angry, and he accused her of hiding information.

For many months they tried to resolve things on their own. Finally, worn out and tired, they called my office to schedule an appointment. In our first session, I asked Lucas a few questions to help me understand his level of trauma. Here are a few of the questions I ask in the first sessions:

1. How are you sleeping at night?

2. How often do you find yourself thinking about Emma's affair?

3. Are you avoiding people and places that you used to go to?

4. Do you feel something is wrong with you because Emma had an affair?

5. How often do you feel anxious since discovering the affair?

6. How often do you find yourself upset or angry at Emma?

After he responded to my questions, Lucas looked at me and said, "It's like you're in my head. How did you know I was dealing with all of those issues?"

I let Lucas know that I have been studying how betrayed partners respond at discovery, and those are some of the most common symptoms people experience; he was surprised. He said, "I didn't know others felt this way, but it makes sense."

I asked him to take an online assessment to help me discover more about his response to Emma's affair. He readily agreed. In our next session, I reviewed his results with him and reviewed each of the five core symptoms of PTSD.

Five Core PTSD Symptoms

In order to diagnose someone with PTSD, there are specific criteria that need to be met. In this section, I will outline the key symptoms from each criterion.

As I move through each area, you may or may not see yourself or your partner's behaviors. I will provide examples of some of the questions for that specific criterion in each section.

Criteria A: Threat to Life

In order to qualify for Criteria A, "The person needs to be exposed to death, threatened death, actual or threatened serious injury, or actual or threatened sexual violence." (3)

Initially, I did not believe that most betrayed partners would qualify for the diagnosis of PTSD because this criterion would disqualify them. However, to discover if there were cases where a threat to life did occur, we asked these questions:

1. How often do you feel violated by your partner's sexual behaviors?

2. How often do you worry that you might contract a sexually transmitted disease because of your partner's sexual behaviors?

3. How often has your partner forced you to have sex with them?

4. Since discovering your partner's sexual behaviors, has s/he hurt, hit, or threatened you?

As the results came in, I was surprised at the responses—over 90% of betrayed partners felt violated by their partner's betrayal. (4) While feeling violated does not qualify as a threat to life, it indicates a strong feeling of disrespect. The next most frequently endorsed question was the fear of contracting a sexually transmitted disease. The results suggest that (60%) of betrayed partners worry about getting a sexually transmitted disease. (5) Since STDs can be life-threatening, I realized that more people than I anticipated would qualify for the PTSD diagnosis. Throughout my career, I have had many clients disclose that they have contracted an STD from their partner. Many have shared how embarrassed they were to ask a doctor or nurse to be tested.

> **Quotes Regarding STDs from Research Participants**
>
> *After the STD infection that nearly killed me, I have no romantic feelings; the thought of him close to me makes me sick.*
>
> *STD was involved in the discovery, and I don't want to be around him or sexual.*
>
> *He has given me three STDs.*

The next question asked about rape within a relationship. This issue is rarely discussed in our culture but is more significant than anticipated. The results indicated that a little over 20% of those who completed the assessment indicated they had been forced to have sex by their partner. When one partner feels it is their right to force their partner to have sex with them, it destroys the relationship. It is controlling and disrespectful to one's partner. As humans, we should never force our will upon another person, and our partners should always have the choice to say yes or no to sexual relations.

And finally, 25% of participants indicated that they had been hurt, hit, or threatened by their partner after discovering their sexual behaviors. Chapter Three discussed the critical role of creating safety in healing and recovery. If at any point your relationship has involved being hurt or hit, or one of you has been threatened, please create boundaries with each other and seek professional support to help you break these patterns.

It is hard to imagine that one in five people have been raped by their partner and one in four are in a relationship with the potential for violence. It is also challenging to think that six out of ten people worry about getting an STD due to their partner's sexual behaviors. These behaviors in relationships will never lead to a healthy relationship.

I am addressing these specific issues because we need to be better. If you want to heal your relationship, these actions cannot be a part of how you interact with your spouse or partner. If you have participated in such activities, I invite you to search deep within yourself and commit to stop your hurtful behaviors. Your partner needs you to recognize the hurt and pain this has created in them. They need you to understand their fears.

If your partner has hurt you in any way mentioned above, please seek help and support. If your partner has engaged in behaviors that put you at risk of getting a sexually transmitted disease, please talk with a doctor about being tested.

Note: This was a challenging section to write. However, the results made it clear that I could not ignore the findings. If you want to see the results and questions in this section, please visit: https://bit.ly/treating-traumat (Criteria A)

Since the diagnosis of PTSD can only be given if all seven areas of PTSD criteria are met, it could be argued that at most 60% of people who experience betrayal trauma could qualify due to the possibility of getting an STD.

However, the other Criteria, from B to G, identified below, suggest that over 70% of individuals are experiencing PTSD symptoms. (6)

Suggested Solutions for Symptoms of Criteria A: Threat to Life

- Establish personal boundaries around safety.
- Seek professional support.

- Consult with a doctor if there is a risk of an STD.

- See *Treating Trauma from Sexual Betrayal*, Chapter Eight, for more solutions.

Criteria B: Recurrent, Involuntary, and Intrusive Memories

In my conversations with betrayed partners, many have discussed experiences where they are in a public setting, and suddenly they experience panic. They explain how being at a park, restaurant, or grocery store can trigger them. Others have told me about frequent nightmares where they dream about what their partner did sexually. They do not realize they are experiencing the key symptoms for Criteria B of PTSD.

Below are a few of the questions from the assessment for Criteria B and the findings:

Question	What Percentage? Minimum Answer Is Sometimes
How often do you have painful memories that remind you of your partner's sexual behaviors?	99%
How often do you have disturbing dreams that remind you of your partner's sexual behaviors?	77%
When your partner tries to get close to you, or you are sexually intimate, how often do you question whether your partner is thinking about you or things s/he has done?	96%
If you are exposed to things that remind you of what your partner has done, how often do you become physically ill (i.e., nauseous, headaches, panic attacks, vomit)?	91%

I thought I had miscoded the answers the first time I reviewed the results. Then, after further exploration, I discovered that these results were accurate. With thousands of participants completing the assessment, I have found that these percentages are correct.

While running an intensive for individuals who have betrayed their partners, I have designated a day where we focus on practicing empathy skills. While reviewing the data, I consider the implications of these results. I think about the person who answered the questions. Then, I share some of these results and ask for their feedback.

Here are some sample questions I ask:

1. What would it be like to have a disturbing dream where you wake up, and your partner cheats on you?

2. Can you imagine what it would be like having your partner attempt to initiate sex with you, but all you can think about is what they did sexually with someone else?

Usually, when I ask these questions, the group's awareness of how their betrayal has hurt their partner increases. On more than one occasion, our group's conversation has led group members to return home and have meaningful conversations with their partners.

Suggested Solutions for Criteria B: Reliving

When clients report they are frequently reliving what their partner did, I conclude that they need to find relief. Such intrusive thoughts can influence every aspect of their life.

Some of the best solutions include:

*   Dream Rehearsal (discussed in a short audio found at https://bit.ly/RYR Chapter Six Support Material)

*   Dealing with core beliefs (discussion found in *Treating Trauma from Sexual Betrayal,* Chapter Nine—Healing Painful Memories)

*   Creating meaningful strategies to interrupt intrusive thoughts (See support material—*How to Interrupt Intrusive Thoughts*)

Criteria C: Avoidance

While reviewing the results with one of my clients, I learned a valuable lesson. She said, "It is hard to be out in public. I feel like everyone is a threat." One of the most common challenges of discovery is losing faith in others. In many cases, betrayed partners struggle to know who they can trust and who they cannot trust. They also struggle to trust their thoughts and emotions. As a result, they attempt to push away or numb out thoughts that remind them of what their partner did.

According to the Diagnostic and Statistical Manual of Mental Disorders (DSM-V), *Criteria C of PTSD* involves the following: Persistent effortful avoidance of distressing trauma-related stimuli after the event. There are two key parts to these criteria: 1) avoidance of anything that reminds you of what your partner did, and 2) avoidance of people, places, or activities that remind you of what your partner did.

Here are some of the questions and results from our assessment of Criteria C:

Question	What Percentage? Minimum Answer Is Sometimes
How often do you attempt to push away memories, thoughts, or feelings related to your partner's sexual behaviors?	98%
How often do you avoid people, places, or activities that remind you of your partner's sexual behaviors?	94%
To what extent do you avoid sexual interaction with your partner since discovering their sexual behavior?	85%

When individuals score high on avoidance, they struggle to be with their thoughts. Over 98% of participants reported attempting to ignore or push away intrusive thoughts because they were too painful. However, while trying to ignore difficult thoughts, most people find them growing with intensity rather than disappearing. This is another example of the Zeigarnik effect described in the previous chapter. The mind continues to think about unresolved issues.

One strategy that may prevent you from avoiding memories, thoughts, or feelings from the betrayal is to pause and evaluate these intrusive experiences. Researchers have discovered that attempting to avoid something in our lives usually makes matters worse for us. If it is something we are afraid of, our fears will grow. If it is a thought, our thoughts about that thing will only increase, not decrease. Therefore, you might find this exercise helpful if you want to respond instead of avoiding unwanted thoughts.

Exercise: I want you to know that this exercise will take courage. However, if you complete it, you will better understand yourself and some of the thoughts you have been avoiding.

Begin by taking a few minutes to write down the intrusive thoughts, feelings, or memories that keep running through your mind. Next, write down two or three things you can do or think when these things come into your mind. Since these thoughts come into your mind even when you don't want them to, you should take control by simply writing them down.

Example: When I think about what my partner did, I will pause and say to the thought, "I see you." Then I will turn some music on, call a friend, or go for a walk. When I feel ambitious, I will write more about the intrusive thought until I have let out my fears and worries. I have learned to face my fear by exploring it. Here's how I did it last time.

Thought: I wonder if he is still acting out.

Challenging Thought: I have had that thought a lot lately. What if he acts out again? What would I do? I know the answer; I will have him leave the house. We have discussed this boundary; I know how I will respond.

This is an example of a strategy I have used with clients who have felt that their thoughts are out of control. By writing down their fears, they generally begin to feel a sense of being in control.

Avoiding People, Places, or Situations that Remind You of Your Partner's Behaviors

The other way that avoidance shows up after betrayal is in relationships. Often, betrayed partners isolate themselves from others because they do not know who to trust. Based on the answers from research participants, well over 90% of those who completed the survey reported that they would avoid people or places that reminded them of their partner's behaviors. When I asked my clients about their experience with avoiding people and places, many mentioned staying away from shopping centers (i.e., malls, shoe stores, etc.), swimming pools or beaches, and religious institutions. These are the places where they feel triggered while observing other couples.

I included one more question from the section that dealt with avoiding sexual interaction with one's partner after discovery. The results indicate that 85% of participants avoid being sexual with their partner, at least in the initial discovery stage. Here's what some of the participants wrote about their approach to sex after discovery.

> *"Too disgusted with my husband to have romantic feelings for him."*
>
> *"I can't look at him the same way, the thought of him touching me makes my skin crawl, and it makes me angry."*
>
> *"Typically avoid interactions or keep things minimal. Occasionally (once a month or two) will want to have sex, but I freeze during sex (can't talk, stop my thoughts, respond, verbalize wants, etc.) and usually cry and feel sick afterward.*
>
> *"Can't imagine ever being intimate again."*

There is a wide range of responses regarding how betrayed partners respond after discovery. In my research, I have found that about 20% of betrayed partners have claimed that their sexual interaction with their partners has decreased or stopped altogether.

Many individuals feel torn, like this person who said, "I didn't want to stop having sex because I thought that would make it more difficult to keep the relationship, and I don't see why I should miss out because of his actions. Also, if he's not having sex with me, where is he getting it? But sometimes I don't want it because I'm so angry and hurt."

In summary, after discovery, many betrayed partners seem confused. Some feel they must fight for their marriage, so they become more sexual. Others feel obligated to have sex because they are married. For these individuals, sex is often emotionally and physically painful. They experience feelings of disgust and get sickened by the thought of being sexual with their partner.

I have observed that it is nearly impossible to predict how betrayed partners will respond sexually after betrayal. Therefore, when betrayed clients ask me if their approach to sex is typical, I say, "Yep!"

I have created an online video, *Seven Strategies for Sexual Reintegration After Sexual Betrayal*, for couples struggling to reconnect sexually after discovery. While you may want to jump online to access that course, I believe that many of you will benefit by first focusing on the steps to healing and recovery included in the next few chapters.

I have found that many couples still engage in sex after betrayal, but deeper forms of sexual integration only come when safety and trust have been re-established.

Let me be clear; I am saying deeper and more enjoyable sex comes as safety and connection increase. We will discuss strategies for improving intimacy, including sexual intimacy, in Chapter Fifteen.

Suggested Solutions for Criteria C: Avoidance

- Avoid isolation and reach out for support. If you do not have meaningful support, consider attending a support group in your area or online.

- Increase emotional regulation skills to help you deal with difficult emotions. Suggestions include 1) Mindfulness; 2) Guided meditations; and 3) Relaxation strategies.

- Additional solutions can be found in Chapter 10 of *Treating Trauma from Sexual Betrayal.*

Criteria D: Negative Alterations in Cognition and Mood

In 2013, the American Psychiatric Association updated the post-traumatic stress disorder (PTSD) symptoms. Their update included a new category that included negative alterations in cognitions and mood associated with the traumatic event(s).

Some of the symptoms included: 1) Inability to remember important aspects of the traumatic event(s); 2) negative beliefs or expectations about oneself (e.g., I am bad, no one can be trusted); and 3) persistent negative emotional state (e.g., fear, anger, or shame). (DSM-V).

This update included critical symptoms that therapists had observed in their clients (e.g., I'm bad because I couldn't prevent my friend from dying, or I can't trust anyone, the world is not safe).

Often after discovery, betrayed partners internalize their partner's behaviors which may include feelings of being unlovable, not good enough, or that the betrayal was their fault. Another common response is for individuals to externalize their experience and conclude that nobody can be trusted or that the world is unsafe.

In the next part below, I include five questions and the results from Criteria D symptoms.

Question	What Percentage? Minimum Answer Is Sometimes
How often do you feel it is your fault that your partner sexually acts out?	83%
Do you feel your partner acts out because you are not good enough?	89%
When in social settings, how often do you feel like you don't belong anymore due to your partner's sexual behaviors?	85%
Since discovering your partner's sexual behaviors, how often do you feel unlovable?	90%
Since discovering your partner's sexual behaviors, how often do you question whether people are safe to be around?	84%

Much like the previous criteria, betrayed clients report elevated symptoms associated with negative cognitions and mood. For each item listed above, 80% of the participants experienced these symptoms at least once, while in most cases, over 50% reported experiencing these symptoms at least half the time or more. In an effort to put this in perspective, if 10,000 betrayed partners complete our survey, 8,000 will feel like they are not good enough or that they don't belong in social settings anymore. When betrayed partners internalize what their partner did, the social and relationship consequences are harmful. Everything we do in life becomes more difficult when we don't feel lovable.

As you will recall, in the chapter on shame, I discussed how negative cognitions (i.e., I am unlovable) hinder the healing process. The influence of betrayal has long-lasting effects when negative beliefs are not resolved. Consequently, one of the key solutions for healing betrayal trauma is to address the negative cognitions and mood.

Suggested Solutions for Criteria D: Negative Cognitions and Mood

- Address negative cognitions (e.g., I am unlovable, not good enough) through treatment methods like eye movement and desensitization and reprocessing (EMDR), Cognitive Behavioral Therapy (CBT), and Internal Family Systems (IFS).

- Address beliefs dealing with trust in others and society. This can be done through creating meaningful connections with others who have been through similar situations and positive experiences with care providers.

- Additional solutions can be found in Chapter 11 of *Treating Trauma from Sexual Betrayal.*

Criteria E: Emotional Arousal and Reactivity

The fifth criterion, emotional arousal and reactivity, includes symptoms such as irritability, angry outbursts, and verbal or physical aggression. Additional signs include reckless or self-destructive behaviors, problems concentrating, exaggerated startle responses, and hypervigilance—constantly assessing for potential threats around you. When these symptoms are elevated, individuals find little mental peace and find that their mind is frequently racing.

Below are a few of the questions from the section from Criteria E. Please note that one of the questions addresses self-harm and other suicidal thoughts.

Question	What Percentage? Minimum Answer Is Sometimes
After discovering your partner's sexual behaviors, how often are you angry when talking to your partner?	98%
How often do you monitor your partner's sexual behaviors since discovery?	91%
How often do you find it harder to concentrate on important things after discovering your partner's sexual behaviors?	98%
Since discovering your partner's sexual behavior, how often have you inflicted physical pain/harm on yourself?	34%
Since discovering your partner's sexual behaviors, to what extent have you had suicidal thoughts?	60%

While the key symptoms of anger, forgetfulness, and monitoring behaviors are elevated (90% or higher for each question), the most important items from this section included the questions about self-harm (34%) and suicidal ideation (60%).

While reviewing these numbers for the first time, I was shocked. I had clients who had shared that they had had suicidal thoughts, but I did not realize that every six out of ten betrayed partners have suicidal thoughts. Furthermore, I did not realize that one in three had inflicted self-harm upon themselves. The emotional pain of betrayal is more than what most people can understand.

The emotional toll betrayed partners experience has been largely overlooked. When individuals cannot slow down their racing minds, their constant anxiety wears them down physically and emotionally. Roy Baumeister, author and researcher, coined the term "ego depletion" to describe what happens when we are out of energy. Baumeister and other researchers have discovered that when our "ego is depleted," we are more likely to cope with unhealthy behaviors (i.e., anger, engaging in unhealthy habits—think ice cream and addictive behaviors). (7)

It has been my experience that reducing the symptoms of Criteria E emotional arousal and reactivity requires consistent effort over time. Furthermore, countering the symptoms described in Criteria E as soon as possible is important. If you are thinking about engaging in self-harm or have suicidal thoughts, please seek professional help and support. An excellent resource in the United States is a new hotline—dial 988 for suicidal support.

If you are experiencing symptoms outlined in this section, here are the top solutions to help you respond effectively.

- Guided meditations (see list of suggestions as found in Appendix K).

- Create accountability and support for the most difficult times.

- Journal when difficult emotions arise (see Expressive writing exercise).

- Additional solutions can be found in Chapter 12 of *Treating Trauma from Sexual Betrayal.*

Does Betrayal Trauma Trigger PTSD?

A few years ago, I wrote an article that outlined each of the core PTSD symptoms and shared the results outlined above. After the article was published in *Psychology* Today, I received many critiques of my work. One person, a professional therapist, indicated that there is no way that sexual betrayal should be compared to the trauma war veterans experience. I wasn't trying to compare the two because they are very different forms of trauma. I was sharing the data from thousands of betrayed partners, demonstrating that the symptoms are very similar.

To validate my findings, in 2019, our assessment of the *Trauma Inventory for Partners of Sex Addicts (TIPSA)* was compared to the Post-Traumatic Checklist

(PCL-5). The PCL-5 has been used to assess individuals for PTSD Criteria B, C, D, and E. The PCL-5 is universally accepted as the standard for evaluating PTSD Symptoms. In our study, we have betrayed partners who take the TIPSA and the PCL-5. When we compared the scores, the results showed very little difference. In essence, the two assessments produced the same results. If a person had PTSD on the PCL-5, they would have similar symptoms on the TIPSA. (8)

Here's my point, a majority of betrayed partners exhibit symptoms of PTSD. If we want to understand the mind of the betrayed, we should look through the lens of PTSD since results indicate that roughly 60% experience Criteria A symptoms, and more than 80% are experiencing PTSD symptoms B, C, D, and E.

> *If a person has PTSD symptoms, the primary focus of treatment should be reducing the PTSD symptoms from their life.*

I hope this chapter has helped you better understand yourself and the specific symptoms you are experiencing due to betrayal trauma. I have outlined the five key criteria of PTSD and offered some basic treatment solutions. If you are experiencing these symptoms, please understand that what you are experiencing is normal. As you reduce the PTSD symptoms, you will experience a deeper sense of healing.

If you have betrayed your partner, I hope that this chapter has opened your eyes to what your partner is experiencing. You may be surprised, but you can help your partner heal in ways you have not considered.

One step you can take is to understand the symptoms described in this chapter. Your awareness of what your partner is experiencing can help you be more patient and understanding. Your partner needs to know that you genuinely understand them. They want you to feel their pain. If you increase empathy and compassion for your partner, the odds of your relationship healing will improve.

I understand that this chapter may have been hard for you to read. Perhaps reading this chapter triggered feelings of shame. If so, seek help to reduce your shame so you can be present with your partner in their pain. My intent is not to make you feel shame; it is to help you increase your empathy and compassion. As your empathy increases, your shame will decrease.

Finally, it is essential to mention two additional questions that are associated with the diagnosis of PTSD. I am sharing these with you so that you have a complete understanding of the PTSD diagnosis.

Duration of Experience

According to the DSM-V criteria, individuals must be experiencing Criteria B, C, D, and E for over a month. In my research, when I asked how long betrayed partners had been experiencing these symptoms, their results indicated that more than 90% had been experiencing these symptoms for longer than one month. Almost 50% reported that they had these symptoms for two years or longer. It is an understatement to suggest that betrayal wreaks havoc on the mental and physical health of those who are betrayed.

Disturbance causes clinically significant distress or impairment in social, occupational, or other important areas of your functioning.

The last PTSD symptom explores how the disturbance (sexual betrayal) influences the social, occupational, or other important areas of your life. When I asked this question to the participants, 93% indicated that sexual betrayal caused significant distress in their lives at least some of the time.

Below are some ways individuals reported their distress and how it influenced their lives:

> *I find it hard to be the parent and grandparent I was before. I feel wrapped up in my little world and sometimes worry.*
>
> *I've lost interest in things I used to do with my children. I'm having a tough time looking for employment because I've lost all my self-worth.*
>
> *I let my thoughts take over my life. If I get stuck on one of the acting-out scenarios, I'll continue thinking about it instead of doing what I'm supposed to do.*
>
> *I am currently unable to work. I quit my job. I became obsessed with what my spouse was doing while I was at work. I couldn't concentrate or focus, and this began to interfere with my performance at work.*

Assessing Your PTSD Symptoms

We have now reviewed each of the symptoms of PTSD that betrayed partners experience. If you have experienced sexual betrayal and want to take this assessment, you can do so by going to the support material for this chapter. This is a free assessment to take, and your answers will contribute to research to help us better understand betrayal and its influence on individuals and couple relationships.

If you want specific feedback on your results, I suggest you seek professional help from a certified sex addiction therapist (CSAT) or certified partner trauma therapist (CPTT). These therapists have been trained to administer these assessments and review your results with you. They can help you understand what to focus on as you move forward in your healing journey.

When I meet with clients who have been betrayed, I use the assessment results to help me create a treatment plan for my clients. It is also helpful for my clients to review their results. Here's a small sample of the type of information that I see when I administer the assessment to my clients.

TIPSA Results:

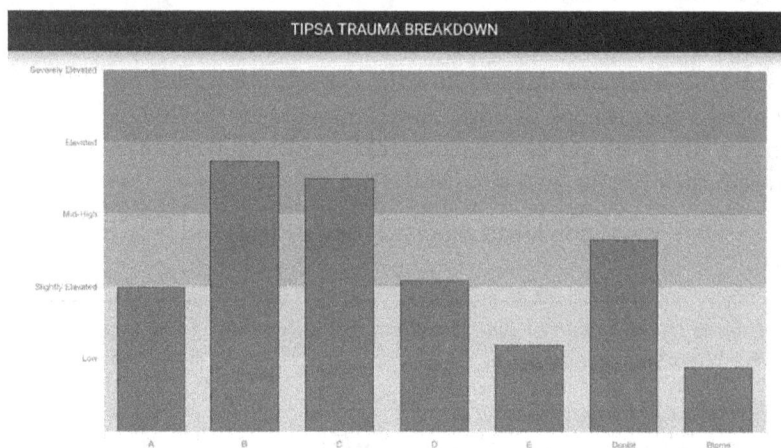

This client's scores were elevated in Criteria B (Reliving the Traumatic Experience) and Criteria C (Avoidance). Their scores were also slightly elevated in Criteria D (Negative Cognitions and Mood).

Based on this information, we want to focus on reducing this client's symptoms in these three categories. However, that does not mean they were not experiencing Criterion A or E symptoms. I would review their responses from these sections with my client to determine if we also needed to address symptoms from those sections.

One more point, in Chapter Thirteen, I will address gaslighting. The two bar graphs on the right side of this image, titled denial and blame, measure gaslighting behaviors which are used during sexual betrayal. I will address these two areas in the chapter on gaslighting.

Helping Lucas Address His PTSD Symptoms

As I reviewed the results from the assessment with Lucas, he began to understand his response to Emma's affair. He no longer felt like he was the only one dealing with these symptoms. He told me he understood what was happening to him.

I could tell his mental wheels were turning, so I waited for him to ask his question. He asked, "So where should I start? I cannot keep living this way!" My response to him was, "Where do you feel you need to start? What issue do you believe is the most critical for you to begin working on from today?" After a brief pause, Lucas said, "I need to be able to focus on work. I find that my mind is constantly wandering, and I can't afford to lose focus." We began developing a strategy so he could focus while he was at work.

Here's the tool I use to help clients narrow down which issue to focus on. I call this the "*What and Why Exercise.*"

Question #1: What's the primary problem with which you want help?

Answer: My mind is racing while at work, and I cannot focus.

Question #2.1: Why is this a problem?

Answer: In my position, I have to focus, or something bad could happen to others. I cannot afford to let that happen.

Note: I usually tell clients to ask themselves, "Why is this a problem?" at least three times, but preferably five times.

Question #2.2: Why is that a problem?

Answer: I could get fired if I make a mistake.

Question #2.3: Why is that a problem?

Answer: I need to provide for my family, and I enjoy my work

Question #2.4: Why would it be a problem if you couldn't provide for your family?

Answer: I would be letting them down. I don't want to let my family down.

Question #2.5: Why would it be a problem if you let your family down?

Answer: I would be doing what my dad did to us. He left us when I was eleven. I don't want to be like him.

By working through this exercise, Lucas discovered that one of his fears was letting his family down. He worried that he would do what his dad had done to his mom and siblings. This insight was helpful to Lucas, but we still had not resolved how he could stop his mind from racing while at work. I asked Lucas about the specific thoughts he was having. After a few seconds, he said, "I think the biggest worry I have is that Emma is going to meet up with her affair partner. This is by far the most common fear that I have."

We again began the *What and Why Exercise* to help him clarify his fear. He had already identified what the problem was. Now we had to help him work through why it was a problem.

Question #1: Why is it a problem if Emma is having an affair while you are at work?

Note: This feels like a dumb question to ask, but it produces incredible results.

Answer: It's not right. I cannot be with her if she continues her affair.

Question #2.1: Why is it a problem if she continues her affair?

Answer: It's just not right. I am working hard while she is screwing someone else. It's freaking wrong.

Question #2.2: Why is it a problem if you are working hard and she continues her affair?

Answer: I have worked hard to get to this point. If she does not value my work and how I provide, then I don't know if I want to be with her. I don't think she appreciates me.

Question #2.3: Why is it problematic if she doesn't appreciate you?

Answer: I will not be in a relationship with someone who does not want to be with me. I want someone who wants me. I may be fooling myself if she cannot respect me and who I am.

Question #2.4: Why is it a problem if she doesn't want to be with you?

Answer: Throughout our marriage, I thought things were going okay. Sure, we had our ups and downs, but I must be stupid not to have known she was cheating on me. I have been wasting my time if she doesn't want to be with me. I deserve to be with someone who desires me.

Often by the time we get to the fifth why, my client's insight has significantly increased. In some cases, they are already experiencing a shift in their thoughts. When we finished this exercise, Lucas said, "I cannot live this way much longer. I need honesty. I will have to ask Emma if she will give up her affair partner. I will explain to her that complete fidelity is what I expect in our relationship, and if she doesn't want to end her affair, I will divorce her.

Next, I asked him, "What if she lies to you again, as she did in the past while hiding her behavior? What will you do? He thought for a moment and said, "I am going to tell her I cannot live with lies or secrets anymore. I will end the relationship if she chooses to continue with her affair. I have to do this because I refuse to live this way.

Note: It is hard for clients to go through this mental exercise. They often recognize the deeper issues and gain more insight by asking themselves why things matter and why something is a problem. For example, in the case of Lucas, he realized that he wanted to be with someone who wanted to be with him. He felt stupid for not discovering her behaviors earlier. He had avoided having a difficult conversation with Emma about his desires and expectations. However, by completing this exercise, he realized that avoiding a difficult conversation was hurting him. He realized she had to be honest with him; she had to choose him and give up her affair, or else they wouldn't be together.

In this exercise, Lucas was able to identify a personal boundary.

We still had not discussed how to handle the intrusive thoughts that came while he was at work. But, over the next few sessions, we developed a strategy to help him respond to the unwanted thoughts. In the next chapter, *Healing the Hurting Heart,* I will discuss how Lucas worked through his intrusive thoughts and other trauma-related symptoms.

Key Takeaways from This Chapter

- In this chapter, we focused on understanding the mind of the betrayed partner. If we want to understand the mind of the betrayed, we must look through the lens of PTSD.

- Based on my findings, over 80% of research participants experienced the following PTSD symptoms: 1) reliving the betrayal; 2) avoidance of people and places and their thoughts; 3) negative cognitions and mood (e.g., I am not enough); 4) emotional arousal (e.g., anger, irritability, thoughts of self-harm).

- In addition, 60% feared getting an STD, and that same percentage had experienced suicidal thoughts.

- Finally, I discussed how to take the TIPSA and the benefits of having your results as you seek professional help.

Chapter Seven

Healing Your Hurting Heart (for the Betrayed Partner)

"My hurting heart is healing. I didn't know how to get through the pain, but I know I can do hard things today. One day at a time, that's where I started."

My client looked at me and asked, "Why won't my pain disappear? I hurt all day long. My mind is racing to the point that I can hardly think of anything else. My sleep is interrupted by nightmares and bad dreams. I can't focus at work because my mind is thinking about what my husband did."

For most of my career, I have met men and women whose hearts are hurting because of sexual betrayal. When clients ask me how to let their pain go, I share what I have learned from other clients whose hearts have healed. I figure those who have been through the healing journey have the most to share.

In this chapter, we will begin by discussing the choices you will need to make to heal. When you picked up this book, you made a choice. You made a choice by reading this far in this book. As you move forward, you will be faced with many options. The decisions you make will influence how you heal.

Some of your decisions will directly influence your relationship. It is common to get lost in questions like, "Can my relationship be repaired?" Or "Knowing what I know now, do I want to move forward in this relationship?" You have probably thought about each of these questions many times since discovering your partners' behaviors. I hope you will heal whether you stay in your relationship or not. This chapter will help you focus on your healing.

After discussing how your choices can influence your healing process, the next part of the chapter will focus on two fundamental principles of healing that my clients have taught me.

Next, I will share twenty core components of the healing process. If you implement these strategies as you work through betrayal, you will have a solid foundation for long-term healing.

I will conclude this chapter by finishing Lucas and Emma's story introduced in Chapter Six.

Choosing to Heal

Have you ever asked yourself, "Am I ever going to get over my partner's betrayal?" I have many clients who ask similar questions from me, "Is it possible to get over sexual betrayal?"

I have put a lot of thought into this question. I don't want to give false hope or misguide someone. I also recognize that those who ask me often feel a sense of hopelessness.

To provide my clients and others with the most accurate response, I began reviewing research to understand if people can get over the hurt and pain of betrayal.

Unfortunately, there isn't a lot of research on the subject. The most helpful finding came from the work of Dr. Peggy Vaughn. Here's what she found in her study with over 1000 participants who had been betrayed:

Your Current Condition (Regardless of whether Still Married or Divorced): Question: Do you still dwell on the affair(s)?	Men	Women
Yes, it's still a pain I carry every day.	56%	55%
While I still think about it from time to time, it's not a constant focus.	30%	33%
No, I've pretty much put it in perspective in my life and moved on.	14%	12%

Source: Dr. Peggy Vaughn (1)

When I first reviewed Dr. Vaughn's findings, I was discouraged. Perhaps you are feeling that way too. After considering these findings' implications, I wondered if there is a way to help clients and others reduce their pain. I began wondering about the 30-33% of individuals still thinking about it, but it's not a constant focus. I continued pondering on the 12-14% who have put their partner's affair into perspective and moved on. How did they do it? How do individuals heal and move on? Is there a secret? If so, can I share it with every individual and couple trying to recover from betrayal?

These questions have driven my work over the past few years. In the rest of this chapter, I will share what I have learned through study and research and what the real experts, my clients who have been betrayed, have taught me about their healing journey.

Principles to Heal Your Hurting Heart

In my book, *Treating Trauma from Sexual Betrayal: The Essential Tools for Healing*, I shared a model for therapists to apply with their clients. The model's purpose was to outline healing solutions and critical steps to take in the process.

The suggested solutions included:

- Seek genuine understanding and create a safe and trusting environment
- Internal exploration: Resolve difficult emotions and hurtful beliefs
- Create a positive support network while reducing negative interactions
- Strengthen your inner-self

In this book, I will highlight essential parts from the model described in *Treating Trauma from Sexual Betrayal* and expound on specific ideas discussed. You can find a copy of this model along with a quiz to see how you are doing in these areas in Appendix F. In the section below, I will outline each solution. However, before I do that, I would like to share two specific traits I have observed in betrayed partners who heal.

Trait #1: Never Give Up

Life is filled with many transition points. How we respond to these specific events or experiences will significantly influence the rest of our lives. Recently, I was reading *B.E 2.0 (Beyond Entrepreneurship 2.0)*.

In the book, authors Jim Collins and William Lazier describe how incredible leaders have responded to significant adversity. I was struck by how many of these iconic figures faced dark times before they emerged to create or do something great.

Collins and Lazier wrote about life's challenges: "Most of us get decked somewhere along the way in life, slammed to the ground, the world looking down on us. And when—not if, when—that happens, we have a choice. Do we get back up? And when it happens again, do we get back up again? And again, and again, and again, and again?" (2) You are likely asking yourself, "Do I get back up again?" I know you do. You keep getting up, and you keep fighting for peace.

Later in the book *B. E. 2.0*, Collins wrote, "When I'm feeling clobbered by events, pounded by setbacks, or just flat-out exhausted from dealing with my own mistakes, I think of Steve Jobs, Winston Churchill, and Tommy Caldwell." (3) Earlier in his book, he shared stories from these three individuals' lives where they had hit rock bottom. Jobs had lost his company Apple, and Churchill at the end of the Second World War and, in his 60s, found himself thrown out of office when his party lost the election. He felt deeply pained but never gave in or up. And Caldwell spent seven years attempting to "free climb" the Dawn Wall, which (if completed) would be the hardest big-wall free climb in history. (To "free climb" means ascending every inch of the cliff under your power by clinging by your fingertips; you use ropes only to catch your falls, not to help you ascend.)" (4)

As I listened to Collins and Lazier describe what these leaders accomplished after their adversity, I realized that these stories paralleled my clients' accounts, who showed this mindset. They never gave up, even though there were many occasions when they wanted to quit, but they didn't.

So, the first principle to healing your hurting heart is never giving up. Keep learning; keep growing. In the end, you will find more internal peace.

Trait #2: Commit to Healing Your Mind and Body

One of the biggest takeaways from my years of research on sexual betrayal is that the stress takes a toll on the minds and bodies of the betrayed. I have seen individuals in their twenties and thirties with ulcers, high blood pressure, and other health-related issues due to stress. As individuals go through the healing process, many who have experienced significant health problems naturally seek solutions by healing their bodies. Clients turn to yoga, mindfulness, and other body-centered solutions as a part of their healing process.

I have observed that when clients engage in mind and body healing, they gain additional strength and confidence to overcome difficult times. Based on my observation, if you want to accelerate your recovery, commit to healing your mind (relaxation training, guided meditations) and body (yoga, regular exercise).

Since constant stress wears down the body, the strategies listed above are some of the most effective ways to relax your mind and body. In multiple studies, yoga, mindfulness, relaxed meditations, and exercise have all been found to help strengthen the mind and body. (5,6,7)

Let's now review the model for healing from sexual betrayal:

Core Healing Solution #1: Seek Understanding and Create a Safe and Trusting Environment (5 Key Components)

1. Model and Find Compassion

Fundamental to your healing is compassion for yourself. Author Christopher Germer described the importance of compassion this way, "The key to compassion is tuning in to the nature of suffering, to understand it in the depths of our being, and to see clearly into its source; but equally important is to be committed to relieve it and to rejoice in the possibility of the alleviation of suffering for all. (8)

Compassion means (com = with) and (passion = suffering). One of the first things you can do in your healing is to increase your self-compassion. This means you avoid judging yourself or speaking to yourself negatively (i.e., I'm so stupid, there is something wrong with me). Instead, acknowledge the hurt and pain you are feeling and avoid all self-criticism. One of the hallmarks of self-compassion is that you are kind to yourself and are less judgmental of your thoughts, feelings, and behaviors.

2. Find Someone to Help You Feel Felt

One of the most critical starting points in the healing journey is to have at least one person who makes you "feel felt." You will know that someone feels your pain. Applying this beautiful concept to the healing journey means you will feel heard, understood, and validated.

3. Seek Information and Get Clear Guidance

Knowledge is power. The more understanding you have about yourself and your partner, the better you can make decisions. Throughout the healing process, information will be your friend.

4. Learn to Listen to and Trust Your Inner Voice

Many clients have shared with me that they felt something was off with their partner, but they couldn't understand what. Then after discovery, what they were feeling began making more sense. You have to show self-trust by pausing and listening to your inner voice when something feels off.

Author of the book *Trust: Master the Four Kinds of Trust*, Ilyanla Vanzant, wrote, "Self-trust the development and mastery of an unwavering, unquestionable inward conviction about your own value, worth, and ability to be, to create, and to enjoy all that you desire in the process of living and learning more about yourself." (9)

5. Establish Goals to Create Hope

A practical step in the healing journey is establishing personal goals. As you create your healing plan (e.g., I am going to do self-care three times a week, I am going to improve my sleep, etc.), you will feel your inner strength grow. This may feel like something difficult or out of your control, but even simple goals can help you feel more in control of your situation.

Core Healing Solution #2: Internal Exploration: Resolve Difficult Emotions and Hurtful Beliefs (5 Key Components)

The focus of the second core solution is internal exploration (awareness). One of the most challenging healing tasks is looking inside at your hurts and pains. This phase of healing is one of the most difficult but also one of the most rewarding ones. As you do the difficult work in this section, you will accelerate your healing. Most of the strategies discussed in this section may need the guidance of a professional therapist.

1. Explore New and Old Wounds

In Chapter One, I introduced you to the *Key Life Event Inventory*. That exercise will help you increase your awareness of how past experiences connect with emotions you feel from your partner's sexual betrayal. I have had clients ask me why they should explore their past experiences when their core pain is associated with their partner's betrayal. I have found that individuals who work through their betrayal trauma from their partner also discover how past experiences (e.g., trauma) bring up old beliefs (e.g., I am unlovable, I am not enough). Often sexual betrayal triggers thoughts and feelings from previous life events, so when you work to heal current events, you will likely bump into past experiences.

2. Identify Triggers

Many betrayed partners become triggered by random experiences (i.e., being at a grocery store, watching a television show, or a song playing on the radio). Developing a plan to respond to these triggers is empowering. More often than not, most partners I have worked with have yet to create a plan, and consequently, when a trigger comes, they need to prepare to respond to it. I have created a short audio presentation to help you respond to triggers: If you want to learn how to respond effectively, visit (https://bit.ly/RYR) Chapter Seven.

3. Address Negative Beliefs About Self and Others

After sexual betrayal, it is common to develop negative self-beliefs. It is difficult to heal when your internal dialogue is critical of yourself. In previous chapters, I discussed strategies that you can use to address negative beliefs you may have. If you haven't taken the time to address your negative self-beliefs, I strongly recommend you prioritize this.

4. Process Painful Memories and Difficult Emotions

Throughout this book, I have emphasized that processing difficult emotions and memories is essential for healing. When our minds replay the same painful thoughts and memories, they seek a solution but cannot find one. A similar approach can help you deal with painful memories and difficult emotions. In Chapter Four, I shared two examples of how clients worked through their shame.

If you would like more examples of processing painful memories and difficult emotions, I suggest reading Chapter Nine in *Treating Trauma from Sexual Betrayal: The Essential Tools for Healing*.

5. Treat PTSD Symptoms

In the previous chapter, I introduced you to the PTSD symptoms often accompanied by sexual betrayal. If there is one thing you take from the last chapter, please remember that your recovery is directly related to reducing PTSD symptoms. As you address each sign, you will feel stronger and more in control of your life, emotions, and healing.

If you are looking for more support to help you reduce negative beliefs, process painful memories, and reduce PTSD symptoms you may be experiencing; I would strongly recommend finding a therapist who specializes in the following treatments:

- Cognitive Behavioral Therapy (CBT)

- Eye Movement and Desensitization and Reprocessing (EMDR)

- Internal Family Systems (IFS)

These are scientifically proven strategies that help individuals reduce traumatic memories and experiences. I will provide additional recommendations in My Favorite Resources in Appendix (F).

Core Treatment Solution #3: Create a Positive Support Network While Reducing Negative Interactions

1. Boundaries

In their book on *Boundaries in Marriage*, Henry Cloud and John Townsend wrote, "Boundaries are not something you 'set on' another person. Boundaries are about yourself." (10) This simple yet true principle guides my betrayed clients toward the path of healing. I have found that many of my clients struggle to establish boundaries because they do not like conflict or because their partner has been critical of them when they have tried to set boundaries.

If you struggle to establish or create boundaries, I invite you to review this statement that I previously shared as you consider what you need for healing.

> "As we draw invisible boundary lines, we are not building walls to keep the enemy out. On the contrary, we keep our lines intact to preserve our relationships! Once we clearly define our boundaries, we begin to communicate openly and directly. And we establish guidelines for what we expect of others—and what we should give them in return. But if we grow up in homes that don't function well in terms of communication or understanding or enter into destructive marriages, boundaries are not respected, and we become confused, vulnerable, and insecure. We don't attempt to defend our rights because we don't realize we have any!" (11)

Individuals who establish effective boundaries are not trying to control their partner. Far too often, I have seen individuals attempt to control their partner's approach to recovery. Usually, trying to control how another person approaches recovery does not work well. Paul Ferrini, the author of *Silence of the Heart*, wrote this about boundaries: "Somewhere there is a decision that honors you and also honors others. Find that decision. Be committed to finding it." (12)

Here's an example demonstrating why attempting to control your partner's recovery is ineffective.

Recently, I was working with a couple trying to decide if they could save their marriage. After a couple of days of observing their patterns, it became clear that the husband would tune out his wife when she brought up things she thought he needed to work on. I brought this to their attention and turned to ask him what was happening when his wife told him what he needed to do to recover. He looked directly at me and said, "I tune her out. I don't need her to tell me what to do." He continued, "My mom did that, and I refuse to be told how to live my life."

His wife was triggering a lot of his childhood issues. While his wife had good intentions, she was pushing him away. As a result, his wife was unknowingly getting the exact opposite results that she wanted. After further discussion, I turned to the wife and said, "I know this is going to be hard, but if you want to have a better relationship with your husband, focus on your personal boundaries and let him identify what he needs to do to recover."

Interestingly, the next day as we continued our work together, she turned to her husband and courageously said, "I have been pushing you to do your own recovery work, and that is not who I want to be. I want to support you but not control you." I looked at him and said, "What does that feel like to hear her say that?" He replied, "That makes me want to be with her."

Note: As you discover more about yourself, you will naturally learn what you can and cannot accept in your relationship. As your awareness increases, your boundaries will be about your healing, not what your partner is or is not doing in their recovery.

If you want to learn more about boundaries in the healing and recovery process. I have recorded a short audio designed to help you effectively discuss boundaries.

2. Establish Close Connections

One of the biggest challenges of sexual betrayal is the ongoing struggle to determine safety. When we don't feel safe, we naturally hesitate to connect with others. Similarly, when betrayed partners need connection the most, they hold back because trusting others makes them vulnerable. What compounds matters is that others do not always know what to do or say.

I asked research participants if they had contacted others for support a few years ago. For the people who answered yes, I asked them a follow-up question, "If you did turn to others, how effective was their support?" I share my findings to give you realistic expectations when you seek help.

Here are a few of the responses I received:

> *It depends. Support groups have been most helpful. Family and friends were not helpful for the most part and mostly dismissive.*
>
> *It was good to tell someone, but it feels very isolating to be in this situation. Everyone's experience is so different. No one understands how I feel.*
>
> *I am on my third therapist. I think it will take some time. Trust is hard, and there is a lot of pain to recover from.*
>
> *My mother told me I was overreacting. Many people told me it was my fault. I find it hard to turn to people for help and feel isolated.*
>
> *Although it was difficult to discuss openly, I realized I had to let it out. I felt I was losing myself and acting like a crazy person. My mom knew something was up. I finally got honest, and she is helping me.*

While each response is different, there are a few things I want to highlight. First, it takes a lot of courage to reach out to others and ask for their support. Second, if one person doesn't respond well, please keep trying. Third, I appreciate the person who said they were on their third therapist. My heart hurts for the person who was told that they were overreacting. Finally, I appreciate a mom helping her daughter navigate through her pain.

Not everyone will know how to help you. However, when you open up and allow others to support you, you will find that a connection will help you heal.

3. Build a Support Team

Usually, when I discuss the importance of building a support team, my clients hesitate. So, I have learned to give them a short exercise. Here's how the exercise works. First, list potential people who might be able to help you in some way. They don't even have to know what you are experiencing. They may be someone you can go to a movie with or exercise with. Second, rank order each person on your list, starting with the person you think could be the most helpful to you. Third, create a plan to reach out to the person identified. Fourth, prepare for your conversation. What will you say to them? What do you want them to know? Fifth, set up a time to meet with them and write about your experience with them. Did it go well? Not so well? What would you do again? What would you change?

This exercise is designed to help you build your support team. I have observed that individuals with a good support team generally heal faster after betrayal.

Additional ways to build your support team include:

- Attending a support group

- Getting a sponsor

- Sharing your experience with friends or family who are understanding

- Talking with a religious leader

4. Inner circle

Choose people to be in your inner circle. A friend taught me this valuable lesson about life a few years ago. He said, "In life, you choose who is on the stage with you, who is in the front row, who is in the back of the auditorium, and who is not in attendance at all." This concept has been of help to many of my clients through the years. By intentionally choosing who is on the stage with you, you will want to ensure you spend more time with them.

One suggestion I make to my clients is to list the people they interact with each day or week. Then identify how close each person is to them (inner circle—on the stage, second circle (in the front row), third circle (in the back of the auditorium), and outer circle (not in attendance). This simple exercise can help you identify if you are spending time with the people who will support your healing.

5. Understand the Spiritual Connection

If spirituality is important to you, staying connected with your higher power can be extremely helpful as you heal. Unfortunately, I have observed far too many people of faith lose confidence in their God because they have stopped trusting everyone. Therefore, if you are a person of faith, I encourage you to remember the spiritual feelings and promptings from your past in which you have felt God's love for you.

Remember that people, including religious leaders, could be better. However, God is perfect, kind, loving, and aware of your suffering. I invite you to do things that will help you maintain your bond with your Higher Power.

Core Treatment Solution #4: Strengthening Your Inner Self

The five suggestions in treatment solution #4:

1. Regain Your Self-Trust

This life gives everyone a dose of difficult challenges. One of the most difficult situations we can face is when someone close to us shakes our confidence. A once-trusted person has made us question our own identity. Many betrayed clients have told me they fear missing the warning signs. Often, after betrayal, betrayed partners question their intuitive responses. They have lost their sense of self-trust.

As you start your journey toward healing, you will discover the importance of trusting your intuition. Author Iyanla Vanzant wrote, "Self-trust is the development and mastery of an unwavering, unquestionable inward conviction about your own value, worth, and ability to be, to create, and to enjoy all that you desire in the process of living and learning more about yourself." (13) The key element discussed here includes an inward conviction about your value and worth. Throughout this book, I have emphasized that healing is about knowing yourself and your true worth.

Self-trust is also about creating boundaries, caring for your needs because you matter, and being true to yourself. Often my betrayed clients tell me they have been angrier than ever. In some cases, they have started wondering if they are just an angry person. My response is that the anger is trying to protect you from being hurt again. Our hurts often come out as anger. As you heal, you will realize that you can trust yourself. You can trust that your thoughts and emotions will help you communicate your thoughts and feelings. When you can trust yourself, your confidence increases because you know who you are and what you will and will not live with.

2. Self-Care

One of my favorite stories about self-care came from a client who had experienced so many challenges. In addition to her husband's betrayal, one of her children had engaged in a questionable behavior so he had to be removed from her home for a while. When I first met her in a group, she said, "I will do anything I can to heal, so please just tell me what to do." Over the next few months, as I got to know her, I realized she was not joking when she said, "I will do anything to heal." This awareness helped me challenge her after a few months to take the initiative to care for herself. Throughout her life, she has been a caretaker. In her childhood, she cared for her mom and younger siblings. Now as an adult, she was taking care of her children, serving her neighbors, and giving to everyone else.

My challenge to her was to identify something she would like to do for herself and then do it. A few weeks later, she came to the group and announced that she would start an art class. She told us she had always wanted to take a class, but other things got in the way. I thought to myself, she is learning to take care of herself; I was excited for her. Life experiences can challenge us and keep us down, but when we keep fighting through adversity, we eventually find more peace and happiness.

One thing I have observed is that for people who regain confidence and make progress in their healing, self-care is a priority for them.

Here are some self-care things I have seen clients doing and how it helps:

- Going to lunch with a friend (helps to stay socially connected)

- Exercise (benefits emotional and physical well-being)

- Focus on getting better sleep (increases energy to carry out day-to-day tasks)

- Getting a pedicure/manicure (helps feel better about self)

- Attends a group (helps develop a support team and social connection)

3. Mindfulness/Yoga

Often, when my clients struggle to reduce their fear and anxiety, I invite them to do mind and body work through mindfulness exercises or yoga. If they tell me they do not have time for these classes, I tell them they are research-based methods for reducing depression, anxiety, stress, and PTSD symptoms. Here's some science to support how these two practices can benefit you.

In a study published in the journal JAMA Internal Medicine, researchers found that practicing mindfulness meditation reduced depressive symptoms by almost 50%. (14) Similarly, another study showed that mindful breathing exercises can reduce anxiety levels by more than 50%. (15)

And in yet another study, researchers found that mindfulness-based therapy was effective in reducing symptoms of post-traumatic stress disorder (PTSD). (16) These studies suggest that regular mindfulness practice can help us become more resilient against negative emotions such as fear and anxiety, as well as increase our overall well-being.

One of yoga's most widely accepted benefits is its ability to reduce stress and anxiety. Studies conducted by Harvard Medical School show that regular practice can reduce cortisol levels—the hormone responsible for stress—by up to 25%. (17) Practicing yoga can also lower anxiety levels by improving focus and mindfulness.

In one study, participants who practiced yoga regularly could better regulate their emotions and reported feeling more relaxed than non-practitioners. Additionally, research indicates that yoga can increase cognitive functioning by improving memory recall and decision-making skills. (18)

As a clinical director of an agency for the past ten years, I have observed that individuals participating in our mindfulness and yoga classes feel more emotionally strong and develop better coping methods when dealing with their partners' betrayal.

4. Resiliency

I had just completed a radio interview with Dr. Al Siebert, an internationally known expert on resiliency, and could not have been more excited. The interview was filled with incredible information about the traits of resilient people. Dr. Siebert shared with our audience strategies on how resilient people make it through challenging times (e.g., holocaust survivors, people who had lost everything through natural disasters, individuals who had significant health challenges, and much more). His ideas were insightful and helped me better understand resilient people.

As we concluded, I asked him if he would be willing to join me again for another interview. He paused and said, "I don't think I can. I have recently been diagnosed with stage 4 cancer and am learning to apply the same resilient principles I have learned from others over the past thirty-five years. I was stunned. He could have canceled our interview, but he shared his wealth of information with others. I followed him over the next few months, and he died about four months after our interview.

His book, *The Resiliency Advantage*, has been a book I have often used since that time. Here are a few key takeaways of what resilient people do when they go through difficulties:

#1. They become flexible rather than rigid.

#2. Resilient survivors handle their feelings well when hit with unexpected difficulties, no matter how unfair.

#3. Resilient people don't wait for others to rescue them; they work through their feelings, set goals, work to reach their goals, and often emerge from the resiliency process with a better life than before.

#4. In crises, they learn to calm themselves and focus on taking the usual actions.

#5. They report that their difficulties have made them stronger than before the adversity. It takes time, but they believe things will work out, and they figure out how to improve their life. (19)

5. Create Genuine Happiness

Some of the signs I look for in healing clients include: smiling, teasing, and having fun again. This is when I know clients are progressing because they are relaxing enough to find joy and happiness again. If it has been a long-time since you laughed and played, I encourage you to give yourself a break from the burdens you have been carrying. You might consider listening to a comedian who makes you laugh or reading a story that reminds you that life can be fun again.

A few years ago, researchers discovered that laughter therapy helped cancer patients in many ways. "Studies have found a variety of positive effects of laughter therapy on anxiety, depression, tension, rage, and general health. It (laughter) has also been found to be useful for insomnia, pain relief, improving pulmonary function, and increasing immunity ([20,21,22,23](#)). When we laugh, it lightens the burden of our difficulties.

Exercise: Even if you are not currently feeling like laughing, I invite you to do some self-care by doing some laughter therapy. In this exercise, I invite you to begin by noticing the tightness and tension in your body. Give yourself a stress score between zero (very little stress) to ten (very high stress). Now that you have your score choose an activity that will make you laugh (i.e., listen to a comedian you like or watch a movie that has made you laugh in the past). After the activity, pause and notice your stress level again. Give yourself a stress score between zero and ten again. How did your tension level change by doing this exercise?

One way to increase your level of happiness is to engage in activities that bring you joy. Such activities include 1) writing in a gratitude journal; 2) giving others compliments; 3) participating in an activity that matters to you; 4) serving others; and 5) engaging in regular self-care.

Note: We have now been through four core treatment solutions that offer twenty strategies to help you measure your progress. If you would like to track your growth, in Appendix (E), you will find a chart that lists each of the twenty items we have just covered. You can score yourself in each area to monitor progress.

The Conclusion of Lucas and Emma's Story

In the previous chapter, I introduced the story of Lucas and Emma. Let's now finish their story. As you may recall, Lucas was reeling from his wife's affair. She had minimized her affair and had been gaslighting Lucas for many months. In a session with Lucas, we went through a "What and Why exercise." In this exercise, we defined the problem and then asked why it was a problem. Lucas gained a lot from the exercise. He realized he was afraid of losing his job and was most concerned about Emma continuing her affair. While he was at work, he was not able to concentrate because he was worried that Emma was still having an affair.

He concluded that he wanted me to help him with two specific things: #1) He wanted help addressing his intrusive thoughts, and #2) he wanted to communicate with Emma that he would not stay in their relationship if she continued her affair. He was creating a boundary so he could begin healing.

Strategies for Dealing with Intrusive Thoughts

A common symptom associated with sexual betrayal is intrusive thoughts. Lucas told me that while he was at work, he couldn't stop thinking about what Emma had done. Then his mind would start worrying about what she was doing while he was at work. He said, "I can't concentrate, and my job requires me to concentrate." So we began developing a plan for responding when the intrusive thoughts began.

Here is a list that we came up with together:

- Recognize the fear/worry and tell myself I will think about these things after work because there is nothing I can do about it right now.

- I can tell Emma what I am experiencing at work and ask if she has any ideas.

- I could practice a relaxation breathing strategy and honor my fear instead of trying to push it away.

- I can think to myself, "If that is what she chooses, I will move on.

Now let's explore how these ideas can help Lucas reduce his worries about Emma while at work.

Idea #1: How to Address Intrusive Thoughts—Recognize the fear/worry.

Lucas's first step was to recognize and accept his fears. Next, he identified what he could and could not control. This concept is referred to as locus of control. "Researchers refer to our perception of being able to influence an outcome as the locus of control. Locus of control is the extent to which individuals perceive that their actions have an influence on the living conditions that they face and the extent to which they attribute their circumstances and rewards to fate, luck, chance, or powerful others, instead of believing that their circumstances and rewards are influenced by their own actions." (24)

Here's how this plays out in marriages. In a 1999 study, married couples were asked about their perception of being able to influence an outcome in their relationship. The researchers found that "Higher levels of marital locus of control were associated with reports of higher positive marital quality and reports of lower negative marital quality. Spouses with lower levels of marital locus of control were more likely to report the presence of marital strains that were linked to lower levels of marital quality." (25) In relationships where individuals reported that their behaviors could influence their spouse, they were happier.

The research suggests that we do better and are more motivated when we believe we can ultimately determine what happens to us. In this case, Lucas became more motivated when he realized that he couldn't control Emma's actions, but he could control how he responded to her behaviors.

Idea #2: How to Address Intrusive Thoughts—Have an open and honest discussion with Emma.

When I asked Lucas about being open with Emma about his fears while at work, he replied that he had been avoiding difficult conversations with her because he did not want any more conflict. He said that he had felt something was off in her behavior before discovering her affair, but he didn't know how to bring it up. He decided avoidance was not helping their relationship, so it was time, to be honest.

Note: I will often role-play with clients because many struggle to communicate their true feelings effectively.

Here's an Example of a Role-Play:

Me: So, what will you say to Emma about the intrusive thoughts you are having at work?

Lucas: I don't know. I will tell her that I can't concentrate at work because I am afraid she is still having an affair.

Me: How do you think she will respond to that?

Lucas: Not very well. Every time I bring up the affair, she gets defensive.

Me: Do you have any idea if there would be a better way to bring it up?

Lucas: I don't; I pay you to help me do it right.

Me: Laugh… Okay…what do you want to say to her?

Lucas: I don't know.

Me: Okay…let's consider the core points you have already mentioned.

- I'm struggling to focus on work.
- I'm worried that you are still having an affair.
- I need to know if you want to be with me or not.

Lucas: That seems about right.

Me: How could you say those things in a way that Emma could hear you without it feeling like you are attacking her?

Lucas: Could I say, "Emma, I have been thinking about our relationship. I find myself struggling at work to focus. I am afraid that the affair is still going on, and it keeps me from focusing. I don't know how to stop these thoughts. My biggest question is whether you want to stay in our relationship.

He then asked, "How does that sound?" Pretty good, I said. Then I asked him what he wanted to happen. He responded that he did want the relationship to work out. I then suggested that he include that thought when he talked with Emma. I said, "If you want the relationship, she needs to know your hopes and desires. She also needs to know that you are struggling to trust her.

In our next session, Lucas told me how his conversation with Emma had been very helpful. His clear and open approach helped Emma understand his concerns. He reported that she didn't feel attacked. She opened up and told him she also wanted to save their marriage. When Lucas asked how she would deal with her affair partner, Emma said that she had stopped talking to the other guy and told him she couldn't talk with him anymore.

When I asked Lucas if he believed her, he replied, "She felt genuine, but I never thought she would have done what she did. I want to believe her, but it is hard. Time will tell. I asked Lucas why he thought Emma was not defensive this time. He replied, "I wasn't aggressive or upset when I approached her. I was prepared and knew what I needed to say. That made it so she could hear what I was trying to say without feeling attacked or accused.

Note: When I role-play with clients, they practice effective communication. I have found that practicing and knowing in advance what you want to say and how to communicate your message effectively leads to positive outcomes. Your confidence grows even if your partner doesn't respond the way you want or hope they will. For example, if Emma had become defensive in this case, Lucas could have said, "I don't want you to feel like I am attacking you. I need your help. I need help to focus on work and could use some ideas. I don't know how to overcome the fears I am having. By enlisting her help, he is inviting her to help him solve his problem. This is an effective problem-solving strategy. (For more information on why this help, please read Chris Voss's book, *Never Split the Difference.* (26)

Idea #3: How to Address Intrusive Thoughts—Practice relaxation breathing and honor my fears instead of trying to push them away.

In one of our sessions, Lucas asked about a strategy he could use when his mind is racing. I suggested that he practice a simple breathing technique that has helped many people relax and reduce stress.

Exercise: Deep breathing can help you slow down and relax, allowing your body to recover from stress and tension. Breathe deeply through your nose and fill your lungs with as much air as possible. Then slowly exhale out of your mouth. Feel how the air moves through your body, calming your mind and body with each breath. Breathe in on a count of four, hold for two seconds, and then breathe out on a count of five. Repeat this cycle ten times to experience the full benefits of relaxation. Pay attention to how your body feels after each cycle, and notice how your breathing may become slower, deeper, and more consistent as you move through the exercise. Acknowledge any thoughts or feelings that arise without judgment, then focus on your breathing again.

Breathing exercises like this can help clear your mind, relieve stress, and help you relax. Researchers have discovered many benefits of practicing a simple breathing exercise like the one above. Some studies have discovered that breathing techniques are effective against anxiety, stress, insomnia, and other physical health issues. (27,28)

Idea #4: How to Address Intrusive Thoughts—I can think, "If that is what she chooses, I will move on because there is nothing I can do about her choice.

In this final strategy, Lucas was practicing letting go of the outcome. While he wanted the relationship to last, he realized that Emma would have to choose their relationship and him. While letting go of the desired outcome is extremely hard, Lucas recognizes that he can't control Emma's behaviors. In this realization, he felt more empowered. He put less pressure on Emma while simultaneously letting her know his expectations. She had to make her choice, and he would respond accordingly.

Key Takeaways from This Chapter

- While healing is not easy, choosing to heal is something you can do for yourself.

- Two common traits of individuals who choose to heal are: 1) never giving up and 2) committing to healing your mind and body.

- A model for healing includes four core components: 1) Seek genuine understanding and create a safe and trusting environment; 2) Internal exploration: Resolve difficult emotions and hurtful beliefs; 3) Create a positive support network while reducing negative interactions; 4) Strengthen your inner-self.

Responding to intrusive thoughts requires a plan. A good plan includes: recognizing when the thoughts are happening, practicing a breathing technique, letting go of the outcome, and talking about the unwanted thoughts can help reduce their power.

Chapter Eight

Understanding the Mind of the Betraying Partner

"How did I get here?"

A group of eight men were gathered together in my office. They were all a little uneasy as it was their first time attending this group. After they sat down, I looked at each of them and said, "It takes a lot of courage to be here. So, I commend you for being here tonight." Then I asked them, "Why are you here? What made you decide to seek help now?" Each of them offered their explanation. The first guy started, "I'm here because of pornography." Another chimed in, "I'm here because of my affairs." "I'm here because sex is controlling my life," another said. Each took their turn, sharing why they had decided to join the group.

After sharing what brought them to the group, I asked them, "Do you think it is possible that sex or pornography isn't the real reason you are here?" They all looked at me, confused. Let me explain; I continued, "While your sexual behavior is the symptom that you have identified, is it possible that there are other explanations besides your sexual behavior? Is it possible your sexual behaviors are being driven by something else?" Now I had their attention.

It has been my experience that most people seeking help to stop their sexual behaviors think that the problem is sex or pornography. While learning to manage sexuality is very important, I have found that their sexual behaviors are only the tip of the iceberg. While it is easy to focus on an affair, sexting, or other behaviors, what drives such actions is very important to consider. Underneath the tip of the iceberg are issues that drive people to act out.

155

Here's an image that illustrates this concept:

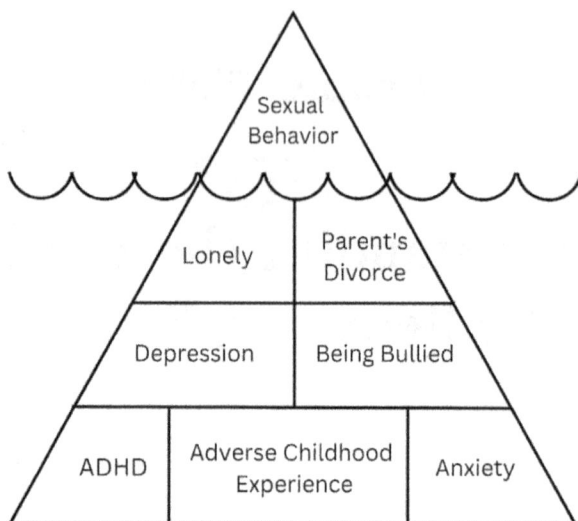

Image created by Megan Gerber, 2023

When I show clients or group members this image, they begin to understand. I explain that their sexual behaviors are one part of what is going on. The image above offers a few ideas about why people act out. Here are some additional reasons:

- Thrill-seeking.
- Caught up in the behavior and lost sight of what matters the most.
- Resentment toward their partner and others.
- Multiple addictive behaviors and sex is just one of them.
- A long history of engaging in sexual behaviors didn't stop their behaviors.
- Dealing with anxiety, depression, or other mental health challenges.
- Traumatic background in which sexual boundaries never existed.

These are just some of the many possible explanations for why someone would engage in unwanted sexual behaviors. While there are many different reasons, there are common themes that stand out. In this chapter, if you have been unfaithful, I hope to help you better understand your behaviors. If your partner has betrayed you, I hope to shed some light on your partner's behavior.

There Is Always a Story

As a faculty member of the International Institute for Addiction and Trauma Professionals (IITAP), I train therapists worldwide. Over the past eight years, the therapists I supervise have brought some of their most difficult cases to discuss with other therapists.

Often the therapists will share one of their most difficult cases with us. As we begin talking about their client's challenges, I invite everyone participating to consider the story of the individual we are discussing. I will ask questions like, "I wonder what would drive a person to meet with a random person to have sex," or "What do you think drove that person to have an affair when they claim love for their partner?"

As the therapists consider these questions, additional questions come up like:

1. At what age was their first sexual experience?
2. What is their sexual history like?
3. What was their relationship like with their mom? Dad? Or other caregivers?
4. Were their parents rigid or controlling?
5. Did they have friends while growing up?
6. Were they bullied in school?
7. Were they shy or reserved while growing up?

As is often the case, the answers to these questions above reveal a story that helps us make more sense of their sexual behaviors. This is one reason why I emphasize to therapists that they need to understand the story of their clients. Much like what I tell therapists while training them if you or your loved one is dealing with unwanted sexual behaviors, I invite you to seek a deeper understanding of what drives these behaviors.

Here's a story to illustrate how understanding the story can help you and your partner.

Eric sought my help because his wife, Jessica, discovered he had been viewing gay pornography. She was confused and began wondering if Eric was gay. She asked him if he wanted to be with a man.

Their marriage had been challenging from the start. Jessica had heard from her friends that after marriage, all men want to do is have sex. She was mentally prepared and was looking forward to being with Eric. However, their honeymoon was nothing like what she had anticipated. She felt like Eric was sexually holding back. She asked him why he didn't initiate sex and if he was attracted to her. He replied that he was attracted to her, but that sex wasn't that important to him. Jessica felt that something was wrong, but she didn't ask further questions.

A couple of years into their marriage, Jessica and Eric rarely had sex, and when they did, it was Jessica who initiated it.

I initially met Eric, and we began discussing his goals. He said, "I want to stop viewing pornography. I don't even understand why I am interested in men. I love my wife, and I am attracted to her. I don't know why I am turning to porn, not my wife.

I began gathering his sexual history. There did not seem to be anything out of the ordinary. His first experience with porn was at age fourteen. He reported that he sought out women at first. As he got older, around eighteen, he said he became curious about men's bodies and began looking up gay porn. When I asked him if anything sexual had happened to him around age eighteen, he couldn't think of anything. We were both interested in his experience and why he started viewing gay porn at that age.

Eric told me he was committed to doing everything he could to save his marriage. I supported his decision but wanted him to keep exploring his past. A few sessions later, he came to my office with the needed insight. He had been preparing to do a disclosure with his wife. While working on a question regarding every sexual activity he had engaged in, a memory from his childhood came up. He told me that between the ages of nine and ten, he and a male cousin had been curious and had touched each other's penis a few times.

Eric told me he had not thought about it since it happened. He said, "I blocked out that experience because I was so embarrassed." He continued, "I think I finally understand what has been happening. I buried those memories because I was ashamed of what we had done. I now realize that I have been holding back because I felt sex was bad. Those early sexual experiences have been hurting me and my marriage for all these years."

Finally, his story was starting to make sense. Eric asked me if he should disclose his experience with his cousin to Jessica. I replied, "I think she deserves to know, but what do you think?" He replied, "I know I need to tell her, but I wonder if she will want to divorce me." I asked him, "How do you think she will respond?" He said, "I honestly do not know. That is what scares me. I truly love her and do not want to live without her. I also realize that I have hurt her deeply by holding back in the bedroom and instead turning to pornography."

In our next session, Eric was prepared to do a disclosure. He began reading his sexual history. Jessica already knew most of the things he shared with her because he had discussed them with her while they were dating. However, when he got to the part where he and his cousin were touching each other, she asked him to stop. It was the moment that Eric feared the most. She looked at him and said, "I wish you would have told me earlier; I could have helped you." In those thirteen words, Jessica had alleviated his fear. He began crying; it was as if the weight of the world had been removed from his back. He replied, "Honestly, Jessica, that memory just came to be a couple of weeks ago. I have been scared to share it with you because I was worried that you wouldn't want to be with me. I love you, and I want to be with you."

Throughout the rest of that session, they gained more insight into his sexual behaviors in their marriage. Eric explained, with his new awareness, that he had been avoiding sex because he thought it was gross or sick. He also explained that he finally understood why he was viewing gay porn. He believed the type of porn he watched was related to what his cousin had done to him.

As additional thoughts came to Eric's mind over the next few weeks, he gained more insight into his approach to relationships. For years, he felt different than other men. They would discuss their sexual escapades, and he would hold back. As long as he could remember, he had been disgusted by sex.

A few weeks later, Eric shared with me that his sex life with Jessica was still challenging, but they were being open and honest about their sexual feelings. Over the next few months, their sex life improved dramatically. Eric also reported that his interest in viewing gay pornography had gone down.

Note: It is important to mention that Eric did a significant amount of therapy to deal with his early sexual experiences. Eric's story illustrates the power of understanding the story. However, simply understanding the story does not change the behavior. Eric did not believe he was gay, but he worried that he might be since he found himself viewing gay pornography. However, his internal confusion was mostly gone after opening up and discussing what had happened with his cousin. Furthermore, Jessica's loving response helped him remove his embarrassment and shame.

It should also be noted that Eric did not believe he was gay. If he had felt otherwise, our conversation would have been different. I would have helped him explore his sexual preference for men and then make an informed decision about his relationship with Jessica.

Now let's explore other stories that help us understand what drives our sexuality.

Common Drivers of Unwanted Sexual Behaviors

What About Attention Deficit Hyperactivity Disorder (ADHD) and Sex

Let's start with ADHD. Throughout my career, I have had many clients dealing with ADHD and hypersexuality. Researchers do not believe that ADHD causes hypersexuality.

However, while ADHD does not cause a person to act out sexually, researchers discovered that individuals who had childhood ADHD were likely to experience earlier initiation of sexual activity and intercourse, have more sexual partners, have more casual sex, and have more partner pregnancies. [1] Dr. Stephen Faraone and his colleagues studied 1001 adults. Those with ADHD endorsed less stability in their love relationships, felt less able to provide emotional support to their loved ones, experienced more sexual dysfunction, and had higher divorce rates. [2] Even though these results shed a negative light on ADHD and sexuality, most individuals dealing with ADHD with proper treatment (e.g., medication and behavioral support) make good progress.

It is important to note that preliminary research suggested impulsivity was the driving factor in hypersexuality. [3] However, the largest sample of adults with ADHD found that poor self-concept was a stronger indicator of hypersexuality. [4] My professional experience with clients dealing with ADHD supports the finding that self-concept (how one views themselves) has more influence than hypersexuality. In addition to addressing self-concept, treatment for ADHD is very effective. If you think you may have ADHD, I encourage you to get tested. Common symptoms include, but are not limited to, the following:

ADHD Predominantly Inattentive Presentation

- Fails to give close attention to details or makes careless mistakes
- Has difficulty sustaining attention
- He does not appear to listen
- Struggles to follow through with instructions
- Has difficulty with organization
- Avoids or dislikes tasks requiring sustained mental effort
- Loses things
- Is easily distracted
- Is forgetful in daily activities

ADHD Predominantly Hyperactive-Impulsive Presentation

- Fidgets with hands or feet or squirms in a chair
- She has difficulty remaining seated
- Runs about or climbs excessively in children; extreme restlessness in adults.
- Difficulty engaging in activities quietly
- Acts as if driven by a motor; adults will often feel inside as if a motor drives them
- Talks excessively
- Blurts out answers before questions have been completed
- Difficulty waiting or taking turns
- Interrupts or intrudes upon others

For more information, please visit: https://chadd.org/for-adults/diagnosis-of-adhd-in-adults/

Adverse Childhood Experiences

To better understand how adverse childhood experiences influence individuals throughout their lifetime, researcher Vincent Felitti and his team gathered data from over 17,000 individuals. They were asked about early life adverse events. Adverse childhood experiences, or ACEs, are potentially traumatic events that occur in childhood (0-17 years). Some of the common experiences they identified include:

- Experiencing violence, abuse, or neglect.
- Witnessing violence in the home or community.
- Having a family member attempt or die by suicide.

Also included are aspects of the child's environment that can undermine their sense of safety, stability, and bonding, such as growing up in a household with:

- Substance use problems.
- Mental health problems.
- Instability due to parental separation or household members being in jail or prison.

In their findings and subsequent research, ACEs are common. In fact, about 61% of adults surveyed across 25 states reported they had experienced at least one type of ACE before age 18, and nearly 1 in 6 reported they had experienced four or more types of ACEs. (5,6)*

*Please note the examples above are not a complete list of adverse experiences. Many other traumatic experiences could impact health and well-being.

After learning about the powerful influence that adverse childhood experiences had on individuals' physical and emotional health as adults, I began wondering about my clients. Did they experience adverse childhood experiences? Did they have more advers e experiences as children? Could that be a contributing factor to their sexual behaviors?

Indeed, individuals seeking help to stop their unwanted sexual behaviors experience more adverse childhood experiences. So, to better understand their childhood, I began administering the ACE inventory to clients coming to our clinic and other clinics throughout the country. Here's what we found. In the chart below, I also included betrayed partners ACE's scores.

Chart: Adverse Childhood Experiences (ACE) Clinical Sample

Number of ACEs	General Pop. Women n=17,000	General Pop. Men n=17,000	Betrayal Trauma Clinical Samples n=712	Sexual Acting Out Clinical Sample n=517
0	34.5*	38.0	28.4	36.4
1	24.5	27.9	21.0	23.0
2	15.5	16.4	11.0	12.4
3	10.3	8.6	12.2	9.7
4 or more	15.2	9.2	26.4	18.5

Of particular note, you will see that both partners had more adverse childhood experiences than the general population. This is significant because higher ACE scores have been related to physical and mental health issues in adulthood. For example, exposure to adverse childhood experiences (ACEs) contributes to seven of the ten leading causes of death in the United States and health risk behaviors, including substance abuse, physical inactivity, and high-risk sex behaviors. (7)

These findings lead me to believe that addressing early life experiences should be a part of helping individuals wanting to stop unwanted sexual behaviors. In my professional experience, most people who have sought my help have experienced at least one challenging experience in their childhood. I share this data to increase awareness of the relationship between past adversity and current sexual behaviors.

If you are reading this book and have higher ACE scores, I invite you to watch a short presentation that I did on this topic. You can find it at (https://bit.ly/RYR) Chapter Eight.

Note: I have observed that most individuals who act out while in a committed relationship have experienced some form of trauma. However, since it is easy to focus on their misbehavior (sexually acting outside of their committed relationship), we do not stop and ask important questions like, "What happened to you?" And "What were you seeking when you engaged in XYZ behavior?" In asking these questions, we can deepen our understanding of what may be driving their sexual behaviors.

Anxiety, Depression, and Sexual Behaviors

When Blaine came into my office, it was clear that he was anxious. As we began talking, I tried to help him feel safe and understood. Throughout the session, he told me that his mind would race, and it would be hard to slow down. I began asking him questions to assess his level of anxiety. Here is a typical list of questions therapists ask their clients regarding anxiety:

Do you experience any of the following symptoms?

1. Feeling nervous, anxious, or on edge

2. Not being able to stop or control worrying

3. Worrying too much about different things

4. Trouble relaxing

5. Being so restless that it is hard to sit still

6. Becoming easily annoyed or irritable

7. Feeling afraid, as if something awful might happen

Questions from GAD-7

Blaine made it clear that he frequently experienced many of these symptoms. While Blaine's primary reason for seeking my help was to address his compulsive sexual desires, his anxiety was so elevated that I wondered if his sexual behaviors were a coping mechanism to escape his racing mind. The more Blaine described his anxiety, the clearer it became that unless we helped him reduce his anxiety, his ability to overcome unwanted sexual behaviors would be nearly impossible.

Blaine is one of many clients I have met over the years who have elevated anxiety levels. After years of helping individuals who struggle with anxiety and compulsive sexual behaviors, I have found that reducing their anxiety makes them more capable of effectively responding to their sexually compulsive behaviors.

It is important to note that anxiety and depression are the top two mental health challenges we face in our society. Therefore, when I work with individuals dealing with sexual compulsivity, I also assess my clients for these issues. Researchers have linked anxiety and depression to hypersexual behavior, and they have been reported as the most common diagnoses among hypersexual individuals. (8,9) Researcher Donald Black and his colleagues reported major depression or dysthymia in almost 14 out of 36 subjects reporting compulsive sexual behavior. (10)

In a research study on the relationship between pornography use and depression, anxiety, loneliness, and life satisfaction, I found that the more individuals consumed pornography, the higher their depression, anxiety, and loneliness got. In addition, their life satisfaction scores were significantly lower than the general population. These findings do NOT mean that pornography makes people more depressed or anxious. It could be the other way around. People who are depressed or anxious may turn to pornography to escape or get away from the complex emotions associated with their anxiety or depression.

In my work with Blaine and other clients dealing with anxiety and depression, I have found that by reducing these symptoms, their ability to regulate their sexual behaviors increases. Some of the most helpful strategies for treating anxiety and depression include:

- Cognitive Behavioral Therapy (CBT)

- Mindful meditations

- Learning about the polyvagal theory and practicing activating the vagus nerve

- Medications (temporary support—not a long-term solution)

- Working to resolve traumas from life experiences— (Talk with a trauma specialist regarding these issues)

Note: As mentioned above, there is always a story. By stepping back and exploring how anxiety, depression, and other issues influence you or your loved one, you are opening up to a deeper understanding. You will be more likely to find solutions that help. For example, I have found that clients who participate in mindfulness activities are less impulsive. Those who practice CBT develop effective skills to help them deal with their mental health challenge and sexuality. I have seen medications help reduce some individuals' compulsive sexual behaviors. My point is this, there are many possible reasons people act out sexually, and there are a wide variety of solutions. If one solution has yet to work, try another or combine multiple solutions simultaneously and see what happens.

Loneliness

In my book, *Treating Sexual Addiction: A Compassionate Approach to Recovery,* I devoted an entire chapter to loneliness. My concern was that stopping unwanted sexual behaviors without meaningful relationship connections is much more difficult.

Regarding the interaction between loneliness and sexually acting out, researchers have found "Loneliness, presence of interpersonal problems and increased vulnerability to stress has also been observed in association with hypersexual behavior. (11) Since loneliness is a form of separation distress that results from failure to have one's basic attachment needs fulfilled, (12) a key solution is to address loneliness."

It has been my experience that there is a link between loneliness and being bullied. My heart hurts for individuals who have been bullied, as it reduces their trust in others and society. Some individuals have shared with me that being bullied as far back as elementary school prevented them from trusting others. As a result, they held back from their peers and never developed meaningful relationships as a child. Often those who are bullied put on a strong face, but they are hurting inside.

I have observed that clients who have been bullied may enter into committed relationships, but they often hold back because they fear being hurt.

As a result, their relationships often feel empty. The unresolved trauma from being bullied continues to prevent them from forming a deep attachment bond.

A more comfortable way to deal with their sexual desires is to turn to pornography or random sexual hookups because these require less risk and vulnerability.

Here are some recommendations for dealing with loneliness as found in my book:

- Unlearn unhealthy attachment patterns—learning to connect with others is a skill. Strategies to address this include a) talking to a friend, b) asking someone to support you as you work to stop your unwanted behavior) and c) learning to reach out for help when you are emotionally struggling.

- Practice deep listening—ask someone, a child, a parent, or your partner to share the emotions and thoughts that they have been having.

- Develop new relationship skills (e.g., empathy and compassion).

- Learn to play again—play is something we can easily forget to do as adults. Playing a sport with a group or joking with friends are all good examples of learning to play again.

- Serve others—service is a powerful way to help others and has an added benefit; it is great for your mental health.

- Seek healthy touch—a powerful way to reduce loneliness is to connect with others through healthy touch. A hug from a child or an embrace from a friend is a good starting point.

Finally, if you want to learn more about loneliness and sexual addiction, I created a free webinar titled *Addressing the Lonely World of Sex Addiction*.

Understanding Your Arousal Template

Have you ever wondered why you are sexually stimulated by whatever arouses you? A variety of factors may influence your answer to this question. Regarding this, a colleague, Dr. David Fawcett, wrote, "Generally speaking, arousal templates are part genetic, part learned, and part cultural." (13).

Below are the three ways he described:

Genetic: Physical health, sexual maturity, fertility, fidelity, facial symmetry, reproductive age, waist-to-hip ratio, and even gender preference are all impacted by genetic markers.

Learned: Our life experiences build on our genetic code. We add to our arousal template through classical conditioning and salient experiences (both good and bad). Learned elements of the arousal template tend to seep in without our knowledge.

Cultural: Environment influences, including family messages, early sexual experiences, religious influences, media (magazines, TV, movies), pornography, gendered messages, and current fashion trends, will also find their way into the arousal template. (14)

Below I have discussed how our arousal template can be influenced: 1) our first sexual experience; 2) the intensity of a sexual experience; and 3) our culture via social media. Here is how these factors play a crucial role in how we develop sexual preferences.

First Sexual Experience

Our first sexual experience will produce strong emotions regardless of what it was (e.g., playing doctor, discovering masturbation, viewing pornography, or unwanted sexual behavior). Whether the sexual event was positive or negative, our initial experience can significantly influence our development. Many clients report returning to their initial sexual experience within a few weeks. When I asked them why, they said curiosity was a big reason for returning to the activity. It is not uncommon for clients to develop their sexual preferences based on these early life experiences.

Therefore, when clients ask me why they do what they do, I ask them a few questions about their sexual history. Often as they share their sexual history, they gain solid insight into at least one part of what is driving their behaviors.

The Intensity of the Sexual Experience

To fully understand our sexuality, we must return to our most intense sexual experiences. Why does this matter? Usually, our mind pays the most attention to unique and intense experiences. If something is highly arousing, it would only be natural for us to try and replicate that experience. As a result, the more arousing an experience is, the more likely we are to return to the associated activity.

Therapists and researchers now believe that our arousal template can change based on our exposure to specific stimuli. Over the past twenty-five years, I have witnessed a significant change in what my clients have been exposed to and at what age they were exposed. For example, early in my career, the J.C. Penny catalog had women dressed in undergarments. My older clients told me that was their first exposure to anything sexual. Today, it is common for clients to share that their first exposure to hardcore pornography was at age nine.

I have often wondered how these differences influence individuals' approach to sex. Some of the questions I have pondered on include:

- How does the brain respond when viewing pornography in a magazine compared to watching an X-rated video?

- How do our bodies respond to sexual activity in which we initiate versus someone else initiating?

- How does a person view their sexuality when their sexual boundaries have been violated by others? I have had many clients share childhood sexual experiences where they were not protected and there were no guidelines. Some examples include a 4-year-old given pornography, a 7-year-old's parents having sex in front of him, and a 13-year-old girl not being allowed to have a bedroom door.

Knowing what is highly arousing in our youth may change or alter as we mature is essential. The idea that our arousal template can evolve fits with research on brain neuroplasticity. Neuroplasticity, also known as neural plasticity or brain plasticity, is a process that involves adaptive structural and functional changes to the brain. A good definition is "the ability of the nervous system to change its activity in response to intrinsic or extrinsic stimuli by reorganizing its structure, functions, or connections." (15)

Based on the rapid changes in technology, our sexuality is also changing. For example, John Gottman wrote an article titled, *An Open Letter on Porn*. In his letter, he wrote, "…research on the effects of pornography use, especially one person frequently viewing pornographic images online, shows that pornography can hurt a couple's relationship. The effect may be true, in part, because pornography can be a 'supernormal stimulus' (see Supernormal Stimuli by Deirdre Barrett)." (16)

Nikko Tinbergen, a Nobel Prize-winning ethologist, described a supernormal stimulus as a stimulus that evokes a much larger response than one with evolutionary significance. One effect of a supernormal stimulus is that interest wanes in normal stimuli. (17) We are witnessing this phenomenon in people not aroused by their partners because they are not as sexually stimulating as the supernormal stimulus of pornography.

When I discuss the idea of arousal templates with clients, it is not uncommon for them to tell me that only a specific sexual activity arouses them (e.g., a specific sexual position). On the other hand, some clients explain that they are aroused by a variety of sexual experiences (e.g., going to a massage parlor, viewing online pornography, or being interested in a specific type of person (i.e., blonde-haired women or mean and aggressive men). In essence, what sexually excites one person may not arouse another person.

It is possible for our arousal template to change from one sexual preference to another based on exposure and intensity of an experience. In essence, a person may be aroused by one type of sexual activity (e.g., viewing a specific type of pornography) and then be exposed to another genre of pornography that unexpectedly provides a highly stimulating sexual experience. As the person seeks out the new type of pornography, they reinforce the new template of arousal. Over time, their arousal template has been altered due to the new sexual stimuli.

There is little evidence that our arousal templates are fixed. However, some sexual fantasies and desires may always be sexually arousing to you. For example, if your excitement is the highest when your partner is wearing a specific type of lingerie, it is unlikely you will lose interest in that.

With the understanding that arousal templates can change, after discovering pornography use or an affair, betrayed partners often question whether they still fit their spouse or partner's arousal template. This may be especially true if individuals are experiencing porn-induced erectile dysfunction (PIED) or erectile dysfunction for other reasons.

As a result, individuals and couples who heal develop a deeper understanding of each other's arousal templates. Moreover, as trust and recovery increase, couples enter a stage where they are more comfortable discussing their sexual preferences. While an open and honest discussion can help, the more important issue is whether each partner is comfortable with the other's template. For example, if one partner wants to engage in sexual activity (i.e., viewing pornography, role-playing, or BDSM) and the other does not, then their differences need to be resolved. This requires two people who want to understand each other and who value one another's experiences. It has been my experience that betraying partners who push their partner to engage with them in their arousal template usually end up creating more hurt and pain in their relationship. For an in-depth discussion on arousal templates, please visit the support content for Chapter Eight at: https://bit.ly/RYR

Note: Gender preference does not equate to arousal template. While there is currently no evidence that our arousal templates are fixed, there is also no evidence that those who are homosexual or heterosexual can permanently alter what gender is most arousing to them. Some people are bi-sexual and claim to have no gender preference.

Cultural Influence on Arousal Template

Over the past twenty-five years, I have observed a significant shift in my clients' sexual behaviors. When I first started doing therapy in the mid'90s, the Internet was just a baby. Most people I met had limited issues with pornography because it was hard to access, but the Internet changed everything. My clients went from viewing magazines to X-rated videos via dial-up modems. Then, as the Internet evolved from dial-up to high flying 5G and 10G connections, the speed and accessibility to the content again changed the landscape. Today, anyone could get on an app and, within a few minutes, be indulging in nearly every imaginable sexual behavior.

I'm curious if our society was prepared for the change (good and bad) that the Internet brought into our lives. Regardless, it is here, and our lives have been significantly altered. One area in which the Internet has changed dramatically is sexual exposure.

I begin this discussion on sexual arousal templates and how they are rapidly evolving due to the Internet. Here are a few examples of what is happening in our society, along with questions I have:

Research	Question
The average child is exposed to pornography by the time they are 12 years of age.	What is the impact of pornography on a 12-year-old brain? How does it influence their sexual development?
73% of teens have consumed pornography	How does exposure influence a child's view of sex? What type of pornography are they viewing? How frequently are they viewing it?
41% of teens have viewed pornography while at school	How does viewing pornography at school influence teens' interaction with their peers?
A majority of teens (52%) who indicated they had viewed pornography have been exposed to aggressive and/or violent forms of pornography.	If over 50% of teens have viewed aggressive or violent pornography, how does that influence their view of sex? What is the arousal template of someone who has only witnessed aggressive sex?

Source: Common Sense Media 2022 Report (18)

In addition to online pornography, the development of apps and gaming devices has made it easy to find sexual encounters. Issues like sexting, hookup apps, and finding virtual escorts are at your fingertips. In the history of humankind, we have never experienced such rapid acceleration of sexual opportunities. While human sexual behaviors have not changed, the speed, accessibility, and intensity of how we engage in sexual behaviors have been permanently altered.

The evidence of these changes can be found in a recent study completed by Common Sense Media. Twenty-five years ago, it would have been hard to imagine that a teenager would take a nude photo of themselves and send it to someone else. In a 2021 study on sexting among youth, here are the results:

- 19.3% had sent a sext.
- 34.8% had received a sext.
- 14.5% had forwarded a sext without consent.

- Females receive more sexts than males.

- Older teens are more likely to send sexts.

- Older and younger adolescents receive sexts at around the same rate.

As reported by Common Sense Media (19)

I have brought up these cultural issues to explain the new norms. However, I hope that my key point is noticed in the cultural shift that is occurring. Regardless of how our culture is changing, we still have to understand our history and our arousal template.

When I train other therapists, I encourage them to help their clients discover their sexual arousal template. I invite them to help their clients explore their arousal template without passing judgment but instead with awareness. We all have personal sexual preferences based on the factors mentioned above. Knowing our personal arousal template can be extremely helpful as you move forward in your relationship.

Exercise: Questions to help you understand your arousal template:

1. What was my first sexual experience? How has it influenced my approach to sexual activities?

2. What is the most intense sexual experience I have ever had? What makes it so intense? Do I find myself seeking out that same type of experience now?

Note: If you want to understand your arousal template, I recommend you find a Certified Sexual Addiction Therapist (CSAT) and ask them to give you the Sexual Dependency Inventory (SDI). Dr. Patrick Carnes created the SDI, which is one of the best assessments available regarding understanding our sexual arousal template. To find a CSAT in your area, you can visit www.sexhelp.com.

Three Examples of Arousal Templates

Now that we have discussed arousal templates, let's pause and ask a few questions. What life experiences have you or your partner had that influenced your approach to sex? By asking this critical question, you can understand more about your partner and why they approach sex the way they do. When we explore our sexual behaviors through the lens of their sexual history and arousal template, understanding our sexuality is simpler than we think - there is always a story.

Here are two short examples of how sexual history and current sex behaviors come together. Steve was introduced to prostitution at age fifteen by some friends.

His friends discovered a few brothels in town where they could pay $30.00 to have sex. After this experience, Steve returned to the brothels as often as possible. After getting married, having children, and developing a promising career, Steve returned to early life experiences by hiring sex workers as an adult in his 40s and 50s. By the time I met Steve, his arousal template had not changed.

Contrast Steve's story with Erica's. Aggressive men aroused Erica. She reported that regular sexual intercourse was boring. When she got into a committed relationship, if her partners weren't sexually aggressive in bed, she would move on to another relationship. You may be able to guess her story. She was abused as a child and came to believe that she should be punished because she was bad. In her case, her self-belief (I am bad and should be treated as such) influenced her arousal template. Emotionally, she felt more comfortable in abusive relationships than in a safe and comfortable one.

Some individuals do not experience sexual arousal. This may also be viewed as an arousal template, but it is usually identified as hypoactive sexual desire disorder (or low libido). There are many possible reasons, including low testosterone, chronic illness, stress, aging, etc.). Here, the key issue to explore is, "Does the person want to have sexual relations, but their body won't perform." Sexual arousal takes into account a person's desire.

Each person has an arousal template, and it is influenced by a variety of factors (genetics, learned behaviors, and our environment). My hope is that this section has helped you better understand yourself and your partner.

Why People Seek Help to Stop Their Sexual Behaviors

Throughout this chapter, I have tried to explain a few of the reasons people engage in sexual behaviors outside of a committed relationship. By now, I hope you can see that it is nearly impossible to describe all of the reasons. If you really want to understand the mind of the betraying partner, it is important to understand the following:

- Their sexual history
- What's underneath their personal iceberg (e.g., ADHD, depression, anxiety, trauma)
- Their arousal template

By understanding these three elements, you will have a better understanding of yourself and your partner. As we close this chapter, let's look at a few additional ways to see into the mind of the betraying partner. There are two questions that are very helpful as we try to understand betrayal.

Question #1: Why do you think you acted out while in your relationship?

Here are some of the explanations I have heard:

- I like pornography
- I couldn't stop myself
- I got caught up and didn't realize I was in trouble until it was too late
- I justified my behavior because I was upset at my partner
- My partner cheated on me first
- I lost sight of what mattered the most

Note: As individuals examine their reasons for acting out, they usually discover there are other things driving their behaviors. For example, a client who said, "I couldn't stop myself," discovered that he engaged in sexual behaviors when he was stressed or overwhelmed. He found that sexual activity was how he would calm his anxiety.

Question #2: What is driving you to seek help now?

Below are a couple of cases that will illustrate the different mindsets.

Zeke sat on my couch in one of our first sessions and said, "I need your help. I am ruining my family. I have repeatedly told myself and my wife that I am going to stop my sexual behaviors. My wife thought the issue was porn, but recently she discovered I had been visiting massage parlors. Initially, I downplayed it, but she started looking at our financial records and found additional visits I had made to the parlors. I know she didn't like the porn, but going to the massage parlors made her question everything I had told her. I don't get it; in every other aspect of my life, I have it together, but when it comes to my sexual behaviors, I feel like I have no control. Why can't I just stop? I honestly feel like my desire is stronger than my willpower."

Zeke wanted help because he couldn't understand himself.

Contrast Zeke's Story with Austin's

Austin came to therapy because his wife told him that he needed to seek help for his anxiety. What she didn't know at the time was that Austin had been using a hookup app and meeting with other women. When he told me his presenting issue was anxiety, I asked if there was anything else he wanted to address. Hesitantly, he said that he had been cheating on his wife. He told me that she would divorce him if she found out and that he didn't plan on telling her. He continued, "She knows I have bad anxiety, but she has no idea that I have been cheating.

When I asked whether he would consider telling her, he replied, "I don't want to lose her." When I brought up the risk of getting an STD and giving it to his wife, he was caught off guard. He hadn't previously thought about that. As I gathered more information about his mental health history and his sexuality, it was clear that he had been dealing with anxiety for most of his life. He was using sex to cope with his anxiety. What he didn't realize was that his sexual behaviors were providing temporary relief, but his anxiety was not going away. While he initially sought help for anxiety, his coping mechanism of sexually acting out had become dangerous to him and his wife.

Initially, Austin was seeking help because of his anxiety and his wife was pushing him to seek help. In cases like this, if progress is going to be made in therapy, the individual needs to shift from an external motivation (to please my wife) to an internal motivation (I need help).

Now Contrast Zeke and Austin's Stories with Heather's Story

Heather grew up in a small farm community where there wasn't much to do. By the time she was fifteen, she had had sex multiple times with different boys from her school. As she shared her story, she told me about being sexually abused by an uncle at age six. After that, there were no boundaries. She learned that she could use sex to get whatever she wanted, so she did. By the time she was sixteen, she was pregnant. She gave the child up for adoption. Not long after giving birth, she met Jack, her first husband. They had a rocky marriage. He was abusive and treated her like he owned her. She resented this and found ways to get him back for being abusive. She began cheating on him out of spite. After five years, their marriage ended. By the time she came to therapy, she felt like she was helpless. She had been through so much trauma that she felt like she was worthless.

Heather came to therapy with an open mind and heart. She genuinely wanted help. She told me that she just wanted to get better. Often individuals like Zeke and Heather make the most progress in the early phase of recovery. Individuals like Austin who seek help usually need more time to change because they are still holding secrets. A key sign that shows real progress is rigorous honesty. When individuals are willing to reveal their secrets with people who are safe, true progress begins in earnest.

Note: I have had many people tell me that after they first discovered their partner's sexual behaviors, they felt that their partner was a monster. They did not feel safe in their presence. However, as their partner worked through recovery, they began to see them through a different lens. They could see their partner as a child. They recognized the signs of someone who was lost, abused, neglected, or bullied. Their awareness of their partner's past didn't take away the betrayal, the hurt, the lies, or the deception, but it did help remove the view of their partner as a monster.

Key Takeaways from This Chapter

- In order to understand the mind of the betrayed, we need to look not at the behavior only (the tip of the iceberg) but at what is driving the behavior.

- Some of the common drivers of unwanted sexual behaviors include ADHD, depression, anxiety, and loneliness.

- By understanding one's first and most intense sexual experience, we can better understand their arousal template. Our arousal template can change over time.

- It is valuable to understand the reasons people give for sexually acting out and the reasons they give for seeking help.

Chapter Nine

The Journey to Recovery: The Process of Changing Unwanted Sexual Behaviors (For Betraying Partners)

"The journey to anywhere begins with the first step."

"It feels like Julie is never going to forgive me. I have been doing everything I can think of to earn her forgiveness. Do you think she will ever get over my affair?" David was expressing his frustration after another fight with his wife. He continued, "I am not sure I can take it anymore. She tells me that I am the worst. She accuses me of cheating on her again, but that would be impossible with the way she monitors everything I do. I swear she knows more about what I am doing than I do."

After listening to David, I asked, "Do you think she believes you will not cheat on her again?" He replied, "Absolutely not. I am sure she doesn't trust me. She keeps telling me she knows I am lying to her every chance she gets. But I'm not."

I said, "Why did you stop your affair?"

David explained, "I stopped because I didn't want to be 'that' guy. I was confused; I probably still am. I want to save my marriage, but I am unsure if it is salvageable. I think I broke my wife. She was not like this before. She was fun to be around. We used to laugh and play. We loved going on vacations together. Now, she doesn't want to do anything with me.

I was trying to get David to focus on himself for a few minutes, not what Julie was doing. "Do you know why you want to save your marriage?" I asked. David replied, "I do love Julie. I want to be with her and the kids, but I don't know if we can keep this up."

When individuals express their sense of helplessness in their relationship, I often validate their concern because I do not know if their spouse will choose to give them another chance. As a result, I introduce them to a psychological construct called the locus of control to help them recognize what they can and cannot control.

In this chapter, I will introduce you to specific steps you can take in your journey to recovery. I will discuss the importance of focusing on what you can control. Then I will share with you some powerful exercises you can take to help you focus on what matters the most to you. I will conclude the chapter by providing solutions successful people take as they stop engaging in unwanted sexual behaviors.

The Importance of Focusing on Your Healing and Recovery

When David said, "Julie will never forgive me," I knew he was starting to feel hopeless in his relationship. Throughout my career, I have met many partners who have betrayed their spouses, telling me they think there is nothing they can do or say to improve their relationship. Indeed, there are times when words or actions may not help improve a relationship. That is a hard reality for some individuals that I have met. However, if you and your partner have read this far, then there is hope for your relationship.

What I will say next is very important if you are feeling hopeless. Focus on what you can control—which is you. You will direct your attention to personal recovery and healing by looking internally. This does not mean you will ignore or avoid your partner. What it means is that you are going to focus on improving your thoughts, emotions, actions, and self-beliefs.

This approach is a psychological concept called the "Locus of Control." Locus of control is a way to describe how individuals perceive the level to which their lives are controlled by external forces or by themselves.

People with an internal locus of control believe they are primarily in charge of their own lives and outcomes. In contrast, those with an external locus of control tend to think that external factors such as luck or fate have a more significant influence on the course of their lives.

It is essential to understand this concept because it can affect many aspects of your life, from stopping your unwanted sexual behaviors to how you approach your relationship. It can even influence your mental health and well-being.

Having an internal locus of control can help you make positive changes in your life. People who believe they are in charge of their destiny are more likely to take the initiative and be motivated to make progress. They may also feel more autonomy in making decisions and problem-solving, which can lead to higher self-esteem and confidence. Moreover, having an internal locus of control can help individuals feel empowered in difficult situations as they are more likely to face challenges head-on.

Trusting Yourself

After introducing the concept of locus of control to David, I asked him, "Do you trust yourself? In other words, do you believe you can stay committed to Julie?" David paused before he answered, "I want to, but my actions haven't yet shown that I can stay faithful."

I then asked, "Do you think Julie can believe in you if you don't know if you can?" David thought about this question and said, "Probably not."

As we continued our conversation, I asked David a few more questions:

Do you think that your behaviors are problematic? Note: If yes, then I will continue to the next question. If not, I want to understand what David hopes to accomplish by coming to therapy.

- On a scale between zero and ten, how difficult do you think it will be to stop your sexual behaviors?

- On a scale between zero and ten, how prepared are you to make the necessary changes to stop your unwanted sexual activities?

- On a scale between zero and ten, how motivated are you to stop engaging in xyz sexual behavior?

David knew his behaviors were a problem. He gave himself a six on how difficult it would be to stop. He further added he never wanted to cheat again but did not feel prepared—his score was a five. He gave himself an eight on the motivation question—meaning he felt motivated to make changes.

Let's pause and reflect here for a minute. We could quickly rush by these scores, but I want to explore their meaning.

Difficulty stopping = 6

Question: What does a five mean? David needs to prepare to make lasting change. He will need to make a concerted effort to make lasting change. At this point a five indicates that he does not feel prepared.

Preparation to stop = 5

Question: What does a five mean? David needs to prepare to make lasting changes. We will need to spend time helping him prepare.

Motivation = 8

Question: What does an eight mean? David's current level of motivation is high. Now is an excellent time to reinforce his commitment and help him develop strategies so he can succeed.

David was realistic in his self-assessment for readiness for change. His answers helped me understand that we needed to focus on helping him prepare. It also helped me to hear David express how hard he thought the change would be for him.

These questions provide a lot of insight; I encourage you to reflect on them often as you go through your journey to recovery. Be aware that your scores will change over time.

Next, I gave David a short exercise. I call it the "What and Why Exercise." I invite you to do this exercise now.

Exercise: What Do You Want to Change?

Instructions: Make a list of things that you want to change. Take three minutes to write down everything that comes to your mind. Once you are done, rank order each item from most important = 1 to least important.

Example:

What I Want to Change	Rank of Importance
Be faithful to Julie	1
Be more involved in my children's lives	2
Stay on task at work and meet expectations	5
Get in better shape	4
Stop spending the money that I don't have	3

In an effort to reinforce David's reason for listing "being faithful to Julie" as number one, I continued this exercise by asking him to write down his reasoning.

Now that you have identified the most important thing you want to change, please write why you want to change that specific thing in your life for two minutes.

Why Be Faithful to Julie

I love Julie. I know that my actions have not shown it, but I do. Even though she makes me feel like I am worthless at times, I can't imagine life without her. She has a fun personality. She is beautiful. She is a good mom. She is creative.

I want to show her that I can be faithful. I am choosing her, and I hope she will choose me again.

I had David move on to the next part of this exercise.

Now review your list and rank order your *whys* from the most important to the least important.

Why I Want to Change	Rank of Importance
I love Julie	1
I can't imagine life without her	5
She has a fun personality	7
She is beautiful	6
She is a good mom	4
She is creative	8
I want to show her I can be faithful	2
I am choosing her	3

Finally, take a few minutes and write about your top three *whys*. Why did you choose these three?

- I love Julie. I have loved Julie since we first met. I know my actions have not shown it, but I still love her. She didn't deserve what I did to her. I want to make it up to her if possible.

- I want to show her I can be faithful. I have let her and my children down. I want to prove that I can be honest and trustworthy. If I think hard about this, I want to prove it.

- I am choosing her. After my affair ended, I realized I had a problem. I had been lying and telling Julie that everything was okay, but it was not. Our relationship was not good because Julie sensed something was off. I resented her because she questioned everything I was doing. I now realize I was not choosing her; I was living a lie. Now, I want to choose her, and I want her to know that I am choosing her.

This exercise helped David clarify what he wanted (be faithful to Julie) and why (because he loved her, he wanted to show her he could be faithful and that he chose her). One thing this exercise did not do was help David figure out how he would prove to Julie and himself that he could be faithful.

I again asked David about his preparation to change. I asked why he gave himself a five on preparation to make the necessary changes to stop his unwanted sexual behavior. He said, "I don't know. I'm not sure how to prepare. What do you mean by prepared?"

The next part of this chapter describes the preparation process in the journey to recovery.

Note: You may wonder if David loved Julie, why would he lie to her, and why would he cheat on her in the first place? I have had many clients, like David, tell me that they love their partner, and as a result, I have thought a lot about what they mean when they say *love*. (If you would like to hear my musings on why betraying partners say they love their partner, please see Chapter 9 support content at (https://bit.ly/RYR)

"We can have the greatest will to do well. But unless we have prepared, it is of little use. Really, it should be the 'will to prepare.' The will to prepare is more important than the will to win."

LaVell Edwards

Preparing to Succeed

To the reader of this book, what steps do you think David could take as he focuses on being faithful to Julie? Perhaps your natural thought is to make a commitment to never act out again. Or maybe you wonder if David has a bigger problem controlling his sexual behaviors and if he should consider seeking professional help.

I ask this question because it is easy for us to tell others we have changed or that we will change, but it is much more difficult to stick to our word when life presents difficult challenges to us. For example, in David's case, how might he respond if his former affair partner reaches out to him? Or how hard would it be for David to stay away from his affair partner if he and Julie had a fight? These are the times that require preparation. By preparing for times like this, when the challenges come, and they will inevitably come, you will know how to respond.

I have realized that many clients want to stop sexually acting out. However, for most of us, halting any behavior is complex. This is especially true if we have been engaging in that behavior for years. After reflecting on the change process, I am convinced that the most effective changes we make come after we have prepared ourselves.

In David's case, he gave himself a five on his preparedness to change for a reason. Based on his answer and in order to emphasize the importance of preparation, I asked David another question:

When are you the most vulnerable to being in contact with your affair partner?

David thought and said, "I think there are two times that I struggle the most. The first is when I have been fighting with Julie. The second is when work is stressful. Sometimes my boss is so critical of me and my team."

Are there other times when you are vulnerable? I inquired. "Yes, when I know that Julie is busy for an afternoon or evening and won't have time to check up on me." I said to David, now that we have identified the critical times in which you are the most vulnerable, we need to help you prepare for when these occasions arise.

#1: Preparation for When Julie Is Upset

Question: How have you responded to Julie when she has been upset in the past? David responded, "Usually, I just sit and listen. However, when she goes on and on accusing me of doing things I am not doing anymore, I eventually stand up for myself and yell back."

I asked, "How does that turn out?" David said, "Not well at all. Julie goes quiet and says, 'You don't care, or she tells me I don't get it.' Then she walks off, and we don't talk for a day or two." I then asked David, "Do you think there is anything you can do to change the outcome in situations like you just described?

David replied, "I have tried everything. I have told her I am sorry. I have sat and listened without becoming defensive. I have even told her that if she thinks I am that bad, she should just divorce me." How did that go? I asked. David said, "Horrible. She accused me of wanting a divorce and that she knew I didn't love her anymore."

Are there times when Julie gets upset and starts yelling at you, but you choose to stay present with her and just listen instead of trying to leave? "Most of the time, I emotionally check out." I may be in the same room as her, but I don't know what to do or say, so I just sit there. Then when she doesn't stop, I get angry and snap back at her.

David made it clear that he really didn't know how to respond when Julie was upset. If this scenario sounds familiar to your relationship, please keep reading. In Chapter Thirteen of this book, the focus will be on helping you and your partner communicate during these difficult exchanges. For now, however, here are three relationship skills I asked David to practice when Julie was upset:

- Think about what she is trying to tell you. Listen carefully, not to the words, but to the fear and worry she is feeling. It may be coming across as anger, but focus on her pain.

- Look at her while she is talking to you. Many people in situations like this look down or away. This can be triggering for betrayed partners because they do not feel you are listening or paying attention.

- Acknowledge her hurt without saying I am sorry. I will have more to say about this in Chapter 12 (Making True Amends—Why I'm Sorry Isn't Working).

Practice Skill: Review this list each day. When Julie is upset, implement at least one of my three new strategies.

Now, I will introduce a couple of new concepts for the following two situations that David wanted to practice. First, we will address the thoughts, feelings, and behaviors David would experience in that given scenario. Second, we are going to have David brainstorm solutions for those situations (e.g., when Julie is busy). Third, David will identify ways to practice one or two of his solutions. And fourth, David will identify the level of difficulty he anticipates we will have with each solution.

#2: Preparation for Times When My Boss Is Being Difficult

Question: What are some of the thoughts and feelings you have when your boss is giving you a hard time?

Thought: It makes me angry. Honestly, I want to quit because he doesn't appreciate the work that I do. I think I would have quit by now if there wasn't other crazy stuff going on in my life.

Feelings: I feel like a failure. No matter how hard I try, what I do is not enough. It's not enough at work, and it is not enough at home.

Question: How have you responded in the past when your boss gave you a hard time?

I used to reach out to my affair partner and complain. Turning to her for emotional support was my mistake.

Practice Skill: Instead of me giving David the suggestion for this one. I invited him to brainstorm different ways to respond.

I honestly need to consider changing jobs. Since that is not an option right now, I will not respond to his negative energy. Instead, I will stay on task and finish my work. If he continues to ride me and my team really hard, I will look for a new job instead of reaching out to my affair partner.

I suggested two more methods of practice:

- Take a break and go for a walk. While walking, think about the things you are grateful for.
- Practice a relaxation meditation within fifteen minutes of the encounter.

Solutions Level of Difficulty:

Practice Skill	Level of Difficulty (1 = Easy / 10 = Hard)
Stay on task and get my work done	4
Look for a new job (not while at work)	1
Will not reach out to my affair partner	2
Go for a walk	1
Practice a relaxation meditation within fifteen minutes of the encounter	6 (It will be hard to find a place to do a meditation)

#3: How to Respond When Julie Is Busy

Question: What are some of the thoughts and feelings you have when Julie is busy?

While I was in the middle of my affair, I would think about finding a way to get together with my affair partner. At times I felt like my emotions would take over, and I would have to contact her. Contacting her was like a drug for me.

Question: How did you respond when Julie was busy?

Whenever I sensed that Julie was going to be busy for the day, I tried setting up a time to meet with my affair partner.

Practice Skill: At this point, David knew the drill, so I asked him to identify things he could do when Julie was busy or gone.

Whenever I feel that Julie is going to be busy, I will plan an activity with my son. We can go for a bike ride or play a video game together. Other possible activities and their level of difficulty include:

• Tell Julie my plans while she is busy.

• Reach out to my friend Steve.

• Work on building a new skill (read a book on building your own business)

Practice Skill	Level of Difficulty (1 = Easy / 10 = Hard)
Do something with my son	4 (He may not be available)
Tell Julie what I will be doing while she is busy	7 (She may not want to hear my plans)
Reach out to Steve	3
Work on a new skill—read a book	1 (This would be fun, and I would feel productive)
Clean up around the house	2 (I can do this, but I won't like it much. However, Julie will like it)

Based on my experience, this type of preparation is rare. Like most of the people I work with, David hadn't thought about how he would respond in such situations. By thinking through these exercises, I have found that my clients are more prepared to respond effectively in crucial moments, such as when they are stressed. Preparation is a powerful way to make changes in your life. Unfortunately, many people overlook this powerful strategy as they attempt to make difficult changes in their life. If you want to be more successful at making a change in your life, I encourage you to follow a similar exercise that I put David through by mentally rehearsing how to respond in difficult moments. These times will feel overwhelming because you already have a set strategy. However, as you practice in advance, it will start to feel natural.

I hope David's story will give you confidence that you, too, can practice how to succeed in difficult moments.

In the next part of this chapter, I will focus on the change process.

The Change Process

We have now identified what David wants to change, and he has identified why he wants to change that specific behavior. We have also introduced the importance of preparing to succeed. Preparation is how you will make lasting changes in your life. Instead of rushing through the preparation phase of change, I want to slow down now and explore how to prepare effectively. This part of dealing with creating change will take time.

Martin M. Broadwell, in his book, *The Four Levels of Teaching,* (1) introduced a concept of how we change. He suggested there are four distinct parts. Here's a diagram that illustrates each section:

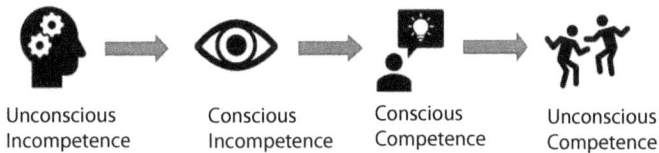

| Unconscious Incompetence | Conscious Incompetence | Conscious Competence | Unconscious Competence |

I have pulled a section from Chapter Four of my book, *Treating Sexual Addiction: A Compassionate Approach to Recovery,* to explain each part.

For the purposes of this chapter, I have adapted Broadwell's teachings and applied them to the recovery process.

Unconscious Incompetence (UI)

During the unconscious incompetence stage, individuals do not understand how their behaviors are influencing their own lives and the lives of others. In other words, they don't know what they don't know.

Many of my clients have reported that, as they work on their recovery, they begin to see how many things they have missed. During the early stage of recovery, they were unable to see how their sexual behaviors had blinded them. As their awareness grew, they began to see the many areas of their life that had been influenced by their actions.

Broadwell suggests, "The individual must recognize their own incompetence, and the value of the new skill, before moving on to the next stage" (2).

Questions to Help Move Out of Unconscious Incompetence:

- How big is my problem?
- How are my actions influencing others?
- What have I been missing because of my actions?
- Do I want to change but do not know how?

Actions to Help You Move Out of Unconscious Incompetence:

- Spend a few minutes writing a response to each of the questions above.
- Take time to reflect on your answers and identify one thing that you will do to change.
- Share what you have learned in the writing exercise with one person and tell them about the one thing you will do to change.

Conscious Incompetence (CI)

The next stage of Broadwell's model is the most difficult. He refers to it as *conscious incompetence*. During this stage, an individual's awareness increases, but their skills do not match their awareness. The individual feels completely exposed and does not know how to respond. This is truly painful. The individual doesn't know how to deal with their own emotions or a spouse's emotions.

I have observed that many people get upset or angry during this stage because they get overwhelmed with feelings of shame and inadequacy. In this stage, individuals begin to see the consequences of their behaviors more clearly but do not possess the skills to keep good on their promises. As a result, many people make promises they cannot keep at this stage. For example, a client like David may tell Julie that he would never have another affair, but his words will not match the internal battle that requires him to believe in himself and that he won't act out again.

The conscious incompetence stage is difficult because most people do not know how to respond when their world starts to fall apart. For example, in David's case, he felt like he was losing his wife and children. How would he respond if he had also been fired from his job due to lack of performance? Where would he turn to when he is under pressure? His old coping habit of turning to sex for comfort can easily return if he is not prepared. In addition, if he has been sexually acting out for years, he may have to deal with his strong cravings and desires to act out.

Questions to Help Move Out of Conscious Incompetence:

How True Are the Following Statements for You?	Please Score Yourself: 0 = Not True and 7 = Very True
1. I want to stop my behavior, but it is harder than I anticipated.	
2. I have tried to quit, but in difficult moments I don't know what else to do.	
3. I am aware of what is happening, and I still choose to act out.	
4. There are times when my desire to act out is so strong that I give in.	

Actions to Help You Move Out of Conscious Incompetence:

- Develop a plan for how you will stop by using the Change 2.0 method (See video Introduction to Change 2.0 at https://bit.ly/change-two).
- Create an action plan for crucial moments.
- Develop a strategy for how you will respond when your desire is low.
- Create a motivation plan.

Conscious Competence

In the next stage, the work of recovery begins. Broadwell suggests that during this stage, "The individual understands or knows how to do something. However, demonstrating the skill or knowledge requires concentration. This is what Broadwell refers to as *conscious competence*. Broadwell writes, "It may be broken down into steps, and there is heavy conscious involvement in executing the new skill." (3) This is when clients learn to respond to stress by reaching out for help instead of acting out. This requires more mental awareness and effort, but clients begin to see progress, and others observing them can see the changes.

I often tell my clients that the *conscious competence stage* can last a long time because new skills take time to develop. I tell them that, as they practice and implement the changes, they will see their progress. Soon, they begin to see how overcoming old habits is not easy, but with the right recovery plan, they can replace old habits with new ones.

I often tell my clients that recovery is much more than being sober. When done right, we become new beings; one who has new knowledge, one who is excited to learn and grow, and one whose quality of life has improved because they are thinking, feeling, and acting differently. This person is finally better at relationships and connecting with others.

A few examples of how individuals respond in this stage include:

- When individuals feel like acting out, they will recognize early what is happening in order to prevent a relapse. Instead of saying to themselves, "I can do this without reaching out to anyone, they will say, "I am going to reach out because I will relapse if I don't." This is often the difference between maintaining sobriety and relapsing.

- Instead of spending time alone, they will reach out to a friend for support.

- They plan in advance how to avoid places of vulnerability.

Below are a few questions to help you assess your level of preparation for change.

Questions to Ask About Conscious Competence:

Preparing to Change	Please score yourself: 0 = Not Prepared and 10 = Very Prepared
1. I have a detailed plan of how I will avoid acting out again.	
2. I have a strategy I can implement when I am stressed.	

3. I have a support team to reach out to when I feel like acting out.	
4. I have positive things to turn to when I am feeling vulnerable.	

Actions to Help You Move Towards Unconscious Competence:

- Review your action plan created in moving out of conscious competence. One way to stay focused on your long-term goals is to keep them in front of you.

- Continue developing habits that lead to long-term recovery (Watch Intro to Change 2.0).

- Be continuously accountable.

In Appendix H, I have included a worksheet you can use to help you create a recovery plan.

Unconscious Competence (UC)

The fourth and final stage of Broadwell's model indicates that "The individual has had so much practice with a skill that it has become 'second nature' and can be performed easily." (5)

During this stage, individuals do many things without thinking about them. This is what is referred to as *unconscious competence*. In this stage, the individual has developed so many positive skills that many things happen on autopilot.

For example, at this stage, an individual will likely reach out to others when they feel stressed. Or the individual might naturally shift attention elsewhere when a fantasy thought arises. Healthy behaviors happen almost naturally because they have become a habit.

One of my clients put it this way, "I just don't think about the things I used to in the past."

It is during the unconscious competence stage that individuals reap the reward of their efforts. They have developed enough healthy habits that they feel confident in themselves and their ability to succeed. Others also sense their energy and feel a difference around them. New knowledge with the right application creates a powerful and lasting change.

Questions to Ask About Unconscious Competence:

- Do I have healthy habits that I am doing without thinking about them?

- Do I find myself doing good things without having to think about it?

- How often do I think a positive thought or feel a positive emotion without having to force myself to do those things?

Actions to Maintain Unconscious Competence:

- Continue developing new habits—commit never to stop growing.

- Identify new passions and purposes to keep your mind growing.

- Lift others with you—your habits can be contagious/bring others with you as you grow.

Note: In this chapter, I touched on how to prepare for the change process. If you would like more guidance on how to prepare so you can make lasting change, I have created a free webinar titled "Change 2.0: *How to Prepare so You Can Make Lasting Change.*" You will find this webinar at https://bit.ly/change-two

Model Your Recovery After What Works

In my book, *Treating Sexual Addiction: A Compassionate Approach to Recovery*, I introduced a concept called "Recovery Capital." Here's the general premise of recovery capital: To stop any behavior, we must focus on improving our quality of life. By approaching change this way, we create a positive energy around change and avoid focusing solely on abstaining from a behavior. Our society, including therapists, has long focused on stopping unwanted behaviors. Now there is a shift to engaging in healthy behaviors as a way to alter undesirable habits.

If you would like to learn more about recovery capital, I will include Chapter One from my book *Treating Sexual Addiction* in the support material for this chapter. It is important to note that those who study successful recovery (from drugs and alcohol) have found that the more recovery capital a person has, the more likely they are to sustain their desired changes throughout their lives.

Recovery Capital is separated into two categories: Personal and Social:

Personal Recovery Capital

People who succeed in recovery create purpose and improve their life skills in order to change their behaviors.

There are five areas in which you can improve your chances of being successful. They include:

- Make sure you have a purpose in life.
- Improve your psychological health—happiness, and well-being.
- Engage in physical activities that increase your energy.
- Avoid risk-taking behaviors.
- Develop your coping skills (e.g., learn how to respond effectively to stressors).

Social and Lifestyle Recovery Capital

The second part of recovery capital focuses on improving social support and creating meaningful relationships. The five key areas include:

- Take actions to help you avoid relapses.
- Get involved in community activities.
- Increase your social support (be accountable to others).
- Engage in meaningful activities.
- Find and create an environment that supports healthy behaviors.

If you want to learn more about how to apply recovery capital as you take steps toward change, I encourage you to read Chapter One of my book.

Model Your Change After What Works

When I meet clients who have been engaging in bad habits for years, many of them feel helpless. They often tell me that they have tried to stop their behaviors but haven't been able to. This is when I introduce them to the importance of modeling their behavioral change using principles that work. There are two overlapping models that I have found to be effective. If you are struggling to stop your sexual behaviors, and don't know where to start, let me share with you what has been effective for thousands of others who have sought help.

First, researchers have discovered that individuals who develop habits around improving their recovery capital increase their chances of sustaining behavioral changes. As a result, I encourage them to start with one recovery capital concept, as outlined above, and then move on to the next one. A second strategy that works hand in hand with the recovery capital model is a task model created by Dr. Patrick Carnes. This model is currently being used by more than 2000 therapists worldwide. Dr. Carnes identified 30 tasks that, if implemented, can lead to sustained recovery.

The first seven tasks include:

- Break through denial
- Understand addiction
- Surrender
- Limit damage
- Establish sobriety
- Physical integrity
- Culture of support

Note: You may be thinking, isn't recovery capital for individuals dealing with drug and alcohol addiction? Or perhaps you are familiar with the work of Dr. Patrick Carnes, whose specialty is sexual compulsivity and addiction. The recovery capital model and the tasks approach can help you even if you are not dealing with an addiction. I have found that these models are effective in creating behavioral changes.

Let me provide two examples using the first two tasks' Dr. Carnes has identified.

The first task is to break through denial. In an effort to help you understand how denial crept into your life, evaluate how your actions have influenced you and the lives of those around you. Here are two questions to consider. I would encourage you to write your response to both questions:

1. How have my actions influenced me physically and emotionally?
2. How have my actions influenced my relationships?

By answering these questions, you are increasing your level of awareness, which is key to beginning the change process (see conscious incompetence). Once your insight has increased, you can turn your attention to altering specific behaviors that will improve your physical and emotional well-being (See conscious competence).

The second task is to understand addiction. While many people reading this book may not be dealing with sexual addiction, understanding the signs of addiction can help you avoid addictive tendencies. The key criteria for any addiction are:

- Inability to consistently abstain.
- Impairment in behavioral control.

- Craving or increased "hunger" for drugs or rewarding experiences.

- Diminished recognition of significant problems with one's behaviors and interpersonal relationships.

- A dysfunctional emotional response.

If you feel like your behaviors have been compulsive and would like to take a short assessment that can evaluate you in these five areas outlined above, the Sexual Behavior Questionnaire (SBQ) is available at:

https://www.humanintimacy.com/course/tsa-book-support

As we conclude this chapter, there are three additional things to consider about the journey to recovery.

- Expect your willpower and motivation to go up and down.

- Successful change begins with simple habits.

- Do something hard every day.

Expect Your Willpower and Motivation to Go Up and Down

In the book *Willpower,* authors Roy Baumiester and John Tierney explain how our willpower waxes and wanes. When our willpower is strong, we are motivated and focused on getting things done and more prone to avoid unhealthy behaviors. However, when our willpower is low, Baumeister referred to this as "ego depletion." While experiencing ego depletion, people's capacity to regulate their thoughts, feelings, and actions is diminished. (6)

So, what happens to us when our ego is depleted? Researchers have discovered that it isn't easy to recognize telltale emotions. However, in experiments, they found that depleted individuals "did react more strongly to all kinds of things. A sad movie made them extra sad. Joyous pictures made them happier, and disturbing pictures made them more frightened and upset. Ice-cold water felt more painful to them than it did to people who were not ego-depleted. Desires intensified along with feelings. After eating a cookie, the people reported a stronger craving to eat another cookie—and they did, in fact, eat more cookies when given a chance. When looking at a gift-wrapped package, they felt an especially strong desire to open it." (7)

Here's the key point. Your success in avoiding unwanted sexual behaviors may be dependent upon your ability to reduce the times your ego is depleted. Furthermore, you will need to discover a plan on how to respond when the symptoms of depletion are manifesting themselves (e.g., strong cravings for a cookie, increased level of sadness).

Historically our society has touted people who are motivated by saying that they are successful. These are the people who get job promotions, lose weight, and overcome bad habits. Unfortunately, this mindset is problematic. If we observe human behavior long enough, some people cannot sustain motivation permanently. Instead, even successful people experience the motivational roller coaster (ups and downs).

So, what is the secret to their success? They have learned to respond when their motivation is low. Instead of beating themselves up, they discover how to rejuvenate by taking a break. These same individuals develop healthy habits that help them stay motivated (e.g., getting enough sleep, eating well, exercising, connecting with friends, being accountable, etc.). By developing healthy habits, they are more likely to stay motivated.

In summary, you should expect that your level of willpower and motivation will wax and wane. The challenge is first to prepare so you can respond when they are low, and the second challenge is to develop healthy habits that keep you motivated.

Successful Change Begins with Simple Habits

The next concept to remember is that most change is done incrementally. Most people do not suddenly make drastic changes to their lives. Instead, they start by making small incremental changes. If we attempt to make big changes too rapidly, we are more likely to fail.Perhaps you may be thinking, I have to stop my sexual behaviors, or I will lose my marriage. That may be true, but it is small behavioral changes that are going to help you reach the end goal of being true and faithful to your partner.

Here are examples of small and simple things you can do to succeed.

Behavior that led me to have an affair: Reaching out to my affair partner when I was frustrated at work.

Small Behavior:

When I am frustrated at work...   I will do two push-ups

I will go for a walk

I will call my friend Tim

I will take a few deep breaths

I will think about my wife

Can you see how these new thoughts and behaviors can help you succeed? While the main objective is to prevent an affair, the smaller steps pave the way for a successful outcome.

Consider that these steps are like training for a marathon. Most people can't walk out the door and run a marathon. Instead, they begin with short runs, followed by adding more distance each week (10%). Over time their distance increases to the point that they can run 26.2 miles. This way, you build muscle memory to help you stop unwanted sexual behaviors.

Do Something That Challenges You Every Day (start small and simple)

One way to make change last is to get into the habit of doing something that challenges you every day. The goal is to prove to yourself that you can do difficult things. Some days the hard thing you do may be getting to work on time. On other days it may be avoiding the donut shop on the way to work. Still, on other days, you may find yourself biting your tongue when a family member does something that drives you crazy. The key point is that by succeeding at one thing that is hard to achieve, you will feel a sense of accomplishment each day.

My invitation to you is to do one thing each day that challenges you.

Here are a few examples of challenging things you can do, ranging from simple actions to more difficult behaviors.

Small and Simple:

- Look in the mirror in the morning and say, "I got this."

- Smile at a family member.

- Think about something you are grateful for.

More Challenging:

- Review tasks you need to get done and make a plan to complete the task.

- Identify an area of weakness and make a plan to improve on that area.

- Study something that pushes you out of your comfort zone.

Even More Challenging:

- Ask your partner to talk with you about their pain.

- Prepare to make amends for how you hurt your partner.

- Call someone who can help you when dealing with a craving to return to your unwanted behavior.

Key Takeaways from This Chapter

- One way to better understand yourself is to identify what you want to change and why you want to change. Once you have done this, you can then prepare to make the changes you desire.

- If you prepare for change, your chances of success significantly increase. You can prepare by learning how to respond in crucial moments, increasing your healthy habits, and expecting your willpower and motivation to go up and down.

- The change process includes a shift from unconscious incompetence to conscious incompetence to conscious competence and concludes with us being unconsciously competent.

- If you want to succeed, model your recovery after what successful people have done. The recovery model is such a model. If you increase your personal recovery (i.e., reduce risks, increase exercise, develop coping skills) and lifestyle recovery (i.e., find a support community, create an environment for success), the odds for your success increase. If you do what successful people do, your chances for change will increase.

Chapter Ten

5 Principles to Rebuild Your Relationship

A principle is a fundamental truth that does not change over time. The Cambridge Dictionary defines it this way, "A basic idea or rule that explains or controls how something happens or works." (1) One of the critical principles of establishing a healthy relationship introduced earlier in this book was the principle of safety. The idea is this: The first principle of human connection is safety. In other words, when we feel safe, our bodies relax, and we can connect with others. Conversely, when we do not feel safe, we put up walls to protect ourselves.

If you had parents who taught you how to create a healthy relationship, you were very fortunate. Unfortunately, our society has been ineffective in teaching us how to create deep, meaningful connections. Parents, who often struggle in their relationships, have difficulty teaching their children how to be successful because they do not have a good model. As a result, many children grow into adulthood without a good model of what to do in their relationships.

As you attempt to rebuild your relationship, I aim to provide you with the foundational principles to help you create a new and improved relationship.

In this chapter, I will provide you with five principles that, if applied correctly, will significantly improve your chances of success in your relationship.

Five Principles to Create Healthy Relationships

Principle #1: Commitment to Integrity

If safety is the foundational principle that allows human connection, integrity is the first principle that helps create safety in relationships. By definition, integrity is being complete, whole, or undivided. (2) It encompasses being honest, truthful, loyal, and committed. As you work to rebuild your relationship, increasing integrity in your relationship is the foundation that can help you heal.

Dr. David Viscott, the author of *Emotional Resilience,* wrote, "If you lived honestly, your life would heal itself." (3) When we are incongruent in our thoughts and actions, we experience internal stress. This usually leads to a myriad of physical and mental health complications. If we are saying one thing and doing another, our lack of honesty will naturally create tension in our lives. I have observed that individuals who come clean and acknowledge their sexual betrayal often end up relaxed after disclosure. There is healing power in confession.

Anna Lembke, in her book, *Dopamine Nation,* shared the research of neuroscientist Christian Ruff and his colleagues, who have studied the neurobiological mechanisms of honesty. "Ruff and his colleagues devised an experiment that invited participants to play a game where they rolled the dice for money using a computer interface. Participants were allowed to lie about the results to increase their winnings. The researchers were able to determine the degree of cheating by comparing the mean percentage of reported successful die rolls against the 50 percent benchmark implied by fully honest reporting. Not surprisingly, participants lied frequently. Compared with the 50 percent honesty benchmark, participants reported that 68 percent of their die rolls had the desired outcome." (4)

What happened next may be one of the more important research findings on honesty that has ever been found. Here's how Lembke described what happened next, "The researchers used electricity to enhance neuronal excitability in the participants' prefrontal brain cortices, using a tool called transcranial direct current stimulation (TDCS). The prefrontal cortex is the frontmost part of our brain, just behind the forehead, and is involved in decision-making, emotion regulation, and future planning, among many other complex processes. It's also a key area involved in storytelling.

The researchers found that lying went down by half when neural excitability in the prefrontal cortex went up. In addition, the increase in honesty 'could not be explained by changes in material self-interest or moral beliefs and was dissociated from participants' impulsivity, willingness to take risks, and mood.' They concluded that honesty could be strengthened by stimulating the prefrontal cortex, consistent with the idea that the "human brain has evolved mechanisms dedicated to control complex social behaviors." (5,6)

You may have noticed the word undivided in the definition of integrity. In my work with betrayal, both partners often report feeling divided. The betraying partner has been living with secrets, and their double life naturally creates a mental division. The betrayed partner, on the other hand, may keep what they are experiencing to themselves because they do not know how others will respond. As a result, both partners frequently seek help feeling the weight of their secrets.

One betrayed partner described her experience this way,

"I didn't dare tell my family what my husband did because I knew they would judge him and tell me to leave. I was ready to leave. When I was around them, I knew I was keeping a secret from them. They knew something was wrong, but I didn't dare tell them."

While you may think of integrity as the betraying partner's issue, the concept of integrity (undivided) applies to both partners in the relationship. The betrayed partner needs to resolve issues that can make them feel dishonest or mentally divided.

Here are two scenarios where this happens:

#1. The betrayed partner has to determine if they are going to tell others about the betrayal. If they hold back to protect the betraying partner, they will likely feel that they are keeping a secret. Then if friends, family members, or others ask how they are doing, their response, at best, will feel like a lie. The result of keeping a secret weighs heavily on the mind of the betrayed.

A few years ago, I met with a couple who had decided that they would not tell their families about the husband's affairs. They determined that it would be best for their marriage. As I sat with the wife, she was extremely sad. She had just spent a few hours with her mom and sisters, with whom she had a great relationship. One of her sisters asked her if she was okay, to which she said, "I'm fine; why do you ask?" Her sister said, "I don't know, you don't seem to be yourself lately, and I am just wondering if you are okay."

She hadn't recognized how the weight of the betrayal was impacting her until her sister pointed it out. It was in that session she determined that she was going to tell her family. After our session, she returned home to discuss her decision with her husband. He was supportive of her decision and asked if she wanted him to tell them. His affirming response and willingness to take responsibility were relieving to her. In our next session, the weight of her burden had been lifted. Her family responded with love and kindness towards both of them and asked if they could be of any help.

Note: I understand that having a supportive family is not everyone's experience. However, the goal is to find a safe person or group of people with whom you can share your burden. This allows you to be authentic and provides emotional support in challenging times. It is important to remember that support can come from many places. Ideally, it should be family support, like the client above experienced. However, when family is not an option, support may come from a trusted friend, a co-worker, or a religious leader.

#2. A second issue betrayed partners need to address is their commitment to their current relationship. Many are wondering if they should stay or leave. The decision to remain in the relationship and work on it is difficult. When clients ask me what they should do, I can't tell them because I don't know what is going to be best for them.

Furthermore, I don't have to live with the consequences of their decision either way.

When we explore their options, they often have a few questions and concerns:

- If I stay, will my partner continue to cheat on me?
- If I leave, how will my children adjust?
- If I stay, can I survive emotionally?
- If I leave, will I be emotionally okay?

While clients are considering their options, they usually are not comfortable discussing their thoughts with their partner. This is an area where they become incongruent in their messaging. It is hard for the betrayed partner to describe the internal battles they are having with their spouse who betrayed them. As a result, many are torn about how much to share with their partner and how much to keep to themselves. As a result, betrayed partners often feel split as they try to make the critical decision about their commitment to the relationship.

Even when betrayed partners make a decision regarding their commitment to the relationship, they often question themselves. They often wonder, "Am I making the right decision?" The consequence is many betrayed partners continue to feel divided and incomplete, which prevents them from being in harmony with themselves. While betrayed partners are not lying or hiding behaviors, their confusion makes it appear that they are not being honest and truthful with their spouses.

Note: If you have betrayed your partner, you may have read the section above and thought, "That is exactly what is happening in my relationship." If so, it is critical to realize that your partner is not trying to deceive you; instead, they are trying to make sense of their own emotions—which have been heavily influenced by your actions. If you want to support your partner and strengthen the possibility of working things out, support your partner as they experience the emotional roller coaster that comes with betrayal. Don't be too surprised if they want you close at one moment and then push you away the other. They may be nice and kind and mean and cold in a short period of time. Please remember these are common behaviors after betrayal. They are struggling to make sense of the emotional chaos that betrayal has triggered. If you can be patient and show compassion during these times, the chance of you and your partner making it will increase.

Integrity for the Betraying Partner

If you have betrayed your partner, becoming a person with integrity in your relationship should be a primary goal. You may be honest and truthful in every area of your life, but in fidelity to your partner, you have slipped. Your behavior does not have to define you. It is what you do moving forward that will determine who you become.

You have likely felt the stress that living two lives puts upon you. Often betraying partners while living with their secrets, they experience elevated pressure and anxiety levels. I have had many clients describe the damaging emotional impact betrayal has caused on them. One of my clients explained it this way, "I couldn't sleep. I knew what I was hiding from my husband. He was working hard and providing for me and the family. Every time I met with my affair partner, I lied to my husband. I would tell him I was spending time with friends when in truth, I was meeting my affair partner. I felt so guilty, but I couldn't stop. I started getting physically sick. I was so stressed. Lying was killing me".

When I ask my clients about their lying and deceiving behaviors, many share their fear of being left by their spouses. Others have told me that they have been lying their entire life, and they don't know why they lie. Usually, those who fit into this category learn to lie in their childhood to stay out of trouble. Still, others have been hiding their behaviors for years, and lying is just one part of the chaos in their lives. They often struggle with multiple addictions.

Regardless of your reason for deceiving your spouse, if you want a better relationship, becoming a person who is honest will benefit your life in many ways.

Researchers have discovered that emotional honesty—radical honesty has many benefits. Here are just a few:

- First, radical honesty promotes awareness of our actions.

- Second, it fosters intimate human connections.

- Third, it leads to a truthful autobiography, which holds us accountable not just to our present but also to our future selves.

- Fourth, telling the truth is contagious and might even prevent the development of future addiction. (7)

While radical honesty is essential to couple healing, for some individuals, simply learning to express honest emotions is powerful. Throughout my career, I have worked with many people who struggle to identify their core emotions. For these individuals, learning how to identify what they are feeling is powerful. As they discover how to express themselves honestly, they show significant improvement in relationships.

Scientific evidence suggests expressing our emotions helps us both physically and mentally. When we have positive or negative experiences, and we choose to share them with others, our mental health increases drastically. In the book, *Opening Up,* Dr. James Pennebaker discovered the power of sharing all emotions. He wrote, "The disclosure of both positive and negative events brings about comparable physiological changes that reflect the letting-go process. All biological changes between expressing good and bad events are not identical, of course. In writing about traumas, people often cry. Disclosing positive events can lead to the expression of smiles and laughter. The central physiological similarity, then, between the disclosure of positive and negative thoughts and feelings is the reduction of inhibition." (8)

Pennebaker's key finding is this: When we have emotions, good or bad, positive or negative, if we do not have an environment to share them with others, we will experience inhibition. When we inhibit emotional expression, we will experience a decline in health. Pennebaker found, "As with traumas, positive events should be talked about and openly expressed. Actively holding them back is another form of inhibition—with all the attendant health risks. (9)

> *If you are holding back emotions (good or bad, positive or negative), your physical health and mental health are at risk.*

In an effort to help you identify your current level of integrity, I have created a short assessment for you:

Personal Integrity Questionnaire (PIQ):

Question	On a Scale Between (0 = Not true and 7 = True)
I engage in secret sexual behaviors that only I know about.	
I am honest with my emotions.	
I am truthful in what I do and say.	
I am honest even in the smallest things.	
I am the same person in private that I am in public.	
I take responsibility for problems I create, and to the extent possible, I try to make things right.	
I keep my commitments. If I say I am going to do something, I do it.	

Exercise: As you review the Personal Integrity Questionnaire (PIQ), give yourself a score between 0 and 70. You will need to reverse score the first item. If you scored a four on the first item, score it as a six. Next, sum up your scores. Higher scores indicate that you feel you have integrity, while lower scores represent the need to improve in this area.

Next, identify one area to improve upon. Use the What and Why exercise.

- What do I need to change?

- Why do I want to change this? Write for three minutes about why you want to improve in this area.

Once you have identified your *'what'* and *'why,'* turn your attention to preparing to change (Review the video on Preparing to Change— https://bit.ly/change-two

How to Improve Honesty and Trust in Your Relationship

If you want to rebuild your relationship after sexual betrayal, creating a relationship built upon honesty and truthfulness is where you should start. The section below will provide steps to help you establish the right foundation for moving forward in your relationship.

Note: The information and resources provided below will take time to digest. The process of preparing and doing a disclosure takes time, effort, and good support. This is especially true for relationships where there have been significant amounts of lying and deception. Please do not rush the disclosure process. My goal for the section below is to explain the rationale for doing a disclosure and to discuss the benefits as discovered in the research.

Prepare and Complete a Disclosure

In recent years, there has been much discussion regarding the efficacy of doing a disclosure after discovering sexual betrayal. Many people wonder if disclosures create more problems than they solve. Others fear that if they disclose to their partner, they will be left. Before I address these issues, let me explain what disclosure means and the process of doing a couples disclosure.

Self-disclosure, or the sharing of personal information with others through verbal communication, is an integral part of relationships. This is especially true when the actions of one person have violated the agreement (spoken or unspoken) between two people (e.g., sexual fidelity). Self-disclosure offers one the opportunity to be honest and truthful about their behaviors.

The disclosure process provides an opportunity for a person to reveal his/her behaviors, thoughts, and feelings that have been hidden from others. Usually, the person who is disclosing works with a therapist to prepare a written document that addresses their sexual history and all sexual behaviors engaged outside of the committed relationship.

Researchers Derlega et al. have written that disclosure can help develop a sense of self and build intimacy within personal relationships. (10) After sexual betrayal, individuals who participate in the disclosure process often increase their awareness and the depth of their challenges.

How a Disclosure Can Help

There may be nothing more difficult than sharing your sexual misdeeds with your spouse. In the therapy world, revealing an affair or other sexual activity outside of the relationship is referred to as "disclosure."

Regarding this, Drs. Deborah Corley and Jennifer Schneider wrote in their book *Disclosing Secrets:* "It is safe to say that all revelations are painful for everyone, often initially traumatic for the partner, and hard for the couple." (11)

So, what is the value of being vulnerable if it is painful for everyone? Multiple researchers have revealed the power of disclosure:

- Drs. Corley and Schneider found that "most couples did not split up after disclosure," which led them to think that the couples who had acknowledged the secrets had a better chance of saving the relationship than those who had not. (12)

- Drs. Corley and Schneider: "...most partners and addicts (over 90% in our study) report they are glad the disclosure happened." (13)

- Dr. Peggy Vaughn conducted research with more than 1000 betrayed individuals. In her research, she discovered that couples who discussed the details of the affair were much more likely to stay together than couples who did not talk about the details. In her study, 86% of couples who discussed the details were still together after an affair. In contrast, only 55% of the couples who didn't discuss the details of the affair were still together. (14)

I have heard over and over that disclosures are effective. I have just shared the research that supports doing a disclosure. However, I am not someone who simply accepts the research. I want to understand why something works. So, I have been creating a personal list of why I believe disclosures are effective. Here's my list:

- A disclosure creates a foundation for honesty and truthfulness in a relationship. In contrast, the previous interactions were based on lies and deception.

- By sharing one's secrets, the betraying spouse can move closer to healing and recovery because they are not carrying secrets of their behaviors.

- There is power in confession.

- The betrayed partner receives the truth so that they can decide about how to proceed in the relationship.

- The betrayed deserve the truth.

- It is hard for the betrayed partner to heal without knowing what happened. Our minds are looking for answers, and when those answers are not forthcoming, we tend to think more about the unresolved issues. (Another example of the Zeigarnik effect).

- It is hard to create deep connections when secrets are being held by one or both partners.

- Being honest may activate the prefrontal cortex. Our prefrontal cortex helps us make better decisions and regulate our emotions. (15)

Resources for Learning More about Disclosures

- *Courageous Love*—Stefanie Carnes

- *Full Disclosure: How to Share the Truth After Sexual Betrayal*—Dan Drake and Janice Caudill

Principle #2: Affirming Worth and Showing Genuine Compassion

At one point in your relationship, you felt genuine love for each other. You may not feel that way right now, but at some point in your past, those intimate feelings were present. You saw your partner with loving eyes. You looked at them with kindness and care. When they were hurt, you were hurt too. You felt what they felt.

Now? These feelings are likely on the back burner. It is hard to feel compassion for someone who has hurt you or who is frequently angry with you. However, if you are going to heal and find joy in your relationship again, it will be important to return to the positive thoughts, feelings, and behaviors that you used to show for each other.

I can hear some of you saying, "I don't know if I can ever feel that way again." That may be true; you may never feel the same way ever again. In truth, that is not what I would expect from any of you. Instead, I want you to create new experiences and memories with each other. In order for you to be able to do that, I want to explore where you are in your relationship and help you understand where you can be.

The principle of affirming worth and showing genuine compassion can help you build a better relationship.

Five Steps to Affirming Worth and Showing Genuine Compassion

Step #1: Identify Your Core Beliefs About Your Partner

- How do you see your partner? Do you see them in a more positive or negative light?

- What do you believe about them (e.g., they are kind-hearted; or they are thoughtless; or they are generally a good person?) Respond to this question: I believe my partner is _____

  _____

- As you reflect on your partner as a person, what do you think drives them to think, feel or act the way they do?

- Do my beliefs about my spouse prevent me from showing compassion to them?

- Am I able to see my partner's misbehaviors as a symptom of some other problem, or do I believe that their character is flawed?

Our beliefs directly influence our behaviors. If we think our partner is weak, we will treat them that way. If we believe that our partner doesn't love us, we will approach our relationship with caution. Our beliefs guide our behaviors.

Now that you have a better understanding of the beliefs you have about your partner, I would like to invite you to think about love and how we manifest love in our relationships.

Step #2: Create True Love Instead of Ersatz Love

Have you ever heard of ersatz love? I hadn't until I met my friend and mentor, Ken Patey. He explained the difference between true (real) love and ersatz love, which has helped me understand why so many people feel empty in their relationships.

Real love is something that can't be faked. It's an emotion between two people that transcends physical and social boundaries, allowing them to share an unconditional bond with one another. In contrast, ersatz love is a shallow imitation of real love—it often comes from misguided intentions or even selfishness and can be easily broken apart without much effort.

The main difference between real love and ersatz love is that genuine feeling of love is based on the principles of trust, respect, honesty, and a true understanding of the other person. On the other hand, ersatz love often fades quickly because it was never rooted in any of these values to begin with. Real love also has the potential to last a lifetime, whereas ersatz love only lasts as long as the circumstances are convenient.

In short, real love is the kind of connection that sustains people through highs and lows and motivates them to grow together. On the other hand, ersatz love is superficial and fleeting. It does not offer any real connection, and it fades quickly. Real love is a commitment, while ersatz love is nothing more than an attraction. Knowing the difference between these two kinds of love can help you identify what type of relationship you are going to create.

Questions to consider:

1. Can I tell the difference between real love and ersatz love?

2. Do I know how to give and receive real love?

Step #3: Remember That All Persons, Including the Self, Are of Infinite Worth and Value

In the middle of betrayal, it is hard to see your partner for who they are. It is also hard to remember your true worth and value. Remembering your true worth is essential if you want to heal. One way to accomplish this is to increase your level of self-compassion. Dr. Kristin Neff, who has studied self-compassion, shares this wisdom, "The research my colleagues and I have conducted over the past decade shows that self-compassion is a powerful way to achieve emotional well-being and contentment in our lives." (16)

This quote is a great reminder of why self-compassion is so important.

> *"Compassion is not only relevant to those who are blameless victims, but also to those whose suffering stems from failures, personal weakness, or bad decisions. You know, the kind you and I make every day. Compassion, then, involves the recognition and clear seeing of suffering. It also involves feelings of kindness for people who are suffering so that the desire to help—to ameliorate suffering—emerges. Finally, compassion involves recognizing our shared human condition, flawed and fragile as it is."*
>
> ***Kristen Neff, Self-Compassion*** (17)

As a therapist, I have had the opportunity to work with individuals from all over the world. I am truly amazed at the incredible people I meet. I cannot emphasize this point enough; we are all of infinite worth and value. If we treat ourselves and others with this in mind, we could solve most of the problems we have in our lives.

Questions to consider:

1. Do I treat myself with dignity and respect?

2. Do I treat others with dignity and respect?

3. Can I accept that I am of infinite worth and value?

4. Do I treat others as if they are of infinite worth and value?

Our relationships can only be as good as we treat each other.

Step #4: Create an Affirming Environment

Everybody creates an environment around them. We can invite people to be close to us through our body language and emotional expressions; similarly, we can push people away just as easily to keep them at a distance. After betrayal, many people get confused because they don't know how to be with their partner. Should I hold back? Should I try to be close? While there aren't easy answers to these questions, there is something that you can do; you can create an environment where healing is an option.

Let me share a powerful story that illustrates the principle of creating an affirming environment.

Robyn, and her husband, Jacob, had come to my office for a couple of sessions. Robyn was frustrated with Jacob's use of pornography in their home. Jacob was busy with work and felt like Robyn shouldn't worry about it. They felt like they were at an impasse. In our next session, Robyn came by herself. She was upset at Jacob. The night before, he had got returned home late from work and grabbed the plate of food she had set aside for him. He went into their bedroom, shut and locked the door, and didn't interact with her or their children other than greeting them.

Robyn said, "I've made my decision. I am going to take my children and stay with my mom for a few nights. I don't want to deal with this anymore. He doesn't pay any attention to me or the children. By coming home last night and locking the door, I know he was looking at pornography. I can't do this anymore."

She had made her decision.

In situations like this, I usually role-play with my client so they can be clear about what they will say. Also, by practicing with them, they are prepared to deal with potential conflict. For example, I may ask a question like, "What will you do if he says, 'I don't care if you leave.' Or 'Fine, you want a divorce? I will give you a divorce.'"

After role-playing a few different scenarios, I asked Robyn this question, "What do you really want Jacob to know?" She thought for a minute, looked at me, and said, "I want him to know that I love him. That I don't want to leave, but I can't live this way."

There it was. Her truth. She didn't want to leave, but she couldn't keep living the way that they were. She went home and followed her plan. That evening when her husband got home, late as usual, he grabbed dinner and headed to their bedroom. She stopped him and said, "Jacob, I am going to take the kids and stay with my mom for a few nights. Nothing is changing in our relationship. The past few nights, you came home late, did not interact with me or the children, and went straight into our room and viewed pornography. I can't live like this. I want you to know that I love you. I don't want to leave, but I can't keep pretending everything is okay when it's not."

She had already packed the kids' bags and had them in her car. The children loved spending time with Grandma, so they were excited for an adventure. She told the kids to say goodbye to Dad and hop in the car while she grabbed her bag. As she got to the door, Jacob was waiting. "Are you sure you want to leave?" he asked. Robyn was at the door; she turned around and said one more time, "I don't want to leave. I love you, but I won't live this way anymore. I hope you will think about what you want in our relationship." With that, she turned and left.

I was scheduled to see them together for our next session. However, Jacob came by himself. I was curious about what had happened and if Robyn had carried through with her decision. Jacob sat down and said, "Robyn left me for a few days last week. I want you to know that I was mad at you." He continued, "Last week after your appointment, she came home and told me she was leaving with the kids for a few days. I was angry and upset at her…and you…and everyone."

I inquired, "You said you were mad at me; what has changed?"

He replied, "When Robyn was leaving, I asked her if she really wanted to leave. She turned around and said, 'I don't want to leave. I love you, but I won't live this way anymore. I hope you will think about what you want in our relationship.' That was it. I don't know how to explain it, but the way she said, 'I love you.' It hit me. She loved me. It was the first time in my life I felt that someone loved me. I knew I had to change since I was pushing the only person who loved me away."

Jacob was finally ready for help. He looked at me and said, "I need help." Robyn had created an affirming environment, and Jacob had felt her love. That was real love in action.

Examples of Affirming Statements with Appropriate Boundaries

- I love you, but I can't keep living this way.

- I believe in you. I can't make you choose to heal or recover.

- I want a better relationship with you; what we have been doing does not work. I hope we can figure this out.

Step #5: Commit to Affirm the Worth of Self and Others

The fifth and final step of affirming worth and showing genuine compassion for self and others is to act. Here's an exercise to help you take action.

Exercise: Affirming Worth and Showing Genuine Compassion

Write down your response to these questions:

1. What can I do to make it easier for others to love me?

   _____

2. I will give myself compassion by doing:

   _____

3. I will show my partner compassion by:

   _____

4. When things are not going well in our relationship, I will remember I am of infinite worth by doing or thinking:

   _____

5. When things are not going well in our relationship, I will affirm my partner's worth by doing:

   _____

Principle #3: Commitment to Growth

Something fascinating happens when individuals and couples truly understand the principle of personal and relationship growth. Let me explain. You don't have to live with personal pain or unwanted sexual behaviors anymore. You can change your relationship; you can change your life. Nothing is fixed; all things can change. You can become better individually and in your relationship.

Because betrayal has been a part of your relationship, you have been forced to learn, change, and adapt. Both you and your partner have had to pause and reflect upon your relationship. Both of you have had to do a self-evaluation, and as discussed in previous chapters, you have had to ask yourself difficult questions (See the Orienting Questions from Chapter One).

Unfortunately, change doesn't necessarily mean that you will grow. Growth is something that you choose to do. Nobody is making you read this book, go to counseling, or seek healing. You are making choices that can lead you to heal and recover.

Personal Growth

As I was contemplating what story would illustrate the principle of growth, I found myself reflecting on a client who started attending one of my groups. Her husband had been cheating on her for many months, and almost at the same time, she discovered that her son had been engaging in illegal sexual behaviors.

After our first group, she pulled me aside and said, "I need you to know that I am willing to do whatever it takes to heal. I can't live the way I have been living. It is killing me. So, if you or your therapists here ask me to do something, I will do it. I just need answers. Over the next two years, I witnessed an incredible transformation in her and her husband's lives. Here are some of the things in which she participated:

- Attended a group for betrayed partners for 18 months.
- Yoga for six months.
- Personal therapy for almost two years.
- Couples counseling as guided by her therapists.
- Family therapy with her son and husband.
- Mindfulness classes.

Near the end of our group, which lasted for eighteen months, I gave the group a challenge to continue learning. She took my suggestion to heart and signed up for an art class. After joining the class, she told our group that she had been wanting to take an art class for many years, but she felt like it would be selfish of her.

One of the ways I track progress in my clients is when their creativity returns. This client had committed herself to change. In doing so, she set an example for her family and our group. I was inspired by her commitment to personal growth.

When I work with individuals who want change in their life, this principle of growth is often the most exciting to them. I have pondered why my clients get excited when we discuss the principle of growth. The answer I have come up with is that our minds are constantly looking for solutions. We want to discover strategies for living better lives. Sadly, we get distracted pursuing behaviors that do not promote lasting joy and happiness.

As you think about your commitment to growth, consider these questions:

1. Am I committed to personal growth and development?
2. What actions have I been taking to improve my life?
3. Are there things in my life I need to remove so I can grow?
4. Am I willing to do anything to become the best person I can be?

Throughout this book, I have tried to emphasize that I do not know if your relationship will make it. Regardless of the outcome, I invite you to become the person you were meant to be. Find your purpose. Find your passion. Then live accordingly.

You do not have to live in a helpless or hopeless situation. As you commit to personal growth, you will feel empowered; you will feel hope.

Here is something I often share with my clients. I hope it helps you.

> *Healthy people develop healthy habits. Healthy habits lead to healthy lives. The secret to success isn't really a secret at all. Make personal growth and development a priority, and you will develop lifelong habits that lead to a meaningful life.*

In this section, I have focused on making personal growth a priority. I firmly believe that your individual development is imperative if you want to have a better relationship. That may sound strange or even selfish to some people. Let me explain why I believe this matters. How can you give yourself to your partner when you do not feel whole yourself? Remember, in the principle of integrity, one of the definitions was whole or integrated. Some people mistakenly believe that self-growth (or self-care) is selfish. When we do our own work to become better people, we become more prepared to create better relationships.

Now let's turn our attention to relationship growth.

Commitment to Relationship Growth

If you want your relationship to last, you will need to nurture your relationship. The couples who succeed in rebuilding their relationship after betrayal transition from monitoring, fighting, keeping secrets, and avoiding each other to more productive conversations, complete honesty, playful interactions, and meaningful time together.

Often when I work with couples, they tend to focus on their problems. Periodically, I invite them to pause and reflect on some of the good things that they have been doing in their relationship. I use a metaphor to explain why this is important.

I grew up on a farm. We had cows, pigs, and chickens. When we went into the field (where the cows were) to play, I sometimes stepped on the cow pie. It was awful. My shoes smelled and were discolored. It was hard to get the manure off my shoes. After stepping in the dung, it would have been easy for me to focus on skip-stepping the cow pies while playing with my family and friends. In other words, I could have kept looking at the cow pie just to make sure that I missed stepping into another one.

By looking up, I saw the flowers, the water that ran through our property, and the beautiful mountains in the background. I didn't ignore the cow pies. I just became more aware of where they were, so I could avoid stepping on them.

As I finish the metaphor with the couples I meet, I encourage them to pause frequently, look around, and enjoy what is around them. I invite them to do things that they both enjoy in an effort to rekindle the love that they once had.

I now invite you to complete this relationship growth Exercise:

Exercise: Activities to Grow Together

Begin this exercise by setting a timer for three minutes. For the first part of this exercise, you both need a pen and paper. Start the timer, and for three minutes, write down activities or things that you would like to do together. Once the three minutes are over, review your list and rank order them from most important to you to least important. Next, share your list with your partner and compare the things that you would like to do. Finally, make a plan to do things on your list (at least one thing a week).

Here are a few principles related to creating growth in your relationship:

- Healthy couples take time to nurture their relationship.

- Couples who rebuild their relationship spend meaningful time together discussing how their relationship will be better.

- Couples who heal grow because they focus their energy on each other.

As you review these principles, consider how you are doing in these areas and make a plan to improve upon them.

Principle #4: Commitment to Agency

We all long to be free to make our own choices. When we sense that others are forcing us to do something, we almost naturally resist being told what to do. However, when we enter into a committed relationship, we establish expectations; some are voiced, while others are not. For most people, fidelity is briefly discussed at the beginning of the relationship, or it is assumed. Therapist and researcher Dr. Peggy Vaughn asked 1083 individuals who had been betrayed how they dealt with the issue of monogamy. Their responses indicate that roughly half (48% women and 54% men) assumed monogamy without discussing it, while another 31% talked about it early in their relationship but did not continue discussing it. (18)

Vaughn's research supports the premise that most people enter a committed relationship expecting fidelity. However, most couples do not discuss what will happen if one partner is unfaithful. As a result, once betrayal has occurred, the betrayed partner scrambles to establish new boundaries. The betraying partner, on the other hand, begins to feel like clamps are being put on them and that they are losing their freedom to choose.

This is where choice and commitment clash. The betrayed partner wants to re-establish safety by asking for total commitment, while the betraying partner wants the freedom to choose. When couples are fighting about agency in their relationship, I often revert back to basic commitment questions:

1. On a scale between 0 (not committed at all) and 10 (very committed), what is your current level of commitment to your relationship? If your commitment level is between zero and three, you are more out than in your relationship. As a result, if your partner attempts to limit or control your behavior, you will likely be resistant. If your commitment levels are high, you will be more open to their suggestions.

2. If you and your partner choose to work on your relationship, are you expecting to be faithful and committed to your partner?

3. How committed are you to being faithful to your partner (0 Not at all - 10 Completely)?

See Commitment Exercise in Appendix I

As you make decisions about your relationship, here are some common guidelines to help you better understand the role of agency. These principles of agency can be a guidepost to help you improve your relationship. If you apply these principles, your relationship will improve. If these principles are being violated, you will struggle to connect on a deeper level with your partner.

Fundamental Principles of Agency

- Choice is essential to healthy relationships. If you force another person to do something against their will, they will either resist or they will shut down (and be resentful). In both instances, your relationship loses.

- You have the right to choose your actions, but you don't have the right to control how others respond to your choices.

- There are always consequences for our behaviors. For example, when we are loving and kind, we draw people towards us. When we are negative, controlling, or unkind, we push others away.

- Personal boundaries prevent us from engaging in unhealthy behaviors that can control our lives (i.e., addictions, infidelity, anger). (See Chapter Eleven)

- When we create mutually agreed-upon boundaries, we increase agency in our relationships. (See Chapter Eleven)

A man or woman forced against his/her will remain the same, still.

Here are some additional ideas to think about as you consider the role of agency in your relationship:

- You can't make your partner stop their behavior.

- You can create personal boundaries about what you will and won't accept in your relationship.

- You can't be unkind and expect to connect

- You can choose to be more loving

- As humans, we seek autonomy. When we believe we can determine the outcome of our lives, we thrive. When we feel like no matter what we do, it won't change the outcome; we feel hopeless or helpless. When we feel like our actions can't change an outcome, we are likely to become depressed.

- If you and your partner no longer share the same values (e.g., commitment to fidelity, commitment to your relationship), any effort to force your partner to conform to your will, will likely be met with resistance. A couple of questions you can ask yourselves are: Do we share the same values? Do we share a similar vision for our relationship?

Note: If your values or vision for your relationship are not similar, the odds of conflict in your relationship will increase. The more aligned your values and vision, the higher the probability you will work through betrayal and other challenges.

Principle #5. Commitment to Trusting Your Instincts and Own Intuitive Responses

The fifth principle for creating healthy relationships is learning to trust your instincts and your own intuitive responses. We all have natural instincts when we are born. Instincts are goal-directed and innate patterns of behavior that are not the result of learning or experience. (19)

While it is easy to identify early life instincts, such as the rooting reflex in infants, it is more difficult to measure our instinctive responses as adults. I have asked many betrayed clients if they have had intuitive feelings regarding their relationship. Many have told me that they have felt that something was not right with their partner, but they couldn't pinpoint the problem. Then, after discovery, they recognize that their instincts were warning them.

Many betrayed partners have said they have had clear impressions or ideas in their minds about how their partner has been unfaithful. Then, in asking their partner if their feeling is right, their partner has lied to them. This has led these clients to mistrust their instincts. However, upon further reflection, my clients realize that their instincts were right all along.

I have also had clients in the middle of a risky situation where they could sexually act out and receive a clear impression that they need to leave. Upon removing themselves from the place, they realized the tremendous risks that they were taking. They viewed this situation as a warning.

Some clients call these impressions instinctive responses or intuitive feelings. I have heard enough of these stories throughout my career that I do not question whether my clients are having them. What I hope to help my clients with is channeling their instinctive responses to help them resolve issues in their relationships.

This chapter will conclude with three ways that you can incorporate instinctive responses as you try to repair your relationship.

Here's a question for you to consider:

Do you believe that your instincts can help you solve relationship problems? If yes, how do you imagine your instincts can help you?

Here are four steps you can take to increase the odds so your instincts can help you solve relationship issues:

1. Slow down—the world we now live in is filled with distractions that keep our minds moving. When we slow down to listen to our internal voice, we may be surprised at what we hear. When clients come to my office, I strongly encourage them to participate in yoga sessions or mindfulness practices. There is solid research to support both of these practices. See the works of Jon Kabat-Zinn, Daniel Siegel, or Thich Nhat Hahn.

2. Meditate on ways to solve your personal and relationship problems. If you want to solve a problem in your life, take the time to reflect on the problem. Then listen to the thoughts and impressions you have. You may be surprised at how much you can feel and hear as you relax.

3. Listen to your inner voice. As you practice listening to your inner voice, pay close attention to your thoughts, emotions, and body sensations. Then ask yourself the questions of your mind:

- How can I overcome betrayal?

- How can I overcome my unwanted sexual behaviors?

- What does my partner need from me?

- How can I show I am trustworthy?

- How can I be better at affirming the worth of my partner?

- How can we grow together as a couple?

- What can I do to support my partner's choices while maintaining my personal boundaries?

These are not easy questions. However, as you slow down, meditate, andlisten to your inner voice; your instincts can help you improve your relationship.

Note: Early in this chapter, I mentioned that by stimulating the prefrontal cortex, you can increase honesty. One way that may be helpful in activating the prefrontal cortex is to meditate. [20]

Act according to your intuition. When you feel impressed to do or say something, act.

A few years ago, I had a client seek my help. As we discussed his relationship with his wife, he was lost on how to help her heal. He felt like he had done everything she had asked him to do, but she wasn't feeling any better about their relationship. I gave him the assignment and questions outlined above. He came back the next session and said, "I realized I had been doing the tasks of recovery. What I hadn't been doing was listening to her. As I reflected on the question, 'What does my partner need from me,' I had the distinct impression that I needed to listen to her. So that's what I did. I told her that I had not asked her about what this experience had been like for her. That night as she spoke, I finally realized what pain and anguish I had created in her."

What a powerful moment for him and for his wife. I believe that the seeds of the solutions to our problems are within us. As you slow down, meditate on ways to solve the challenges you face, listen to your inner voice, and act accordingly, you will be surprised at the power of your own intuitive responses.

> *The answer is not in your head; it will come from your heart.*

Key Takeaways from This Chapter

- There were five principles that were discussed in the chapter: 1) commitment to integrity; 2) commitment to affirming worth and showing genuine compassion; 3) commitment to growth; 4) commitment to agency; and 5) commitment to trusting your instincts and own intuitive responses.

- The first principle of integrity is being whole or complete. After betrayal, complete rigorous honesty helps activate the prefrontal cortex.

- The second principle of affirming worth and showing genuine compassion begins with self-compassion. We discussed the power of your beliefs and how they influence your perception of yourself and your partner. All persons are of infinite worth and value.

- The third principle is the commitment to growth. We began by discussing personal growth. One way to improve your relationship is to begin with self-growth.

- The fourth principle is a commitment to the agency. The key elements include: 1) Choice is essential to healthy relationships; 2) you can choose your actions, but not the consequences; 3) there are always consequences for our behaviors; 4) personal boundaries protect us from addictions; and 5) relationship boundaries help us sustain healthy relationships.

- The fifth and final principle is learning to trust your instincts and your own intuitive responses. A solid strategy to accomplish this is: 1) slow down; 2) meditate; 3) listen; and 4) act.

Chapter Resources:

Information on applying the five principles in your relationships: Chapter 10

https://bit.ly/RYR

Chapter Eleven

Creating New Boundaries– Why Your Values Should Guide Your Boundaries

Create Boundaries to Save Yourself and Your Relationship

When I asked Mike how he was doing, he wasn't too happy. He said, "Amber is driving me absolutely crazy. She is monitoring everything I do. The other day while discussing details about my trip to New York, the one where I went to a massage parlor, she accused me of hiding other behaviors. I feel like everything I do right now is under a microscope. Just last night, she handed me a long list of boundaries that if I don't follow, she will request that I move out. I'm ready to quit."

I asked Mike, "What was going through your mind while conversing with your wife? Mike replied, "I felt overwhelmed. I know I made a mistake, but I don't know if I will ever be able to regain her trust." I asked, "Have you ever felt this way before?" Mike thought for a few seconds and said, "Yeah. I often felt this way with my mom. While I was growing up, I felt like no matter what I did; it wasn't enough for her. My room wasn't clean enough; my grades weren't as good as she wanted them."

I commented, "So you have felt this way before? What do you think the difference is between your mom and your wife?" "I'm not sure," Mike replied, "I guess my wife doesn't nag me like my mom. However, it feels that way right now."

I asked another question, "So how did you respond to your mom when you were younger?" Mike said, "I ignored her and avoided her as much as possible. I learned to hide my behaviors as much as possible."

Interesting, I was thinking out loud. "Do you think that subconsciously your wife's response to your betrayal is reminding you of your mom?" Mike replied, "I hadn't thought about it that way. It makes sense."

"How do you think that influences how you interact with your wife?"

Mike responded, "That's a good question. I think I just tune her out like I did my mom."

"And what does that do to your wife?" I inquired. "It makes her super angry. When I tune her out, she gets so mad."

I continued, "What do you think would help you and your wife in situations when you want to tune her out?" "I have no idea," Mike replied. "Maybe, if I could see my wife for who she is instead of feeling like she was acting like my mom." "That's an interesting idea," I said. "What would that be like for you?"

Mike replied, "It would be hard. I feel like all she tells me is that I am not enough." I followed up with another question, "Who do you think your wife is trying to tell you?" Mike said, "Hmm, I haven't thought about that. I know I have hurt her. I guess she is trying to stop me from hurting her again."

I asked, "Why do you think she is trying to implement all of those boundaries?"

Mike replied, "I used to think because she wanted to control me. Maybe it is because she wants to make sure I don't hurt her again."

I replied, "I'm guessing you are right. You are beginning to understand her more. The important thing we will need to work on is staying present with her instead of reverting back to early responses associated with your mom."

Note: This was just the beginning for Mike. Initially, he thought the issue was Amber's controlling behaviors and a long list of boundaries. He learned that Amber creating boundaries was her way of seeking safety. She wanted their relationship to work out, and the boundaries were the only way she knew how to stop her pain.

Over the next few sessions, he would learn to observe what Amber was trying to say rather than reacting. We discussed the importance of staying present with her instead of checking out. I had him reiterate what his wife was saying just to make sure that he understood. We discussed the importance of reducing his shame (the little boy feeling that he's not good enough). Then, I had him practice empathy and compassion exercises, as found in Chapter Five. As Mike changed, so did Amber. She saw that Mike was genuinely listening to her. He was also showing remorse and commitment to her. For Mike, the big change came when he realized he was interacting with Amber the way he did with his mom.

Amber's Boundaries

After discovery, Amber couldn't make sense of Mike's behaviors. She had so many questions, but Mike wasn't giving her answers. All he had told her was that he had gone to a massage parlor. When she asked for more details, he was hesitant but ended up telling her. She had so many questions; was it his first time visiting a massage parlor, had he had sex with anyone, and had he engaged in any other sexual activities she didn't know about? He told her no, but she did not believe him.

Amber started looking online for support. She didn't want to tell her family and friends because she was embarrassed by what Mike had done. Unfortunately, the more she read, the more worried she became. After reading so many stories of betrayed partners, Amber began wondering if Mike was minimizing his behaviors. Had he lied to her about the extent of his sexual behaviors? Her fears increased because Mike had stopped responding to her questions. He said, "I have told you everything. Why do you keep asking?" Amber felt stuck. She couldn't wrap her mind around what Mike had done, and he wasn't helping. They were at an impasse.

One day while reading a blog, she found an article that discussed the importance of setting boundaries after betrayal. This was a new idea, so she printed out the list of boundaries from the blog. She thought that maybe this would help their relationship. Amber further hoped that Mike would accept the boundaries. It was a long list. But when she shared the list with Mike, he responded defensively.

"Are you kidding me," he replied. "Are you ever going to get over this?"

Amber got angry and accused him of lying to her. She knew he was hiding something from her.

Mike retorted, "It doesn't matter what I say; you won't believe me." And with that, he left.

A couple of days later, Mike came for the above-mentioned session.

Let's now review Amber's response. Based on the information we have; it would be fair to say that she is experiencing many of the PTSD symptoms discussed in Chapter Five. As a reminder, the five key symptoms are:

- Threat to life—fear of getting an STD (Not sure if she worried about this)
- Reliving the events—nightmares, intrusive thoughts (Most likely)
- Avoidance—avoiding people and places (Yes, this is happening)
- Negative cognitions—I'm not safe, I am stupid; I am unlovable (Most likely)

- Emotional arousal and reactivity—anger, can't sleep (Yes, this is happening)

Amber was likely experiencing four of the five PTSD symptoms. And like most people in this situation, she didn't know what to do. Given this information, it makes sense that she was willing to try anything that would help. She hoped that creating boundaries would help Mike recognize that something had to change. Instead, when she approached him, it backfired, and they got into another fight.

While I didn't work with Amber, I have worked with many people in such circumstances. While helping her understand what she was experiencing (PTSD), I would simultaneously want to help her create effective boundaries. Below are the steps I would take to help her with her PTSD symptoms.

Here's what this would look like:

- Assess for PTSD symptoms (to learn more, see https://www.bit.ly/RYR—Chapter Six)

- Discuss the Zeigarnik effect so Amber realizes what is happening. She's not able to finish the story.

- Attend to the PTSD symptoms (work on symptom reduction) (see Chapter Five and my book Treating Trauma from Sexual Betrayal)

- Help her prepare for a discussion with Mike about their relationship.

- Help her establish boundaries based on her values (I will explain this process next)

The next section of this chapter will focus on a key principle that I believe is the most effective way to live life. I will outline the concept and discuss how they could influence a couple like Amber and Mike.

Why Values Should Determine How We Live Life (and Act as Our Boundaries)

Values are the principles that help us decide right and wrong and guide us on how to act in various situations. If I were to ask you to reflect on your core values, what would they be? What values have helped to guide your life? If you pause and reflect on this question, you will identify what matters the most to you.

I am going to break our core values into two areas: 1) personal values and 2) relationship values.

Personal values are the principles that influence and guide your life. Your thoughts, feelings, and behaviors affect them. Since we are imperfect humans, even though we have core values, we don't always live by our values. When we go against our core values, we experience stress because we have broken our boundaries. This creates dissonance, which is "inconsistency between the beliefs we hold or between our actions and beliefs." [1]

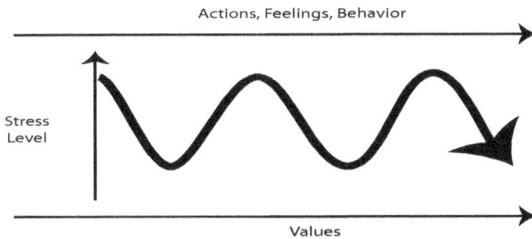

To reduce our stress, we have two options. First, we can lower our values to match our thoughts, feelings, and behaviors; second, we can improve our thoughts, emotions, and behaviors to align with our values. The further apart our actions are from our values, the more dissonance we will feel.

Some of the most common personal values include:

- Personal growth
- Community contributions
- Good health
- Meaningful relationships
- Wealth
- Fame/Recognition
- Image

I have chosen to focus on personal and relationship values for this chapter on boundaries. I want to emphasize the importance of pausing to evaluate what matters the most to you in your life and your relationships. If you and your partner will identify your core values, you will discover whether you and your partner share common values.

Here are questions you will want to ask regarding your personal and relationship values:

1. Am I being true to myself?

2. What are my core values? What do I value the most? Am I living true to these values?

3. Am I committed to being faithful in my relationship?

4. Do I expect my partner to be faithful to me?

5. What level of connection do I want to have in my relationship? (Level of connection includes: 1) openness; 2) vulnerability; 3) honesty; 4) lifting my partner up; and 5) willingness to resolve problems.

Amber's Core Values:

Since I will be asking you to do this assignment, I have included an example of core values so that you have an example:

- Amber's Personal Values—What Principles Will Guide My Life?

    1. *Be true to self:*
    ◊ I will avoid being angry.
    ◊ If I say I will do something, I will do it.
    ◊ I won't engage in behaviors that don't align with my values.
    ◊ I will discuss my boundaries with Mike and keep an open mind.
    ◊ I will work to improve my sense of self-worth.
    ◊ I will increase my self-compassion.

    2. *Be physically healthy (emotionally and physically):*
    ◊ Eat well—improve my diet.
    ◊ Exercise—three times a week.
    ◊ Incorporate mindfulness into my daily routine.
    ◊ Go to yoga at least once a week.

    3. *Contribute to society:*

◊ The best way I can contribute is to teach my children and help them feel loved.

◊ Serve others, friends, and family—lift them up.

◊ Participate and be effective at work.

- Amber's Values in Her Primary Relationship

1. I value fidelity—I will be faithful.

2. I expect my partner to be faithful and value fidelity.

3. Treat my partner with kindness and love—I can love and still have boundaries.

4. Help my partner when they need support.

5. Be aware of my partner's emotional needs.

> *Values are the principles that help you to decide what is right and wrong and how to act in various situations.*

Mike's Core Values:

- Personal values—What Principles Guide My Life?

1. *Be true to self:*

◊ Do what I say I'm going to do.

◊ Be a person who has integrity.

◊ Act consistent with my values.

◊ Avoid conflict.

2. *Be physically healthy:*

◊ Take care of my body (exercise—ride my bike or cross-train 3x a week).

◊ Eat well—I need to stop eating out.

◊ Improve my sleep.

3. *Find a good balance between work and home:*

◊ Be a good provider—take care of my family's financial needs.

◊ Work hard—be creative on the job.

◊   Spend time with the children, be attentive.

◊   Play games with my children.

- Mike's Values in His Primary Relationship

    1. I expect myself to be faithful and true moving forward.

    2. Be caring and compassionate.

    3. Be a person that Amber can turn to.

    4. Be reliable.

    5. Be supportive.

Once you have identified your core values, the next step is to evaluate how to best incorporate them into your life. This is where you will identify how to implement personal and relationship boundaries. For example, if I were working with Mike, I would want him to review his values and then identify boundaries that would help him stay true to those values. Here are a few of the questions I would want him to address:

1. How will you measure doing what you say you are going to do?

2. How will you eat better? What's your plan to improve in this area?

3. What will you be doing when you spend more time with your children?

4. How will you measure being faithful? What does that mean to you?

Let's now turn our attention to how boundaries help us maintain our values.

How Boundaries Help You Live Your Values

I have observed throughout my career that almost all of my clients are coming to my office due to boundary violations. As children, many of these clients were abused, bullied, asked to take on an adult role, or dealt with a parent's addiction. As an adult, they deal with similar boundary issues: abuse, addiction, and betrayal.

There is a long list of boundary violations we can experience. The sad consequence is that when boundaries are breached, negative consequences follow. If you are like many of my clients, you have never been taught the importance of establishing boundaries.

In Amber's case, she had never thought about establishing boundaries. She had assumed that Mike would be faithful. Her response, by creating a lot of boundaries, was her way of protecting herself. She wanted to make sure that Mike didn't hurt her again. Unfortunately, Mike interpreted her efforts as a way to control him. As a result, her desire to create boundaries was met with opposition.

Sadly, when many people think about boundaries, they feel internal resistance. They feel that they are restrictive. If this is how you have experienced boundaries in the past, my hope in this next section is to help you see the power of establishing guidelines in a positive light. Boundaries can be the key to living a life aligned with your values and beliefs.

Here are just a few of the many benefits of creating boundaries:

First, you will feel more in control. Second, you will experience an increased sense of self-worth, and third, you will develop confidence that influences your relationship approach. On the other hand, if you have never learned how to create boundaries, you will likely feel a lower sense of control. You will feel like you can't influence your own life, which can trigger feelings of hopelessness and helplessness.

When we cannot establish boundaries in our personal life or relationships, we will likely experience Learned Helplessness. Dr. Martin Seligman discovered the concept of Learned Helplessness in 1965. His study showed that when animals are presented with an unavoidable shock, they will stop trying to escape it, even when allowed to do so. This phenomenon became known as Learned Helplessness and has been studied extensively in animal and human research. Learned helplessness has been linked to depression, anxiety, other psychological disorders, and physical health problems such as chronic pain and cardiovascular disease. (2,3,4)

By learning to implement boundaries, your actions will reduce feelings of helplessness. Below is a quote that expresses the power of boundaries.

The Importance of Boundaries

I believe that in recognizing and respecting our boundaries, we affirm ourselves, our rights in all our relationships, and the rights of others. When we fail to defend ourselves, when we fail to stand up for ourselves under attack, we lose some treasured part of ourselves—our integrity, belief in ourselves, the real "I" at the core of the inner self, and each time this is a little death. And when we fail to respect the rights of others, we inflict losses, large and small, that may shake the core of the lives of all we touch. (5)

Setting Psychological Boundaries: A Handbook for Women

My intent in writing this next section of this chapter is twofold.

First, you can establish values as outlined in the beginning of this chapter, but if you don't have boundaries in place, it will be hard to live according to your values. There is great healing power in creating personal boundaries. As you learn to apply guidelines in your personal life, you will gain confidence and a better sense of autonomy. If you have been struggling with unwanted sexual behaviors, you will learn that your success will depend on aligning your boundaries with your values. If you have been betrayed, you will learn that boundaries will improve your confidence. As you establish personal boundaries, you will feel better about yourself and your life.

Second, when you learn how to apply boundaries in your relationships, you will have clear expectations of each other. You won't be guessing what your partner wants or needs from you. Unfortunately, many couples realize that their personal boundaries are misaligned after years of fighting and arguing. By having an open dialogue about the guidelines, you want in your relationship, you take out the guesswork. Then as a couple, you can decide whether you can move forward in your relationship.

> *The strength of your relationship is only as strong as the boundaries you create.*

The next part of the chapter will focus on how you can create personal and relationship boundaries. In my conversations with couples, most of them report that they do not like discussing limitations. When I ask them why, they tell me that they usually get into a fight or argument when they talk about relationship guidelines. If this is the case for you and your partner, I invite you to let me walk you through the process of establishing boundaries. I hope to change your mind so that you can both see the benefits.

Let's get started.

General Guidelines for Creating Personal Boundaries

If you have never been taught about boundaries, here are some general guidelines.

The first step to creating healthy personal boundaries is understanding who you are and what matters the most to you (Review section above). If you do not understand your values, beliefs, and limits, it is hard to communicate them effectively with others. Therefore, a good starting place for you would be to make a list of things you want—and don't want—in your life. Identify situations or circumstances in your life in which you feel you need to establish boundaries. This could include anything from how you want people to treat you in relationships to how much time you are willing to devote to certain activities or tasks.

Here are a few questions you might consider asking yourself:

1. What do I value the most in my life?
    1. What brings me the most satisfaction in my life?
    2. What behaviors do I need to remove from my life to feel free?
    3. What boundaries in my life are working?
    4. What areas of my life need boundaries?

The second step is to practice implementing your boundaries. In step one, you created a list; now it is time to start practicing saying "No" when something doesn't align with what you wrote down. I find that it is easier to discuss personal boundaries than it is to implement them. Therefore, you may need to practice in your mind the boundary you are trying to establish before you are comfortable implementing it with your partner or others. Remember that setting boundaries doesn't make you selfish; it gives you the freedom to prioritize what matters most in your life without feeling guilty or overwhelmed by external expectations or obligations.

Here are two examples of people establishing personal boundaries:

The Boundary for Betraying Partner:

I am going to remove all apps on my phone that I have used to act out.

Step #1: Identify the app or apps that need to be removed.

Step #2: Remove the app.

Step #3: Report to someone what you did.

Step #4: If I desire to download the app again, I am going to _____ before I do.

The Boundary for Betrayed Partner:

I am going to do three things a week for self-care.

Step #1: I am going to brainstorm ideas that would be self-care activities for me.

Step #2: I will identify the three most important self-care items I wrote down.

Step #3: Create a plan for when I am going to do the self-care activities.

Step #4: Share my plan with someone so I am accountable.

Step #5: Do my self-care activities and evaluate how they influence me.

> *Boundaries aren't something you do to another person. Boundaries are something you do for your own self-care, well-being, and protection.*
>
> **Vicki Tidwell Palmer, Moving Beyond Betrayal** (6)

The third step is to continue evaluating your boundaries to make sure that they are in alignment with your values. If you are consistently breaking your own boundaries, you will be stressed. In life, we are a work in progress, which means we need to evaluate our lives and make adjustments to make sure we are living according to our values. For example, if your family is your priority, it's important to make time for them. On the other hand, if all of your time is spent taking care of your family, you may need a break to do some self-care to stay strong mentally. The key point is to check in and do some introspection to make sure your boundaries are in harmony with your values.

The Key to Setting Boundaries Is Knowing Yourself

Below are specific examples of how to create particular boundaries to guide your healing and recovery. I provide these detailed examples so you can see how boundary setting works.

Personal Boundaries for the Betraying Partner

If you are the betraying partner and want to rebuild trust in your relationship, here are things you will want to remember:

1. You will be more effective at establishing trust if you create your own boundaries. Betrayed partners want to see their spouses engaged in their own recovery. If they are the ones doing the work (e.g., setting up therapy appointments, encouraging you to read a book, or listening to a podcast), they will begin to feel like you don't care. As you are proactive, your spouse will see that your heart is changing.

2. Acting out is a boundary failure. In order to stop your unwanted behaviors, you will need to develop clear boundaries. You will need to identify specific situations in which you crossed boundaries and then establish specific guidelines for each situation you violated (e.g., I will not spend time alone with people with whom I could act out). Remember, these need to be your boundaries, not your partners. Make sure to write your plan down.

Here's an example of how one person developed their new boundaries:

A few years ago, I was working with a man who had betrayed his wife on multiple occasions. Some of his affairs began while on the job. As we discussed the times he was vulnerable, it became apparent that he needed to establish workplace boundaries. I helped him create strategies he could use at work. Here are a few of the things we came up with:

- He began by avoiding the sexual banter that was common at his place of work.

- He left his door open while meeting with customers.

- He talked with a trusted co-worker about his desire and asked if he would remind him if he were engaging in anything that was inappropriate. (Accountability is an effective way to create boundaries).

This client was successful because he identified when he was vulnerable, and he created boundaries to protect himself. By mentally rehearsing his boundaries and then carrying them out, he and his spouse gained confidence.

1. Accountability makes boundaries more effective. One effective way to ensure you keep your boundary is to tell someone what you are doing. This will keep you honest and will lead to personal growth. When we are accountable to others, we are allowing others to help us succeed.

2. Boundaries are not to control you; they are to give you more freedom. When you were acting out, you probably didn't care about boundaries. That is what happens when you are in a sexual trance. However, when you come back to reality, you realize that you are not free at all. There are almost always consequences for engaging in sexual behaviors outside of your relationship.

Exercise for Creating Personal Boundaries (Betraying): In this exercise, you will be asked to identify three things: 1) What boundary you will create; 2) Why you need to create this boundary; 3) How you will keep your boundary; 4) When you will begin keeping this boundary.

What	Why	How	When
I am going to avoid getting online or looking at apps on my phone when I am alone.	I often relapse when I am alone. If I'm not online or on my phone, I can't relapse. Another reason why this matters to me is that I want to be better. I want to stop giving in to my impulses.	When I am alone, I will: 1) read a good book; 2) do a chore around the house that needs to be done; 3) review my personal goals; 4) call a friend or accountability person if I am feeling vulnerable.	I am going to start now. In order to do that, I need to: 1)find a good book to read. I will do that this weekend; 2) I have wanted to organize the garage. I will plan on spending 2 hours in the garage the next time I am alone; 3) I am already reviewing my personal goals each day, so that will be easy; 4) I will call my friend, David, and will tell him in advance so he knows when I am going to be alone.

Notice that a lot of detail is put into this exercise. Clear details provide the necessary structure for long-term success. Our brains like clarity and need to know the expected path.

Personal Boundaries for the Betrayed

As a betrayed partner, you will need to reflect on your life and what you have learned about boundaries. Unfortunately, as a society, we have not done a good job of teaching people how to identify their values and then establish limits or guidelines around those values. As a result, when boundaries are crossed, many people have a hard time knowing how to respond.

In the classes I teach and the groups I run; I often discuss general guidelines for creating boundaries. In many instances, individuals who have experienced betrayal and other forms of trauma generally struggle to identify their personal boundaries. In an effort to help clients consider what is common, I provide the following suggestions:

- I will make choices for myself and my personal healing.
- I deserve respect.

- I am separate from others and will make decisions that will help me maintain my dignity.

- Any traumatic event or events that have happened to me were a violation of my rights.

- I am not responsible for others' choices, but I am responsible for the choices I make.

- Being happy and being myself are my fundamental rights.

- What would you add? _____

As you think about these suggestions and create your own, I invite you to be as specific as possible. For example, how would others show you respect? As you create your list of boundaries, your confidence will increase. However, remember that your boundaries are about you and not about what your partner should and should not be doing.

Here's a case scenario: Jamie and Adam have been separated for two months. They are reconsidering getting back together. Here are two examples that demonstrate the differences in how you can approach setting boundaries.

Client A: The only way I will allow you to move back home is if you are attending a 12-step group, seeing a counselor, and doing your dailies. If you aren't willing to do these things, I don't want you back home.

Client B: I would like for you to move back home. However, I want to know what you are doing to avoid repeating your behaviors. If there is one thing I have learned about myself over the past two months, I can't go through this again. So, as we consider moving back in together, I need to know what your strategy is to avoid hurting me again.

Notice that Client A is telling their partner what to do. In contrast, Client B chooses to ask their partner a reflective question, "What are you going to do?" This is followed by an honest expression, "I don't know if I can go through this again." Then the conclusion, before we get together, I would like to know your strategy for recovery. As you will recall, this fits well with the Principle of Agency discussed in Chapter Ten.

Below is an example to help you identify and design your boundaries:

Exercise for Creating Personal Boundaries (Betrayed): In this exercise, you will be asked to identify four things: 1) What boundary will you create; 2) Why you need to create this boundary; 3) How will you keep your boundary; 4) When will you begin keeping this boundary with specific details?

What	Why	How	When
When my partner relapses, I will not sleep in the same room until we re-establish new boundaries and expectations. I will need to know your recovery plan. I will not be around you if you insult or threaten me.	I need to feel safe. I don't want to be in a relationship in which my partner is not faithful and committed to me. I want my partner to know that I don't want this kind of relationship. I hurt every time my partner acts out. I feel like I am not enough. I need them to know that I can't keep doing this.	In the past, I have been afraid of creating boundaries. Usually, when we have discussed boundaries, we have either fought, or I have shut down. I need to learn to follow through on the boundaries I make. I will mentally think through each conversation we have had and recognize that even if we do argue or fight, I am going to stay true to myself. How will I do this? 1) I will identify my bottom lines; 2) I will make my boundaries clear to my partner before a relapse; 3) If there is a relapse, I will take a few minutes and review my personal plan of action.	I am going to start preparing now, but I am not ready to carry out my boundaries. I need to think through them first. What boundaries am I committed to that I will enforce if they are broken? If there is a relapse, I will ask that we sleep in different rooms. I can do that now. I don't want to be touched by my partner if there is a relapse. Talk with them about this now. Things I want to think through before we talk about them: 1) How will I respond if my partner lies to me? 2) What is the best response if my partner continues relapsing? 3) I need to learn how to speak my truth without reservation.

Creating Specific Relationship Boundaries

If you want specific ideas, you should have a look at Vicki Tidwell Palmer's book, *Moving Beyond Betrayal*. In this book, she discusses four primary types of boundaries and adds a fifth. According to Tidwell Palmer, the four primary boundaries are:

- **Physical**—Physical boundaries are about how close you allow others to get to you physically and the access you give others to your personal property.

- **Sexual**—When your sexual boundaries are functional and intact, you know how to express your sexual needs and wants, as well as how to set limits with your partner about sexual activity that isn't comfortable for you.

- **Listening**—The listening boundary is about taking in what you hear and deciding what you think and how you feel about what you've heard. When the listening boundary is functional, you will know how to sort through what you hear and how to protect yourself from taking in others' emotions or any data that isn't true for you.

- **Talking**—The talking boundary involves the ability to share your thoughts and emotions in an honest, authentic, and relational manner. (7)

According to Tidwell Palmer, there is also a fifth type of boundary. She refers to this as the personal energy boundary—which is an intuitive or "felt sense" of another person. She describes it this way," ...sensing someone's personal energy is when you're with a person or in a group of people, and you experience emotions that seem to come from nowhere or that aren't congruent or consistent with your own mood or internal state in the moment. When this happens, you may be sensing other people's thoughts and/or emotions—their personal energy. (8)

Here are some additional boundaries that couples have found helpful as they work to create a safe environment where their relationship can grow. I have adapted these ideas from the work of Henry Cloud and John Townsend (9):

- Space Boundaries—*provide distance between you and your partner:*
  - ◊ Physical separation (e.g., sleeping in different rooms or locations for a period of time.
  - ◊ No touch for a designated period of time.
  - ◊ No sexual contact for a designated period of time.

- Time Boundaries—*provide a pre-planned time away from your partner:*

◊ If communication gets heated, take a break (e.g., 30 minutes).

◊ No contact for a set period of time (e.g., 24 hours).

◊ No sex for 30, 60, or 90 days—usually, couples do this to reset their sexual relationship. It also gives them time to reflect on their relationship without feeling sexual pressure. This works well for some couples and not well for others. (10)

- Emotional Boundaries—*may be necessary if emotions are running high:*

◊ Take a break (at least 20 minutes) if one partner is criticizing, using contempt, or is emotionally flooded. Researcher John Gottman uses this term to describe what happens in a couple's relationship when one or both partners feel overwhelmed and unsafe. He has found that people in a flooded state respond in a "nasty-nasty escalating exchange." They are in a psychological state of insecurity. They are feeling flooded, and there is no escape. (11) (See Video: *"Why You Can't Solve Problems While Flooded."*).

◊ If any form of yelling or insults, we will stop the conversation.

◊ When we can share emotions and feel that they will be heard, that will be progress.

(See *Seven Rules for Fighting*—Chapter Fourteen.)

What Should We Do When We Don't Agree on the Boundaries?

I am often asked by couples what they should do when they can't agree on the boundaries. For example, what is the right answer when one partner wants the other to move out of the room after a relapse and the partner refuses to leave? Or what should a couple do when one partner wants to abstain from sex and the other one doesn't? The right answer is to identify your core values and live consistently with them. If you ask your partner to leave the bedroom after a relapse, what is the value you are choosing? In this case, it is the value of safety. You are creating boundaries in the following areas: 1) safety; 2) space—physical; and 3) sexual.

If your partner asks you to leave the bedroom due to your relapse, but you do not leave, then you should consider the values that have guided your decision. Perhaps you feel that your partner is overreacting. Or maybe you feel like you are being rejected. Can you identify what core value is guiding your behavior?

One Directional Boundary vs. an Agreement

Suppose you and your partner cannot agree on the boundary. In that case, what should be done? You create a one-directional boundary. In essence, you are choosing to maintain your boundary (e.g., leave the bedroom). However, you cannot force your partner to leave the room. Therefore, in this case, you would leave the bedroom and sleep in another room. You are enforcing your boundary, but your partner is not in agreement. This is referred to as a one-directional boundary. In situations like this, you cannot expect your partner to support your decision. However, you are staying true to your boundary.

The alternative to a one-directional boundary is an agreement. This implies that when couples come to an agreement, in essence, one partner identifies their boundary, and the other one agrees to it. For example, in the case above, the partner who sexually acted out would agree to leave the bedroom for a designated period of time if they acted out.

Clearly, when couples are in agreement with the boundary and associated consequences, they have a better experience. The key difference is that the boundaries are clear, and both partners are in agreement on the consequences.

When Your Values Do Not Match

I recently talked with a group of therapists about some of their everyday concerns. One therapist brought up an issue to which they didn't know how to respond. Here's the situation. The client they were working with was uncomfortable doing a sexual act with their partner. Their partner was insisting that they perform sexually, or that meant that they didn't care about them. I have experienced similar circumstances with clients, so I am guessing that some of you reading this book may be experiencing a similar issue.

I have often contemplated how to respond when my clients cannot agree on critical issues surrounding their relationship. While this book mainly focuses on sexual betrayal, couples often discover that they disagree on more than sex. For example, many couples seek guidance to help them deal with issues like, parenting, finances, where to live, in-laws, spiritual differences, how to solve problems, and much more.

My conclusion is that couples who have significant differences in their values are at the greatest risk for conflict and relationship termination. When your values are not aligned, out of necessity, you have to spend extra time trying to negotiate your challenges. As I see it, you and your partner will then have a few options:

1. *Adapt to match your partner's values*—You will need to be careful if you choose this option to avoid losing your own identity. Do you agree to keep

the peace in your relationship? Will you resent your partner if you align with their values?

- *Your partner adapts to meet your values*—You may get your way, but is your partner generally in agreement, or are you going along to avoid conflict? If they agree but are silently suffering, they may end up resenting you.

- *You and your partner come to an agreement on shared values*—In this case, you both make adjustments to your personal values to improve your relationship. Both partners are focused on strengthening their relationship.

- *You and your partner no longer share common values*—When it is clear that your values are no longer aligned, you have to make some difficult choices. You can choose to stay in your relationship, recognizing that you no longer share the same values, or you can end your relationship. When couples choose to stay together when their values are not shared, they still need to identify what they will and will not accept. These are the core values that they live by (e.g., I won't stay in this relationship if you have another affair, or I won't be in a sexless marriage).

It has been my experience that couples who choose to stay together after betrayal generally realign their values. They are open about their hopes and desires for the relationship. In many ways, the betrayal has forced them to communicate more authentically. I have observed that individuals who first identify their values and then discuss them with their partner are more effective at staying true to themselves.

Key Takeaways from This Chapter

- As you identify your core values, you will be more effective in establishing your personal and relationship boundaries.

- Your boundaries should be guided by your values. When you violate your own boundaries, you will experience dissonance (stress).

- There are different types of boundaries: 1) physical, 2) sexual, 3) listening, 4) talking, 5) personal energy, 6) space, 7) time, and 8) emotional.

- Relationship boundaries can be one-directional or an agreement. When you are implementing a one-directional boundary, you cannot expect your partner to always follow your boundary.

- You and your partner may not share common values. If this is the case, you will need to make a conscious choice of how to respond. By being open and honest about your values, both of you can make better decisions regarding your relationship.

- Remember, the strength of your relationship is only as strong as the boundaries you create.

Chapter Twelve

Why I'm Sorry Isn't Working

"Not having a workable way to say 'I'm sorry' to the relevant person(s) can lead to long cycles of mistrust and conflict."

On many occasions throughout my career, I have had a betrayed partner express their frustration when their partner says, "I'm sorry." Initially, this response caught me off-guard. I thought, "Isn't telling the person you have hurt that you are sorry a good thing?" Then, when I asked for more information, I learned about the timing of when "I'm sorry" was said by the betraying partner. I discovered that the betraying partner often expresses their sorrow when their partner is upset or asking for more information. In situations like this, "I'm sorry" means very little. Their partner is already hurting, and "I'm sorry" says little.

When the words "I'm sorry" don't help, it is common for the betraying partners to say something like, "You are never going to forgive me, are you?" or "Are you ever going to get over this?" It is these types of responses that make betrayed partners get even more upset.

In my work with betraying partners, most of them tell me they don't know what to say when their partner is upset. This is when I share with them the strategies for apologizing. In her book, *A Good Apology*, Molly Howes shared the following: "The more important the relationship, the more crucial making a good apology can be, and the greater the cost of failing to employ one. Love does not mean never having to say you're sorry; love requires you to learn how to say you're sorry well. (1) Molly Howes then suggests four core strategies to make a good apology.

The Four Steps of a Good Apology

It doesn't take a lot of effort to tell someone that you are sorry. In fact, we often hear people say "sorry" for the simplest of things. As a result, the word may have lost its meaning. So, imagine that we removed the word "sorry" from our vocabulary. What do you think would be an effective way to let someone know that we are _____? I almost used a word that should not be spoken.

Consider an event from your past where you felt like you hurt or harmed someone. Now imagine that you want to express to them how much you regret your behavior without using that word.

What would you say to them? This simple yet effective exercise can really make you think. Perhaps, if we all tried to eliminate that word _____ from our vocabulary, we would be more clear in how we communicate when our actions have harmed the other person.

Another way to reclaim the word "sorry" would be to follow the word with a specific explanation of why we are sorry. For example, I'm sorry I was late; I should have planned better. That was not being respectful of your time. The word "sorry," when used by itself, does not say much and leaves the person to whom you are apologizing wondering what you are sorry for. In contrast, by offering specific details of why you are sorry, the word can reclaim its intended purpose.

According to Molly Howes, expressing our regret should not be our first approach. Instead, in her four steps to a good apology, she suggests the following process:

- First, you must come to understand the other person's injury, including the effects of your actions. This usually involves asking questions and listening.

- Second, you must articulate a sincere statement of regret. You must acknowledge what you did and how it affected the other person. This is no small feat for most of us, especially when we didn't intend to hurt someone.

- Third, you must make reparations. This can include material restitution, although that's less likely to occur in relationships.

- Fourth, you must make a convincing plan to prevent the problem from happening again. (2)

In this next section, I will address these steps in depth.

Step #1: Ask Questions and Listen

I mentioned earlier that I often role-play with my clients. I have found that this practice is essential for many who don't know how to express themselves accurately. I believe that in many instances, individuals say, "I'm sorry" because they don't know what else to say.

When we role-play, I tell them that the first step is to ask questions and listen to their partner's responses. I explain that this is the first step. When trying to repair a relationship wound that you have created, it is essential to consider the pain you have caused. Perhaps you struggle with this first step because you are afraid of what your spouse will say to you. You may fear that your partner will yell or criticize you. In many instances, you may be right. However, by genuinely listening to your partner's pain, you are creating an environment where they can work through their anger. If you can work through your shame and listen to understand your partner, you will accelerate the healing process.

As a result, we work to reduce their shame before we focus on implementing the steps for a good apology.

Once betraying partner have the skill of staying present and listening to their partner without becoming defensive or dismissive, they are in an emotional place to genuinely hear what their partner is telling them. Often this first step is overlooked, and this is why many betrayed partners do not feel heard.

When it is clear that my clients are prepared, we move on to the next step.

Note: I recognize that betrayed partners can also hurt and offend their significant other. These same four steps can be used by betrayed partners as they express their regrets and make amends.

Step #2: Articulate a Sincere Statement of Regret

It is hard to express heartfelt regret after a sexual betrayal. In fact, speaking from experience, it takes time and a lot of self-reflection to come to the partner you have betrayed and offer a sincere statement of regret. One way that I work with my clients to help them develop their statement of regret is to have them remove the words "I'm sorry" as they express their remorse. Often clients struggle to say what they feel without saying, "I'm sorry."

It takes time to come up with alternative statements like these:

- I deeply regret what I did to you.
- I feel bad for how I hurt you.
- I was wrong and shouldn't have done what I did.

These statements show more personal insight. If you are the betrayed partner, how do these words sound to you? When I go through this exercise with couples, betrayed partners shake their heads in agreement. They want to hear the words, "I deeply regret," "I feel bad," and especially, "I was wrong."

Step #3: Make Reparations (As Much as Possible)

The word "reparations" refers to "the act of making amends, offering expiation, or giving satisfaction for a wrong or injury." If you aren't familiar with the word expiation, it is "the act or process of making atonement for something." (3) I have given significant thought to how a person can make reparations after sexual betrayal. While there are no easy answers, I share my thoughts below:

- Take care of your own issues (e.g., work on your recovery, make a plan, stay committed to your healing).

- Focus on becoming the best person you can be.

- Increase in your understanding and application of empathy and compassion.

- Acknowledge the harm you have created—more than once.

- Take action to prevent the behavior from happening again (e.g., talk with a counselor or attend a 12-step group if your behaviors have become compulsive).

- Be accountable—follow through on your commitments and be accountable for your actions moving forward.

- Seek feedback from your partner on your progress. Ask the question, "What am I missing?"

Remember that making reparations is a process that will require ongoing effort. It's important to prioritize your partner's needs and feelings. As you become patient and understanding, you create a safe environment where they can work through their emotions. Ultimately, the goal is to repair the harm caused by your actions and work towards a resolution that promotes healing and restoration.

Step #4: Create a Convincing Plan to Prevent the Problem from Happening Again

While your words are part of a good apology, your actions carry much more weight. This statement, "Show me, and only if you have to, use words," should be your focus. Your confidence should increase as you focus on stopping your unwanted behavior. However, if you are in the early stage of recovery, you may not have a solid plan in place. At times like this, you will need to be honest with your partner by telling them that you are developing your plan. You will want to give serious attention to creating your recovery plan. For more information on creating a solid plan for healing, see Chapter One of *Treating Sexual Addiction: A Compassionate Approach to Recovery*.

I have helped many clients create their recovery plans, and when they put in the time and effort, their confidence increases. I often ask them this question, "How prepared on a scale of 0 (Not at all) and 10 (Completely) do you feel to make the changes you desire?" Their answer is usually an indicator of their readiness to succeed. My suggestion is to create a plan that you believe in. Can you give yourself an eight, nine, or even a ten on your recovery plan? If not, why not. If yes, what have you done to prepare?

If you feel that something is holding you back, I invite you to consider what Dr. Joe Dispenza, author of *You Are the Placebo* suggested. He wrote, "When you learn new things and begin to think in new ways, you are making your brain fire in different sequences, patterns, and combinations. That is, you are activating many diverse networks of neurons in different ways. And whenever you make your brain work differently, you change your mind. As you begin to think outside the box, new thoughts should lead to new choices, new behaviors, new experiences, and new emotions. Now your identity should also change." (4)

> *The best way to predict the future is to create it—not from the known, but from the unknown.* (5)
>
> **Dr. Joe Dispenza**

I invite you to create your recovery plan. Make a plan based on your personal values that were discussed in Chapter Eleven. As you gain confidence in your plan, your partner will sense a change in you. By creating a plan, you are showing your desire to be a better you.

When It's Better Not to Apologize

In her book, *A Good Apology*, Molly Howes suggested that there are times when an apology can make matters worse. Your timing and your mindset could have a significant influence on the outcome. If you are not attuned to your partner, you can add to their pain. In an effort to help you avoid attempting to apologize at the wrong time, below I share Molly Howes' list. I have also included a few of my own ideas about when it's better not to apologize.

- When you are still acting out.

- When you are hiding behaviors.

- When it's only for your benefit.

- When you don't mean it.

- When it would hurt the other person.

- When the person doesn't want to hear from you.

- When the person can't receive it.

- When a person demands too many apologies.

- When your apology is never-ending.

- When you haven't done anything wrong. (6)

Video Support Discussing "*When It's Better Not to Apologize*." https://www.bit. ly/RYR (Chapter Twelve)

Making Amends

Jeff and Monica had been in therapy for one year after she discovered that he had engaged in multiple affairs. They both had been working hard to heal and recover; however, their relationship was at a crossroads. They had been living apart for nearly 18 months, and it was time to decide whether they would get back together or divorce. In my office, Monica looked Jeff straight in the eyes as she said, "I am very anxious, but I am going to move towards reconciliation. You better not hurt me again." Jeff teared up and said, "I don't want to hurt you again. I don't want you to regret your decision."

Monica turned to Jeff and said, "What are we going to do when we are together and run into one of your affair partners?" Jeff replied, "I will just get out of there." Monica responded, "What do you mean? We can't always run from our problems. And that isn't the only issue. I want to know what you are feeling and thinking. Are you feeling shame? Are you reminiscing about what happened between the two of you? How am I going to know what you are feeling?"

These questions made Jeff think for a minute, but he didn't have a good answer. I asked him what he considered a good response would be in such a situation. After thinking for a minute, he said, "I'm sorry." She looked at him and said, that isn't enough. So, I asked him if we could role-play so that he would have a plan of what to say to Monica if they encountered one of his previous affair partners. Jeff eagerly accepted my suggestion.

Before we began our role-play, I reminded Jeff of these guidelines:

- Listen to your partner's concerns so they feel heard.

- Acknowledge your partner's hurt and pain.

- Own your part—be specific about how your behavior contributed to their hurt.

  ◊ Let them know that they didn't deserve to go through what your betrayal did to them.

  ◊ Give your partner space. As you make amends, it's important to respect your partner's boundaries and give them space if they need it.

  ◊ Avoid pressuring your partner to forgive you or trying to force a resolution.

Jeff then began, "Monica, I haven't been good at listening to your concerns. I understand you are concerned about how I will respond when we bump into one of my affair partners. I know that when that happens, it will hurt you. I should not have done what I did. You didn't deserve that."

Monica felt like that was a good start. She still didn't know the best way for them to respond when seeing one of his affair partners. Jeff stepped up this time and said, "I want you to know I don't want to be with them. I want to be with you. I feel awful about what I did and what I have put you through. In moments like those, I want you to know that I choose you." This response from Jeff was compelling because, earlier in the day, Monica had shared with us that she felt like she was not enough for him. Jeff's response, "…I choose you," was something Monica had been wanting to hear for months. She began crying, and Jeff did as well.

I feel privileged to witness these tender moments of vulnerability and remorse. Another outcome of this experience was something that came to my mind. I thought Monica could share some of her other triggers with Jeff so that he could think about how to make amends when those triggers come. I presented the idea to them.

Here's the assignment I gave them.

I asked Monica to write down some of her most difficult triggers and share them with Jeff. It was then Jeff's job to write an amends statement to each one of them. Monica loved the idea because she had felt for so long that Jeff didn't understand her hurts and pains. Since then, this assignment has been called Crucial Moment Amends.

At the beginning of our work together, most of my clients' struggle knowing what to say in those crucial moments. For years, I have role-played with clients so that they know how to respond when their partners are triggered. By mentally rehearsing effective ways to respond, many clients and their partners reported significant improvement in their relationship.

Since that original experience, I have given significant thought to the importance of helping my clients know how to respond effectively to their hurting partners. I have found that having a plan in place prevents poor responses in highly charged moments.

It is common to get defensive and react poorly in difficult emotional moments. However, by developing a plan, my clients become more prepared for such moments. In addition, as they seek to understand their partner's pain in difficult moments, their partner is more likely to see their desire to make amends.

Many betrayed partners have told me that they have been wanting and waiting to feel heard. Finally, their partner is listening and responding to them.

The critical point is this, by preparing to make Crucial Moment Amends, my clients know in advance how to be with their partner in their pain. By preparing for highly charged emotional moments, they know how to respond effectively. The challenge is applying these tools during difficult times.

How to Make Crucial Moment Amends

In your relationship, there will be times when your actions can help you and your partner heal, or they can trigger a cascade of negative events. These are crucial moments.

The focus of this chapter has been to provide some of the best strategies for making amends. Below, I will provide three common scenarios and two examples for each situation.

Scenario #1: When the Betrayed Partner Is Feeling Triggered

Betrayed Partner: I just had a horrible dream. My whole body is shaking. I still can't believe you cheated on me.

Betraying Partner's Not-So-Great Response: Are you ever going to get over this? I don't know what else I can do. I'm not sure you can forgive me.

Betrayed Partner: Please don't talk to me. You have no idea what you have done. Will you just leave? I can't believe how insensitive you are.

Betraying Partner's Not-So-Great Response: I'm sorry, but you keep bringing up what I did. I want to move on, and all you do is talk about the past.

Betrayed Partner: So now you are blaming me for bringing up the past? You are unbelievable. Just get out!

Betraying Partner's Not-So-Great Response: Okay! I'm out of here.

If you are like most of my clients, you will relate to the dialogue above. Unfortunately, most couples do not know how to get out of this unhealthy cycle. Below is a dialogue of how a couple could more effectively respond to the betrayed partner's bad dream.

Betrayed Partner: I just had a horrible dream. My whole body is shaking. I still can't believe you cheated on me.

Betraying Partner's Better Response: Wow! It is hard to see how my behaviors have hurt you. I was so caught up in what I was doing that I didn't see how much pain it would create for you. You deserved better. Is there anything I can do to help now?

Betrayed Partner: You really want to help? You have no idea how much you have hurt me. And yeah, I do deserve better. You can't take back what you have done. So, I'm not sure if there is anything you can do to help.

Betraying Partner's Better Response: I do want to make things right. What I did was so wrong. You have every right not to trust me. I know it doesn't help to say it now, but I am committed to being a better person. I want to earn your trust again. I want to be with you.

Betrayed Partner: You are right; I don't trust you. I don't know if I can ever trust you again. You want to be a better person now? You should have thought about that before your affair.

Betraying Partner's Better Response: You are right! I should have thought about the hurt I was creating for you. I deeply regret the way I hurt you. I do hope someday to regain your trust. For now, my focus is on becoming a better person. I do feel bad that you keep having bad dreams.

As you read through this dialogue, how do you think the betraying partner is doing?

If you are the betrayed partner, what do you think and feel about these responses? Would they help you? Please write down your answer and discuss your thoughts about the betraying partner's responses above.

If you are the betraying partner, what are your thoughts and feelings about these responses? Some key elements to consider as you learn to respond:

Crucial Moment #1: Respond to the trigger—bad dream:

- Acknowledge the pain—It is hard to see how my behaviors have hurt you.
    - ◊ Validate your partner—You deserve better.
    - ◊ Be willing to help if your partner desires—Is there anything I can do to help now?

Crucial Moment #2: Respond to this statement: You really want to help? You have no idea how much you have hurt me. And yeah, I do deserve better. You can't take back what you have done. So, I'm not sure if there is anything you can do to help.

- Express true desire—I want to make things right.
- Acknowledge your wrongful behavior—What I did was wrong.
- Awareness that trust is earned—I don't expect you to trust me. I want to earn your trust.
- Your intention—I intend to become a better person.

Crucial Moment #3: You are right; I don't trust you. I don't know if I can ever trust you again. You want to be a better person now? You should have thought about that before your affair.

- Admit your mistake—You are right. I should have thought about my behaviors.
- Express regret for your actions—I deeply regret the way I hurt you.
- Revisit your desire to regain trust with no expectations—I hope to earn your trust someday.
- Your intention—I will focus on becoming a better person.
- Come back to the initial problem—Acknowledge the bad dream (How do you feel about the dream?—I feel bad that you continue having bad dreams).

If you are the betraying partner, this example may seem difficult for you to do. It will take work to prepare your mind to respond effectively. However, if you practice and take into account the key principles outlined above, you can learn to make crucial moment amends.

If you are the betrayed partner, my hope is that these examples help you too.

Sometimes we don't know how to discuss these difficult issues. It is my desire that these examples help both of you realize that you can break out of the unhealthy patterns that you have likely been engaged in.

Below, I have two more scenarios. I invite you to review each situation and try to think through how you would respond. You may want to review the concepts discussed in the section above.

Scenario #2: When Your Partner Is Upset or Angry

Your Partner: I hate you! You have ruined my life. You have taken everything from me. Are you happy? Was it worth it?

I'm a little curious. Before you read the two responses below, I invite you to think about how you would respond to your spouse in this situation. Please don't read on until you have written down your response.

Your Not-So-Good Response: If you hate me so much, why don't you just file for a divorce? You are just an angry person.

Your Better Response: I don't know what to say. I wish I had a good response. I have hurt you. There are no excuses for what I did to you. I should have made better choices. You deserve better treatment from me.

Scenario #3: When Your Partner Is Asking Difficult Questions

Your Partner: Why did you sleep with them? Are they better than me? Did you enjoy the sex? Why did you even come home after sleeping with them? Why did you have sex with me after sleeping with them? Did you not consider that you could give me an STD?

Before you read the responses, I suggest that you reflect on how you would respond. Then write down what you think would be a decent response.

Your Not-So-Good Response: Which question do you want me to answer? You don't even give me a chance to respond? Obviously, there is nothing I can say that will please you.

Your Better Response: Among the questions you asked, which one would you like me to begin with? I am willing to answer your questions. Let me begin by saying my actions were wrong.

An Essential Step to Couple Healing: Address Your Regrets

If we are honest with ourselves, we recognize that we have done something that has hurt or offended our spouse. While some offenses are more egregious than others, we should do everything possible to correct our wrongs when our behaviors offend our loved ones. We are demonstrating our desire to repair the relationship by addressing our misdeeds. The challenge many of us face is acknowledging our mistakes and correcting them with the people we love the most.

We tend to hurt the people we presume to care about the most. If you want to heal and repair your relationship wounds, I have created a short exercise to help you and your partner address your regrets. My purpose in creating this exercise is twofold: First, an essential step in your healing is identifying behaviors you want to change or improve. Second, based on the Zeigarnik effect (See Chapter One), we know that unresolved issues do not entirely disappear. When we handle our misdeeds with our partners, we create a relationship without unresolved issues. By acknowledging our faults, we can find inner peace.

Before I have you and your partner go through a regrets exercise, I want to revisit the importance of activating our ventral vagus. In Chapter Three, I introduced the Polyvagal Theory. The theory, as founded by Dr. Stephen Porges, suggests that the autonomic nervous system in humans has three branches: the sympathetic branch, the parasympathetic branch, and the ventral vagal branch. The ventral vagal branch is important for social bonding, helping us to feel safe and connected in relationships.

Polyvagal Theory suggests that when we are in an environment of safety, the ventral vagal branch is activated. This helps to control our sympathetic nervous system, which is responsible for fight-or-flight responses. When the ventral vagal branch is activated, it can help us be more emotionally regulated and connected with those around us. Thus, ventral vagal regulation is key in enabling healthy social bonding, allowing us to feel secure and connected within relationships. (7)

Please do not continue this exercise if you are currently unable to access your ventral vagus. Here are a few questions to help you know if you are able to access your ventral vagus in your relationship.

1. Can you genuinely smile at your partner?

2. Are you able to use a melodic voice with your partner?

3. Can you maintain eye contact with your partner?

4. Are you comfortable engaging in healthy touch with your partner (e.g., holding hands, a long embrace, a meaningful kiss)?

If you do not yet feel comfortable engaging with your partner in these ways, that is okay for now. This would likely indicate that there is an unresolved issue between you and your partner. You may need to discuss the barrier with your partner before completing this exercise. However, if you can't put your finger on why you cannot engage in the four behaviors above, you may benefit by asking yourself the following questions:

1. Which of the four behaviors above is most difficult for me? Why?

2. Which of these behaviors can I improve upon?

3. Is there something my spouse could do for me that would increase my desire to engage in these behaviors?

If you want to improve your chances of accessing the ventral vagus in your relationship, I strongly suggest you practice each of these four elements: 1) facial expression—smile; 2) tone of voice—a pleasant tone; 3) maintain eye contact; and 4) healthy touch.

Now that you have prepared your mind to access the ventral vagus branch, you are prepared for the regrets exercise. Below you will find the five-step process.

Step #1: Take three minutes and write down your behaviors or thoughts that you regret in your relationship.

Example: *Betraying Partner*

1. I regret…

2. Being selfish and not thinking about how my actions would impact you.

3. Sexually acting out.

4. Lying to you.

5. Making you feel like there was something wrong with you while I was acting out.

6. Getting angry when you asked me if something was wrong.

Example: *Betrayed Partner*

1. I regret…

2. Not listening to you when you wanted to talk about stress at work.

3. Yelling at you.

4. Hiding my emotions and not telling you my true feelings.

5. Calling you names when I found out about your affair.

6. Not trying to understand how your childhood has influenced your life.

Step #2: Review your regrets identified above. Then order them by identifying your biggest regret and move downwards until you have placed each regret in order.

Step #3: If you could have a do-over, what would you do differently? Be as specific as possible. Also, list how you will handle situations like this in the future.

Example: *Betraying Partner*

I regret that I was being selfish while acting out. If I had a do-over, I would think about how my actions would hurt you and others. In the future, I am going to think more about you during the day. If I feel vulnerable, I will remember how my actions hurt you in the past.

Example: *Betrayed Partner*

I regret that I didn't listen to you when you were stressed. If I had a do-over, I would make sure that we had more time each day to talk. In the future, I want to be more intentional about how we communicate. I will also try to understand the stress you are feeling.

Each of the first three steps is for you to complete on your own. Now it is time to share what you have written with your partner. Two more guidelines: 1) The betraying partner should go first, and 2) before you move onto the fourth step, make sure that you have prepared mentally. (See strategies for increasing ventral vagus listed above.)

Step #4: Begin by sharing each step outlined above with your partner. Once you have reviewed your list, ask your partner for feedback. Be open to their thoughts and ideas. Be aware you may not have identified all of the ways your actions hurt your partner. You can ask your partner to share with you other ways your actions have hurt them. Make notes and, at a (specified) later time, go through Step #3 again. Once the betraying partner is done, the betrayed partner should share their list following the same guidelines.

Step #5: Discuss how this experience was for you. What was it like writing down your regrets? What did you learn about yourself? Did this exercise help you understand more about your partner? If yes, explain your answer. If not, why not?

My Commitments: Being a Person with Relationship Integrity

In this chapter, we have discussed strategies to help you repair your relationship. We will now conclude with a final strategy designed to improve the conversation between you and your partner.

The "My Commitments Exercise" was created to help couples who are ready to repair their relationship. The objective is to help them identify their commitments as they move forward. I do not recommend this exercise if you have not completed a full disclosure and an impact letter. I have found that this exercise is most helpful to couples who have been doing their personal work and who are ready to move toward a deeper connection.

If you are not ready, that is okay; you can come back to this part of the chapter at a later time.

7 Questions About Your Commitment to Your Relationship (Betraying Partner):

1. What commitment are you making to yourself about your sexual behaviors?

2. Are you ready to fully commit to your partner? In other words, are you ready to stop sexually acting out?

3. Have you prepared to succeed in this commitment? Write down your answer.

4. How will you show your commitment to your partner?

5. If there is one thing you worry about with making this commitment, what would it be? How will you overcome your concern?

6. What do you want your partner to know about your commitment to this relationship?

7. Are you ready to commit to making a better relationship with your partner?

7 Questions About Your Commitment to Your Relationship (Betrayed Partner)

1. What commitment are you making to yourself as you approach healing in your relationship?

2. Are you ready to fully commit to your partner? Simply put, do you feel safe enough to give your heart to your partner?

3. Have you prepared to succeed in this commitment? Write down your answer.

4. How will you show your commitment to your partner?

5. If there is one thing you worry about with making this commitment, what would it be? How will you overcome your concern?

6. What do you want your partner to know about your commitment to this relationship?

7. Are you ready to commit to making a better relationship with your partner?

Now that you have answered these questions, I invite you to incorporate your answers in a letter to your spouse. You can expand on each of these items. It may take you some time to ponder and reflect on your answers. As you prepare your letter, you might think of additional commitments you want to make to your partner. If so, add them to your letter. As you prepare your letter, I encourage you to be sincere and share your real intent toward your relationship. Finally, identify the true desire of your heart and express it through words to your partner.

Once you and your partner have completed your letters, identify a special date on which you will read your letter to your spouse (e.g., May 24th). You might want to dress up and visit one of your favorite restaurants. You can plan a mini-vacation, or you may choose to invite people who have aided in your healing and recovery to a special event where you will read your commitment letters to each other.

Key Takeaways from This Chapter

- It may be best to avoid the words "I'm sorry" when you are attempting to apologize. If you do use these words, be specific and explain why you are sorry.

- An effective way to repair relationship wounds is to use Molly Howes' four steps of a good apology: 1) Ask questions and listen; 2) Articulate a sincere statement of regret; 3) Make reparations; 4) Create a convincing plan to prevent the problem from happening again.

- There may be times when you are not ready to apologize. You can create more distance between you and your partner if you attempt to apologize before you are ready. By mentally preparing, you can increase the odds that your relationship will last.

- Crucial Moment Amends happen when you respond well in difficult moments. When emotions are high, it is often hard to stay focused on what matters the most to you. If you can step back and genuinely listen to your partner, you can make Crucial Moment Amends.

- Address your regrets. An effective way for couples to rebuild their relationship is to become vulnerable with each other by sharing their regrets. A five-step exercise was provided, which included how to share your regrets.

- A final way to work towards amends is to share your commitments with each other. Identify your new commitments, write a letter, and plan a special day or evening to share your new commitments with each other.

Chapter Thirteen

Gaslighting No More

When couples seek my help because they feel stuck and cannot progress toward healing, they give common reasons. One of the most consistent challenges they face is deception and lying during the betrayal. Betrayed clients often ask if it is possible to overcome the lies and hidden behaviors that their partner used while sexually acting out.

There is no easy answer to the betrayed partner's question. Let me explain why while I ask you to consider a few questions:

1. How can a betrayed partner move on mentally if they can't determine whether their spouse is honest with them?

2. Is it possible for betraying partners to be honest when they don't yet trust themselves?

3. How can betraying partners demonstrate that they are being honest and truthful now when they claimed they were telling the truth while acting out?

4. What do betrayed partners need from their partners to feel safe again?

After researching how betrayal influences individuals and their relationships, the answer to these questions may be the most critical issue for couples to resolve in the healing process. In this chapter, I will address these questions so you and your partner can understand the importance of addressing the lies, manipulation, and deception as you attempt to rebuild your relationship. This chapter will not be easy to read. Nevertheless, if you and your partner can resolve the issues discussed, there is a good chance your relationship can be healed.

In 2005 when I began researching the effects of sexual deception on betrayed partners, my initial question dealt with post-traumatic stress disorder (PTSD). At that time, I realized that if betrayed partners were experiencing PTSD, it would be essential to identify factors that would possibly increase their symptoms. As I listened to my clients and reached out to colleagues, specific themes rose to the top. A few of the most frequent responses I received were:

- Adverse childhood experiences (e.g., neglect, abuse, parents' divorce).

- Other relationship traumas (e.g., previous dating relationships).

- The relationship dynamics with their current partner (e.g., denial, blame, and deception).

- Personal addictions (e.g., alcohol, drugs).

- Mental health issues (e.g., anxiety, depression).

While other factors contribute to a betrayed partner experiencing PTSD symptoms, these are some of the most common ones brought up by clients and other professionals. Over the past few years, as thousands of betrayed partners have shared their experiences with me through my surveys, each of these issues has consistently shown to be relevant in discussing what elevates an individual's PTSD symptoms.

However, when I review the data from clients who have come to our office or from random individuals who have taken the survey online, the findings show that those with high levels of gaslighting experience are the ones with the highest level of PTSD symptoms. Let me put this in another way, the number one predictor of PTSD symptoms is the amount of gaslighting a person experiences in their relationship. Based on these research findings, I now believe that one of the most critical issues couples have to address is the gaslighting that occurs when the betraying partner acts out sexually.

It is essential to note the other four items listed above (e.g., adverse childhood experiences, other relationship traumas, etc.) also add to the manifestation of PTSD symptoms. While training therapists, I often ask them which of the five items listed above contributes the most to PTSD symptoms. They usually guess adverse childhood experiences or gaslighting.

> *The number one predictor of increased PTSD symptoms in betrayed partners is the amount of gaslighting a person experiences in their relationship.*

Note: Between 2005 and 2013, I was gathering data on my website using a scale titled Denial and Blame. These two ideas came from clients who shared their stories of betrayal with me. They talked about how their partner would deny their behavior and only come clean (or partially clean) when they are caught. Or in other cases, the betraying partner would blame them when they acted out sexually. I did not hear the term gaslighting until 2013 while attending a conference for professionals learning to treat sexual compulsivity and addiction. When our instructor used the term gaslighting and described what it was, I instantly knew that the Denial and Blame Scale I had created was measuring gaslighting behaviors.

The Definition of Gaslighting

As I write this book, the term gaslighting is frequently used in media, the internet, and other outlets. It is especially being used in many contexts where there is sexual betrayal in relationships. This brings up a concern for me. If we are going to discuss gaslighting, we need to make sure that we have clearly defined what it is and what it means. Since the word has gained popularity, I believe it is being used in a vague, undefined way. For this reason, I want to review the definition and share the questions we use to measure gaslighting in relationships.

Gaslighting is a form of manipulation and deceit used to control another person or gain an advantage. It is a psychological tactic that involves making someone else doubt their own memories, perception, and judgment by undermining their intelligence and credibility. Gaslighting can be done by simply denying that something took place, telling the other person they are crazy or paranoid for thinking the way they do, and trivializing their feelings. Gaslighting can also take more subtle forms, such as feigned forgetfulness or confusion and playing mind games. Over time, these tactics erode the self-confidence of the person being gaslit. In many instances, being gaslit leads to feelings of worthlessness, hopelessness, and despair.

Denial, Blame, and Deception Scale (Gaslighting)

When I began researching the effects of sexual betrayal on individuals and their relationships, I had not considered the amount of lies that go into sexual deception. Now having reviewed the results of thousands of people, it is clear that gaslighting plays a significant role in deciding whether a couple will heal and recover or not. There is no other way to say this; if gaslighting is present in the relationship, the relationship cannot heal.

In the following section, you will find the questions and frequency with which betrayed partners report being gaslighted by their partners.

Denial Scale (Gaslighting)	Never	Sometimes	About Half the Time	More Often Than Not	Always
How often does your partner deny their involvement in pornography or other sexual behaviors?	17.91%	20.98%	12.27%	27.55%	21.29%
In your relationship, how often has your partner been open and honest about their struggle with pornography or other sexual behaviors?	40.15%	40.64%	10.53%	6.36%	2.33%
How often has your partner looked you straight in the eyes and denied they were viewing pornography or sexually acting out?	10.10%	16.59%	9.55%	35.56%	28.21%

Even when you have evidence regarding your partner's sexual behaviors, how often do they lie to you?	12.18%	20.99%	11.66.%	29.71%	25.48%
If your partner ever disclosed their sexual behaviors, how often have they told you only half the story?	5.71%	14.66%	12.61%	31.77%	35.65%
To what extent has your partner claimed to have stopped sexually acting out, but later you discovered that they hadn't stopped at all?	18.11%	18.05%	10.44%	23.73%	29.67%
How often has your partner told you that you were crazy to cover up a lie they have told you?	31.50%	18.65%	10.07%	18.22%	21.56%

How often did your partner hide the amount of money they spent on their sexually acting-out behaviors?	41.48%	16.53%	5.05%	7.61%	29.32%

Note: Here are some of the highlights that stand out in these findings: Roughly 67% of betrayed partners report only being told half the story (more often than not or always). Even more challenging is that only six percent of betrayed partners report being told the full story upon first disclosure. Other key findings include: 68% of partners have been told that they were crazy to cover up a lie; 78% report being lied to even when they have evidence; and almost 90% report that their partner looked them in the eye and lied to them.

Blame Scale (Gaslighting)	Never	Some-times	About Half the Time	More Often Than Not	Always
How often has your partner blamed you for their sexual conduct?	31.68%	24.75%	13.48%	16.54%	13.54%
How often would your partner say that your relationship problems were because of your personal issues?	23.80%	20.98%	13.62%	21.17%	20.43%

How often has your partner taken responsibility for their sexual behaviors rather than making you feel their problems were because of you?	23.87%	31.27%	15.79%	16.28%	12.79%
To what extent have you felt like something wasn't quite right in your relationship, but your partner would tell you it was because of your insecurities?	10.05%	15.87%	10.85%	28.86%	34.38%
How often has your partner told you that if you were more sexual, they would not have to view pornography or act out in other ways?	50.86%	20.16%	6.92%	10.97%	11.09%

Source: Skinner, K. B., (2023)

Note: Here are a few key findings that I have gathered from the blame section:

- Roughly 68% of betrayed partners report that their partner blamed them for their sexual activities outside of the relationship.

- 76% report that their partner told them that their relationship problems were due to the betrayed person's issues.

- 13% of acting-out partners take responsibility for their sexual indiscretions.

- 90% of betrayed partners have felt like something was off in their relationship but were told it was because of their insecurities.

- Lastly, 49% have been told by their partner that if they had been more sexual, they would not have acted out.

These findings make it clear that denial and blame are common strategies used by betraying partners. It would be fair to say that most individuals who are being sexually deceptive have used one or more of these gaslighting behaviors. If you find these results triggering anger or other uncomfortable emotions in you, please take a few deep breaths. If you are feeling shame because you used these tactics, I invite you to take courage and be open and receptive to the ideas shared through the rest of this chapter.

Now that we have looked at the research regarding gaslighting, let's turn our attention to finding solutions. Below are the general guidelines I use as I work with couples where gaslighting has been used during and after betrayal.

Let's explore each of them.

Three Steps to Help You Deal with Gaslighting

Step #1: The only way to heal is through complete truth and honesty.

For the Betraying Partner:

As discussed in Chapter Ten, one of the five principles of healthy relationships is a commitment to integrity. If you have denied, blamed, or deceived your partner to cover up your sexual deception, and you desire to heal your relationship, begin by evaluating the ways and methods you used to cover up your behaviors. This is not an easy exercise, and it will require you to look at your actions.

One way to identify the behaviors used to gaslight your partner is to review each of the items from the Denial and Blame Scales above. I have created an exercise that can be found in Appendix J. There is a writing exercise in the appendix designed to help you prepare a statement to share with your partner. As you write the document, you may want to consult with a professional therapist and read the letter to your partner with the therapist's guidance.

For the Betrayed Partner:

Based on my research findings on gaslighting, I believe that exploring how gaslighting has influenced you is essential for your healing. If you avoid addressing how gaslighting has hurt you, it will be more difficult for you to reconnect with your partner. Therefore, I have included a document with questions regarding gaslighting for you to consider. Here's a word of caution for you. In the exercise your partner will complete, I will ask for specific details of how they lied, deceived, and manipulated you. In essence, I will ask them to be absolutely vulnerable with you.

Word of Caution: If you do not desire to reconnect with your partner or if you already know that you want a divorce, it may be best for you to move on without going through this exercise. You already know that they lied to you and that they manipulated you. Ask yourself how knowing that information would help you heal. The only time I recommend couples going through a divorce to complete this exercise is if the betraying partner wants to clear their conscience and the betrayed partner wants to know the whole truth and believes that learning about the lies will help their healing.

Remember, the goal of this exercise is to help individuals heal. It allows the betraying partner to become completely transparent. They are revealing their deceptive playbook. For the betrayed partner, this exercise will often help answer questions about the betrayal they have been thinking about.

Step #2: Couples need to engage in a three-step process: 1) doing a complete and full disclosure; 2) the betrayed partner writing an impact letter; and 3) the betraying partner writing an emotional restitution letter.

In this book, I will not address this three-step process as it is discussed in-depth in the following resources:

- Carnes, S. (2020). *Courageous love: A Couples' Guide to Conquering Betrayal.* Gentle Path Press.

- Drake, D., & Caudill, J. (2019). *Full Disclosure: How to Share the Truth After Sexual Betrayal: (A Comprehensive Guide for the Disclosing Individual): Includes Volumes 1, 2 & 3.* Banyan Therapy Group and McKinney Counseling & Recovery.

Below I will share a new exercise I have specifically created for couples to address the gaslighting behaviors in their relationship (See steps three through four).

Step #3: Both partners prepare to engage in a discussion regarding the gaslighting behaviors.

It may take some time to fully prepare yourself to discuss the gaslighting behaviors. While doing the third step, "The Emotional Restitution Letter," you will be addressing some of the gaslighting behaviors. However, I believe by addressing the specific ways that gaslighting was used in betrayal, you are addressing the biggest barriers to healing. I believe many couples want to rush through this process. They want to be done with it quickly since reviewing deceitful behavior is painful. Here are a few things you can do to prepare for the discussion of gaslighting behaviors:

- Make sure that at least a disclosure and impact letter have been completed. You may choose to include the gaslighting letter in step two—part three (emotional restitution).

- Much like preparing for disclosure, you will need to pause and reflect on the specific gaslighting behaviors. (See Step One above)

- Make sure both partners are emotionally prepared to discuss gaslighting and its impact on your relationship.

Step# 4: Both partners need to seek a deeper understanding of how the gaslighting has influenced them.

In the next step, I invite both of you to reflect on how the gaslighting has influenced you and your relationship personally. Here's a short example of what it might sound like for both partners:

Betraying Partner:

I realized that while I was acting out, I engaged in the following deceptive behavior: I lied to you on multiple occasions about where I was and what I was doing. In particular, I told you I was going with my business partner when instead, I was meeting up with my affair partner. That was one of the ways I lied to you.

What lying did to me: I realized that I had created so many lies that I couldn't differentiate between the truth and a lie. I didn't realize how stressed I was getting while living a life of lies. Only when I came clean did I realize how sick it was making me both physically and emotionally. I developed high blood pressure and ulcers because I was living a lie. I was also more anxious. Clearly, my actions influenced the way I was with you. You didn't deserve any of this. I regret my behavior.

272

Betrayed Partner:

The betrayed partner will now take this information and write a response:

For the longest time, I thought I was going crazy. I felt something was off, but each time I approached you, you told me that I was making things up. You told me that my fears were related to my family relationship, which infuriated me. What you did was so wrong. It made me angry at you. Now that I know, I realize I yelled at you because of these acts. I don't know how to move on right now. I do appreciate you finally acknowledging that you were lying and deceiving me. You are right; I didn't deserve it. But how can I trust you, knowing that you lied to me?

Betraying Partner's Response:

You have every right to be angry at me. What I did was wrong in every way. I can't change what I did in the past, but I can focus on who I am going to be moving forward. I have been evaluating my core values and the type of person I want to be. I realize I have work to do, and these are the things I am working on:

- I will be a person of integrity. I do not want to lie to you or anyone.

- I want to be a person who you can rely on.

- I will do what I say I am going to do.

- I am going to avoid putting myself in vulnerable situations. If I find that I am feeling vulnerable in any way, I am going to acknowledge what I am feeling and reach out for help.

I realize that it will be hard for you to believe these things I am saying. I hope that, over time, I will regain your trust. You have every right not to trust me. I hope with time, my actions will show you that I am striving to be honest.

Note: It is my suggestion that if you are attempting to rebuild your relationship, you will want to address many of the gaslighting behaviors that were used. You can do so by following the steps outlined in steps three and four above. Please be aware that if you find yourself frequently fighting and arguing, you will likely need to go through this exercise with a professional therapist. If you choose to do this exercise on your own, you may need multiple conversations to go through all the ways gaslighting was used. I recommend completing this exercise when both partners have prepared and are emotionally regulated. You may need to find your mentally safe place before going through this exercise.

> If gaslighting triggers the highest levels of PTSD symptoms, treatment should focus on helping couples address this most painful issue.

In the remainder of this chapter, I will address two things. First, we will look at some of the most common barriers couples face when they try to deal with gaslighting that occurs in the relationship. Second, I will suggest strategies to help you both mentally prepare for the disclosure of gaslighting behavior.

Barriers to Addressing Gaslighting in Relationships

When couples attempt to address gaslighting in their relationship, the conversations rarely go well. Why? Because neither partner has prepared for the emotional intensity such a discussion creates. Below is a common scenario of a couple attempting to deal with gaslighting behaviors. The dialogue illustrates what often happens when the betrayed partner attempts to deal with the aftermath of sexual deception.

Jenny, the Betrayed Partner:

"I can't believe you lied to me. You hid your behaviors, looked me in the eyes, and told me you weren't sexually acting out. You deceived me. How can I possibly believe anything you tell me?"

When Jenny stopped, her husband, Tom, looked at her with a helpless look. Jenny had just laid out some of the ways he had hurt her, and he had no idea how to respond. Let's look at a few different options.

Tom, the Betraying Partner:

Unhealthy Response #1: Stay silent until Jenny gets really upset and starts yelling. Then accuse her of yelling all the time.

Unhealthy Response #2: Say, "You are right. I am a lousy husband. You should just divorce me since I am so rotten."

Unhealthy Response #3: Accuse Jenny of not being available by saying to her, "I wouldn't have done what I did if you had been around."

Each of these three responses are Tom's way of fighting back. In the first scenario, his silence will upset Jenny more. Eventually, he will use her anger against her. In this situation, both partners are upset and will start fighting. The outcome will be extended disconnection.

In the second response, Tom is playing the victim. He is hurting Jenny by agreeing with her and playing the martyr. This is referred to as fighting from the one-down position. It is not attending to her pain; instead, the focus is on how bad he is, "I'm a lousy husband. You should just divorce me since I am so rotten." When this happens, the betrayed partner feels unheard and invalidated. The betraying partner is making it about themselves. This is an example of how a person uses their shame to influence an outcome.

In the third response, Tom turns the tables on Jenny and blames her for his behavior.

In each of these situations, healing is stymied. The relationship cannot be repaired because the pain is not being addressed. Instead, the betrayed partner feels hopeless, and the betraying partner feels shame. If we look at this from the polyvagal theory perspective, both partners are in the sympathetic arousal state and are in fight or flight mode. John Gottman refers to this as being "flooded." [1]

When it comes to relationships, being "flooded" is a term used to describe the overwhelmed feeling that can occur during conflict. This type of flooding occurs when one person in a relationship experiences intense emotions such as fear or anger and becomes completely overwhelmed with the situation at hand. When this happens, the individual may not be able to think clearly or respond in an appropriate manner, leading to further conflict and a downward spiral in the relationship.

Or if things really escalate, one partner may shut down.

Here is a list of barriers that need to be resolved or eliminated:

- Resolve shame (e.g., I'm a lousy person, just divorce me).

- Avoid blaming by taking responsibility (e.g., I wouldn't have, if you would have…).

- Remember, silence doesn't solve the problem and, in many instances, creates more anger in the betrayed partner.

- Continued denial or minimization of behaviors (e.g., telling half-truths, it was just one time).

Now let's explore more effective responses to Jenny's statement:

"I can't believe you lied to me. You hid your behaviors, looked me in the eyes, and told me you weren't sexually acting out. You deceived me. How can I possibly believe anything you tell me?"

Tom's Effective Responses:

Effective Response #1: Sometimes, I can't believe it, either. It was wrong and is something I regret every day. I hid my behaviors, and I lied to you. I understand if you don't believe me right now, I hope someday that I can regain your trust. I regret hurting you. I am ashamed of my behavior and want to do my best to make amends for hurting you.

Effective Response #2: I deeply regret lying to you. When I looked you in the eyes and lied, that was horrible behavior. I was deceptive. I hope that someday I will be able to earn your trust. In the meantime, I am committing to do all I can to right my wrongs.

Effective Response #3: There are days when I pause and reflect on my behaviors. They were wrong, and you didn't deserve what I did to you. One of my biggest regrets is that I looked at you and lied when you wanted the truth. That was absolutely wrong.

If we evaluate each of the three responses, there are common themes. In the first response, we see acknowledgement (e.g., I did lie), no expectations (e.g., I hope to earn your trust), and regret (e.g., I regret hurting you).

In the second response, he begins by expressing regret and is specific (e.g., regret lying to you). He continues with a specific issue that Jenny brought up (e.g., when I looked into your eyes and lied…). Then he acknowledges his deceptive behavior (e.g., I was deceptive), and then concludes with his desire and commitment (e.g., I hope to earn your trust, and I commit to doing all I can).

In the third response, we see increased self-awareness (e.g., I reflect on my behaviors) which is followed by acknowledging his hurtful behaviors (e.g., they—meaning his behaviors—were wrong, you didn't deserve what I did). That is followed by expressing a specific regret (e.g., looking at you and lying).

In the next chapter, I will provide additional examples of how to make amends. I will also explain why I recommend that you avoid using the words "I'm sorry" when you acknowledge your mistakes. However, before we move on to the next chapter, I want to provide effective strategies to help you prepare to discuss gaslighting.

How to Mentally Prepare for a Discussion on Gaslighting

A few years ago, I started asking individuals to describe the patterns they experienced in their relationship (See Chapter Two, where I discuss the Karpman Triangle). I began realizing that Stephen Karpman was right. People argue and fight in predictable patterns. Unfortunately, they do not realize that they are stuck in an endless loop until one or both partners feel hopeless.

In many cases, couples have told me they fight about similar issues. I want to review the idea that we fight in patterns because it is likely what you have been doing when you attempt to discuss gaslighting in your relationship. I am convinced that most couples are not emotionally prepared to discuss gaslighting, and as a result, they continue to fight about the same unresolved issues.

Below, I offer a few ideas to help you and your partner prepare for disclosure and discussion on gaslighting behaviors.

#1: Be Emotionally Ready—The goal is to prepare yourself for a difficult conversation. The chance of being effective increases when your mind is open and your heart is in the right place. Strategies for effective emotional preparation include a) deep breathing; b) regular relaxation; c) guided meditations; d) humming; and e) the basic exercise—See Appendix K to learn more about each of these exercises.

If you want to repair your relationship, mentally working through one or more of these activities will improve your energy which will be felt by your partner, even during a difficult conversation. On the other hand, if you are angry or defensive while communicating, the most natural response from your partner will be to fight, flee or freeze. It requires significant discipline for a person to stay mentally engaged while they are feeling attacked. This is one of the reasons most people respond poorly when they feel attacked.

In the examples above, I provided effective and unhealthy responses. The only way to effectively respond when you feel attacked is to activate your prefrontal cortex. This is most effectively done through the activities described above since they will help you activate the ventral vagus nerve. This will require practice and effort.

If both partners are working to access their ventral vagus, the odds of working through difficult issues dramatically increase.

Note: If you are wondering whether betrayed partners can communicate about gaslighting without being angry or critical, I would say that the most effective conversations I have witnessed have been when partners discuss their hurts from a calm place. There is power in discussing the anguish of the soul in an authentic way without anger or animosity.

#2: Attune to Self—As you look internally, you start noticing your thoughts, emotions, and physical sensations. By listening to these signals, you are developing the self-awareness skill of attunement. As you improve your level of self-attunement, you will notice thoughts that lead toward connection and thoughts that lead to fighting or fleeing. You will recognize when your emotions are elevated, signaling the need to take a break before attempting to discuss important issues with your partner. Finally, as your awareness increases, you will identify tightness and tension within your body, a signal to you that you may need to take a break.

As you practice self-attunement, you prepare yourself for the next step, which is attuning to your partner. If you struggle with attuning to yourself, it will be more difficult to attune to your partner and others.

#3: *Attune to Your Partner*—When we are attuned to our partner, we can readily pick up their emotions. If something is wrong, we detect something is off and address it. If we are misattuned, we miss what our partner is trying to tell us through their words, expressions, and body language. We also miss emotional expressions as well. In contrast, if we are attuning to our partner, we recognize their body language and notice facial expressions signaling frustration or hurt. In addition, we pay attention to their words of choice. If we are attuned to our partners, they will "feel felt," as Dr. Daniel Siegel suggested in his book *Mind* (2). When we feel felt, we experience emotional bonding. We experience being seen and heard without being judged. When this happens in relationships, both partners experience true intimacy—the feeling of being felt, heard, and seen.

#4: *Mental Rehearsal*—If you want to improve your communication skills, one way to practice is by mentally rehearsing your conversation. Mental rehearsal is a powerful tool when it comes to learning how to communicate more effectively. It involves imagining yourself in a situation and practicing the responses you would like to make. Through this practice, you will become better at recognizing certain scenarios and responding with what you have rehearsed in your mind. Mental rehearsal will also help you build confidence as you develop your communication skills.

Betrayed Partner's Mental Rehearsal

Imagine how you would talk with your partner about gaslighting in your relationship. Think through how your partner might respond. Then consider how you could effectively communicate with them. As you mentally work through different situations, you will come up with ideas that can help you improve your ability to communicate your desires in difficult moments.

Betraying Partner's Mental Rehearsal

Consider an experience where your partner is talking with you about your gaslighting behaviors. What would be an effective response? What have you done in the past that worked? What didn't work? How could you respond if you do not know what to say? I encourage you to give significant attention to this process. Only through practice will you be prepared for the time when it happens again. As you develop your communication skills through mental rehearsal, your partner will see your progress. They will be more likely to open up to you because they sense your genuine effort.

Rebuilding your relationship after sexual betrayal requires effort and desire. When couples ask me what they can do to heal, I provide them with as many ideas and tools as I can. I want them to succeed. However, I have come to the conclusion that healing is not possible as long as gaslighting is still happening. The possibility of healing increases significantly when couples explore the role of gaslighting in their relationship. The betrayed partner needs to share how it influenced their thinking and their trust. The betraying partner needs to do everything possible to make amends for their gaslighting behaviors. By reviewing the exercise found in *Appendix J*, you are increasing your chances of healing. As a reminder, the process of talking about gaslighting is emotionally charged. For this reason, I invite you to frequently review the examples I have provided. If you want to heal, prepare your heart and mind so that you can deal with one of the most painful barriers to couple recovery.

Key Takeaways from This Chapter

- Gaslighting increases post-traumatic stress responses in betrayed partners.

- If couples want to rebuild their relationship, they need to address the gaslighting behaviors (an exercise to address gaslighting can be found in Appendix J).

- Denial and Blame Scales reveal that gaslighting is common during and after betrayal. One of the best ways to repair the relationship is by discussing how gaslighting was used in the relationship. Examples were provided on how you can do that.

- Three steps to help you deal with gaslighting include: 1) complete truth and honesty; 2) working through a step-by-step disclosure process; and 3) both partners must be willing to discuss gaslighting from an emotionally regulated state of mind.

- There are common barriers that prevent an effective resolution to gaslighting. Examples of effective and ineffective responses were provided.

- If you are prepared to discuss gaslighting in your relationship, you will increase your chances of rebuilding your relationship. Specific things you can do to prepare include: 1) be emotionally ready; 2) attune to self; 3) attune to your partner; and 4) mentally rehearse before having your conversations.

Chapter Fourteen

How to Create the Moments That Will Change Your Marriage

"Love is a Choice: Make It Every Day"

Every day we make decisions regarding our lives. Some choices leave lasting consequences, while others become insignificant. But have you considered how we make these decisions about our lives?

For example, have you considered what type of person you want to be in your relationships? Have you thought about what you wish your family or friends would say about you at your funeral? Questions like, "What type of person do I want to become? Or "What can I do to become my best self?" These questions are easy to ask but complicated to answer.

As the author of your life, you have been writing your story. You may or may not like the story you have written so far. I am confident that if you are reading this book, your story has undoubtedly been filled with challenges.

As you read this chapter, I invite you to contemplate your story. How will you answer the question about overcoming the adversities of life? What decisions will you make today that will impact your posterity and future generations? As you face your burdens, you are the creator of your life story. In this chapter, I will explain two concepts: 1) There are specific moments that can quickly change the trajectory of your life. I will provide ideas on how to create and respond during these critical times, and 2) How healthy habits can help you start healing moments to jump start relational healing.

The Power of Moments

In each of our lives, some moments stick out. You remember your first day on a new job, your first kiss, driving your first car, or when you were praised for doing a job well. You also remember the difficult moments that you wish you could forget. Our lives are filled with moments that change our lives for good and bad.

In this section, we will focus on specific moments in your life and your relationship that can determine the outcome of your relationship. We will then discuss how to create healing moments for you and your partner. We will conclude this section by discussing things you can do to increase positive moments while decreasing negative ones.

Have you ever wondered what drives people to change their behaviors? As a therapist, I often wonder why some people change, and others do not. I have also contemplated why some people suddenly shift their behaviors while others move towards change at a turtle's pace.

Here are other questions I have considered: 1) What motivates people to change? 2) Are there things a person can do to accelerate the change process? 3) What helps people stay motivated so that they can make lasting changes in their lives?

These are questions I am going to invite you to consider in the exercise below. In a moment, I will invite you to consider some of the previously mentioned questions regarding change and motivation, but first, please consider the following two stories.

Story #1: Aaron Was Hiding from Himself

The day I realized I was being stupid was the day my desire to change began. I was all alone thinking about my life. I wasn't happy. I had betrayed my wife, and my children would hardly talk to me. I wasn't the person I thought I would be. For years, I had been blaming my wife for my unhappiness. I used her lack of support as my excuse to act out sexually.

In the beginning, I turned to pornography. Eventually, that wasn't enough. I began looking for other sexual encounters, and they weren't hard to find. The problem is I was never satisfied. While my wife had become my scapegoat, I was avoiding my own emotions. My double life was killing me. There was nobody to talk to. I felt trapped. I wanted to stop, but how?

I'm not sure exactly what woke me up, but that day, it finally registered in my brain that I was wasting my life away. My heart began changing at that moment. No more stupidity. No more blaming my wife for my behavior. It wasn't her fault that I was escaping into meaningless sexual encounters. It was me. I had to look at myself honestly. When I did, I couldn't stand the person who was looking back at me in the mirror.

Initially, I refused to look at him. He had become a person I didn't recognize. Then I realized I had ignored his pain. Avoidance of my past and numbing out was not the answer. It was time to wake up and become the person I always imagined I could be.

I am awake today. The cost of living blind for all those years is hard for me to think about. My wife and children have suffered so much because I wasn't willing to deal with my issues earlier in life. I have done my best to make amends with my wife, but she is still hurting. I wish I could take her pain away. Can I have a do-over? Can I ever make it up to her and my children?

Exercise:

1. As you look at this person's story, what do you think motivated him to change?

2. Are there things he could do to accelerate the changes he needs to make in his life?

3. What can he do to stay motivated?

4. What can he do to repair his relationship with his wife and children?

I hope you took the time to answer each question.

Here are my answers:

1. *What motivated him to change?*

While it wasn't clear what led up to that day, he did say, "I didn't like myself." I believe he was reviewing his life and realized he was heading in the wrong direction. When we pause and reflect on our lives, we often gain more insight. For him, he began taking ownership of his actions and stopped blaming his wife. He also realized that he had unresolved issues from his past that he needed to address.

Key Concept: As self-awareness increases, so does our capacity to make change. By reflecting on his life, he realized he was not the person he wanted to be. Sometimes it is hard to look into the mirror of life, but he did. The path ahead was neither easy for him nor for his wife and children. The alternative to waking up would likely have been divorce and estrangement from his children.

2. *Are there things he could do to accelerate change?*

Ideally, he would have recognized earlier in life that he had unresolved issues that needed to be addressed. However, once he began the change process, there are many things he could do: Here's a short list:

- Do a self-assessment by asking these questions:
  - ◊ What kind of person do I want to be?
  - ◊ What do I need to do to change?
  - ◊ What is motivating my change?
- See orienting questions from Chapter One.
- Prepare to do a full disclosure with the wife.
- Create a recovery plan.
- Find a person with whom he can be accountable for his behaviors (a sponsor).
- Participate in a support group with others struggling to stop unwanted sexual behaviors.
- Develop healthy habits (i.e., eat, exercise, sleep, meditate).
- Eliminate situations where he is vulnerable to returning to previous behaviors.
- Talk with a professional counselor and focus on unresolved issues from his past.
- Reduce his shame.
- Increase empathy and compassion.
- Be a person that can look in the mirror (a person of integrity).
- Create meaningful relationships.
- Serve others.
- Do everything he can to make amends with his wife and children.

3. *How can he stay motivated?*

It is difficult to stay motivated. In fact, you should expect that your motivation will wax and wane. As a result, you have to be prepared for when your motivation is low. Some of the best things you can do to stay motivated include:

- Be consistently accountable to others—many people find support, and then when things go well, they stop reaching out. Successful people stay accountable.

- Continue to develop healthy habits. By developing good habits, you are reducing the likelihood of returning to unhealthy behaviors.

- Create a vision for your future and engage in behaviors that help you become the person you envision yourself becoming (e.g., a good dad, a better husband, an owner of your own business.)

- Keep your goals and desires in front of you. Successful changers frequently review their path. As a result, they are less likely to stray away from their goals.

- Create a plan for when your motivation is low. For example, you could write down five things you will do when your motivation is low. Then when you find yourself struggling, you already have a plan in place. By preparing for days when your motivation is low, you are more likely to succeed.

4. *What can he do to repair his relationship with his wife and children?*

Making amends after sexual betrayal requires consistent efforts, and it may be one of the most difficult things you will ever do. You have to be prepared for your partner's skepticism. Betrayed partners are often slow to accept the efforts of their betraying partner due to previous experiences with broken trust. As a result, patience is required. Throughout this book, I have listed many reparation activities. I will review some of them here:

- Amends begins with creating a safe environment. (See Chapters One and Two) The process of creating a safe environment takes time and includes many different parts. They include:

- Being honest and truthful (See Chapter Ten)

- Listening to your partner and seek to understand their pain (See Chapter Twelve)

- Acknowledging deceitful behaviors

- Preparing a full disclosure and share it with your partner (See Chapter Thirteen)

- Increasing your skills in empathy and compassion (See Chapter Five)

- Acknowledging and address gaslighting behaviors (See Chapter Thirteen)

- Improving your capacity for intimacy (See Chapter Fifteen)

Now add your ideas to this list. Once you have combined the lists, I would encourage you to identify the top two or three things you can focus on.

As you focus on the behaviors listed above, you will be creating an environment where moments of healing can occur within yourself and your partner. Remember, the change process begins by recognizing your inner desires to be the best self you can be. Once your desire for improvement begins, you can strive to have a better relationship with your spouse.

Story #2: Nathan Was Stuck and Couldn't Move On

I found myself getting angry all the time. I never used to get upset like that. After a while, I could hardly stand being around my wife. After she cheated on me, I couldn't look at her without thinking about her actions. In my mind, all I could see was her with her boss. I wanted to kick or punch something. For the longest time, I couldn't stop the thoughts of her cheating from taking over my mind.

One day, my wife and I got into a huge fight. I accused her of still being involved with her boss, even though she had left the company. She looked at me in disbelief and said, "If you can't believe me after all I have done to change, I worry that you will not be able to get over this."

I yelled, "How can you expect me to believe anything you say after you lied to me for so long?" She responded, "You are right. I can't expect you to believe me. I hope someday you will see that I am trying my best to earn back your trust. What I did was wrong. Every day I regret doing what I did. I wish you could see into my heart; I want to be with you. Not just with you, I want to be happy with you."

I don't know what it was, but the way she said, "I want to be with you. Not just with you, I want to be happy with you," my head and heart felt something different. That was a turning point for my healing. I had been so focused on how she had wronged me that I had missed the things she was trying to do to repair our relationship. Not long after our argument, I began making a list of the ways that her betrayal had changed me. As I reviewed my list, I realized that I had lost a part of myself. I did not want to let her betrayal determine the type of person I was going to be. That day, I decided to focus on the things I knew I could control.

Here is a list of things I can focus on:

- Get more sleep. I had become anxious to the point that I had stopped sleeping well. I think that influenced my emotions because I was always tired.

- Resolve the painful memories that keep running through my mind. When they come, I will remember the day my wife told me she wanted to be with me. If the thoughts persist, I will reach out and tell her I am having a hard day. She reassured me that she would be there for me if I had a difficult time.

- I need to talk with someone besides my wife so I don't feel alone (find a friend or family member who knows what I am going through).

- I need to stop beating myself up. Since discovering the betrayal, I have struggled to feel like I was good enough.

- I need to figure out how to deal with my anger. This should be my top priority because it only pushes my partner away.

If this person were in my office, together we would review their betrayal trauma and PTSD symptoms and create a plan for reducing each symptom. In addition, we would create a plan to focus on each of the items listed above.

Here are a few pivotal moments in Nathan's healing that we would look for:

- When his sleep improved, this would indicate that his nervous system was starting to relax.

- He identified that he was having painful memories (i.e., flashbacks or nightmares). He may benefit from participating in a few sessions of EMDR, the Somatic Experience, IFS, or ART. For a description of each of these treatments see this chapter's support material.

- Nathan really needed someone to talk to besides Ashley. One key behavior we would look for is for him to find someone he can confide in. Isolation and feelings of being alone are common after sexual betrayal, so this would be a big step for him. By finding a person whom he could trust, he would put less pressure on Ashley for his support.

- Negative self-talk is a key barrier to long-term recovery. Therefore, Nathan's progress could be measured by a shift in beliefs. His beliefs would alter from not being good enough to knowing he is enough.

- The way Nathan expressed his anger in his relationship was a big barrier to their healing. Every time he got upset; he would call her names. His progress in this area would include: 1) avoiding personal attacks; 2) identifying the core emotion driving the anger (i.e., hurt, sadness, etc.); and 3) communicating to his wife the underlying emotions. He would also incorporate healthy ways to identify his emotions (i.e., journaling, thinking through what he was trying to communicate, etc.).

Note: While there are additional areas of healing that Nathan would eventually work on, these are the ones he first identified. If you are attempting to heal from betrayal, it is essential that you focus on the specific areas you want to change. If you would like assistance identifying issues for you to focus on, I would recommend taking the *Trauma Inventory for Partners of Sex Addicts (TIPSA)*. You can find it in the support material for Chapter Six, or you can have a trained therapist administer it to you and review your results (See www.sexhelp.com)

How to Create Crucial Moments for Lasting Change

Over the years, I have wondered about the timing of when people choose to change. For example, why do some people try to stop lying and cheating only when they are caught? Or why do other people disclose part of what they did and not the whole truth? Why would they only do a partial disclosure when they could be free by telling the whole truth? On the other hand, why do some betrayed partners choose to move towards reconnecting while others keep their partner at a distance? Or how do some betrayed partners create effective boundaries while others try to control their partner?

As I have contemplated the various responses betraying and betrayed partners display, I have found a few common themes individuals and their partners display when they heal. I will discuss these observations below.

Crucial Moment for Couples #1: Safety Through Honesty

Honesty from Betraying Partner

There is no connection without safety. There is no safety without honesty. Therefore, when betraying partners choose to be honest, regardless of the consequences, they begin their attempt to repair their relationship. They also begin their personal journey for lasting change. Throughout this book, I have discussed the importance of being rigorously honest and becoming a person of integrity. My favorite moments as a therapist come when individuals let go of their fears and become completely vulnerable. They become honest with their partner, their accountability team, and others with whom they are close. They accept and try to live honestly, as per the quote from Dr. David Viscott, "The truth had the power to heal, to protect, to guide. Living in the truth was living free and at one's best." (1)

Honesty from the Betrayed Partner

For betrayed partners, honesty is very different from their partner. They do not have to disclose their misdeeds. However, their honesty in relationship healing is also critical. They have to decide if they are willing to work toward relationship repair. (This may take months or longer, depending on the information they receive in a disclosure and the recovery efforts of their partner.) If they choose not to remain in the relationship, for them, honesty is saying, "I do not want to move on with you." If they choose to stay, they still need to communicate how they will approach their relationship (i.e., what are their boundaries, expectations for closeness, and desire for closeness).

As betrayed partners work through their pain from betrayal, many discover areas of their lives that they want to change. As a result, I have had many clients say something like this, "As I have watched my partner be honest, I have realized that I need to explore my own life. I recognized that I could have been better in my relationship. No, I didn't cheat on my spouse, but I could have been open and transparent when I felt something was off. Instead, I pulled back, and when my partner asked what was wrong, I wouldn't discuss my concerns. I now know that I must be honest with how I am feeling. It's okay to say, 'I don't agree' or share my opinion."

When both partners feel safe enough to share their genuine feelings without hesitation or concern, they have accomplished another feat for healing and recovery. It takes a lot of courage to be vulnerable and share your deepest feelings and emotions with someone who has betrayed you. If you want to measure progress in your healing journey as a couple, ask yourselves this question, "Are we comfortable enough in our relationship to have an open and honest dialogue with each other? Or does one or both of us feel the need to hold back?"

How to Create an Environment Where You and Your Partner Can Open Up?

It should be expected that both partners' desire for relationship repair will fluctuate. Therefore, even the most honest expressions (e.g., I'm all in, I can't commit right now, or I will do anything to earn back your trust) can and will change. What both partners need to heal their relationship is consistent communication. This will help you and your partner share thoughts and emotions related to your relationship (i.e., I'm worried, scared, hopeful, excited).

Some couples implement the FANOS (FANOS) method to improve communication in their relationship. FANOS is an acronym for Feelings, Affirmations/Appreciations, Needs, Ownership, Struggles/Sobriety. One person checks in while the other listens without questions or comments. Then the other person checks in the same way. If you choose to implement this method in your relationship, I recommend that you sit close to each other and maintain eye contact during your check-in.

Once you and your partner have established a safe environment, FANOS is one of many potential check-ins you can use. Another strategy you can use is a basic needs check-in.

When we are born, our most basic needs include:

- Healthy touch

- Eye contact

- Facial expression (i.e., a smile)

- Tone of voice

- To be nourished

When these needs are met in our childhood, we are more likely to create healthy attachments with our caregivers and others. When these needs are not met, we are more likely to turn to unhealthy coping mechanisms. The need for these forms of connection never stops. Individuals of all ages benefit when their basic needs are met.

In the early stages of healing and recovery, it probably didn't feel safe to have these needs be met by your partner. It is hard to look your partner in the eye when you have been betrayed. It is hard to look at your partner and smile when you have been betrayed. Healthy touch? That's not a possibility, either. Most couples are not using a soothing voice when they discuss betrayal. As a result, in the early stage of recovery, most couples feel empty because their basic needs are not being met. Thus, when they desire the most comfort, their basic needs are not being met. This is one of the many reasons why individuals and couples feel so alone right after discovery. This is why it is essential to have support from a trusted friend, family member, or support group in the beginning stage of healing.

As couples move towards healing and recovery, they renew their connection by implementing their basic needs back into their day-to-day lives. If you would like to learn more about how you and your partner can practice reintegrating the basic needs into your relationship, I have created a few exercises to help you practice. I have created an online course titled *"Five Steps to Stay Connected: Daily Exercises for Couples Trying to Heal from Infidelity."* You can access this course for free at: (https://humanintimacy.com). As a reminder, these exercises are best applied when you have created an environment where you want a deeper connection.

You will know that you and your partner are healing when you can discuss almost anything. This is the type of environment where you can grow together through self-expression. You can open up because you are not afraid to do so. This could be a goal for your relationship, "Create an environment where we both feel safe sharing our thoughts and ideas with each other. We want to be ourselves in the presence of each other."

Here are additional moments where I have observed honesty and trust as couples rebuild their relationship:

- Completing a full disclosure (betraying partner)
- Preparing and doing an impact letter (betrayed partner)
- Creating an emotional restitution letter (betraying partner)
- A recommitment ceremony
- Crucial moment amends

Crucial Moment for Couples #2: Address Fears

If possible, imagine that you and your partner are sitting down and having a good conversation. Recently, you have been having better conversations, so you decide that now is a good time to share something with which you have been struggling. The challenge is you don't want to create a problem. However, in the end, you choose to bring up the issue since you believe that your partner cares about you and that they want to help you resolve your concern. So you say, "I have been having a really hard time lately with thoughts and fears about your sexual betrayal. I wanted to bring it up because I have been struggling. Do you have any thoughts or ideas?

If you are the betraying spouse, how would you respond? (I encourage you to pause here and ask yourself these questions:

1. How would I feel if my partner shared their concern with me this way?
2. How would I respond?
3. How would I have responded in the past?

Now imagine that you say this to your spouse, "Thanks for sharing. It seems like these thoughts have been coming up more recently, is that right? I'm here if you would like to discuss what you are feeling or thinking. I want you to know that you can share your concerns with me at any time.

If you and your partner could communicate this way, how would you feel about your relationship? I share these examples because I believe that it is the type of communication that will heal your relationship. In order to be effective, as this couple is, you and your partner will need to feel safe sharing difficult emotions with each other. You will need to trust each other on a deeper level.

If you want to learn to communicate more effectively, you will need to learn how to overcome your personal fears and worries. We fear that our spouse will reject what we are feeling or thinking. Perhaps these fears stem from past experiences. If in the past you have shut your partners' emotions down, I encourage you to 1) Acknowledge and take responsibility for your past behavior (i.e., in the past, I became defensive and didn't listen to your concerns); 2) ask your partner to share their concerns with you. In other words, give you another chance by sharing their difficult emotions. Express your commitment that you will seek to understand without becoming defensive; and 3) validate your partner's concerns or feelings (i.e., thanks for sharing, I understand that these feelings will come because of my behaviors).

A good goal for your relationship could be:

Goal: We want to create a relationship where we can be honest with each other by sharing our concerns and fears with each other without reservation.

Crucial Moment for Couples #3: Avoid Elevated Conflict

World-renowned relationship expert Dr. John Gottman has discovered that he can predict with a high probability if a couple will stay together or divorce. He used the term "four horsemen of the apocalypse" to describe four key behaviors between couples that can indicate the potential for later divorces. These are stonewalling, criticism, contempt, and defensiveness. (2) While all relationships experience some level of conflict, when these four behaviors start to become more common, it can be a sign of deeper issues that can lead to the breakdown of the relationship. In studies conducted by Dr. Gottman, he discovered that couples who consistently exhibit stonewalling and criticism are at higher risk for divorce than those who don't. (3)

Note: If you are not familiar with the term stonewalling, here is a good explanation: Stonewalling is a response style in communication characterized by withdrawing from the interaction or conversation without providing any feedback or response. Stonewalling can take many forms, including refusing to engage in the conversation, giving silent treatment, or physically leaving the conversation or location.

Defensiveness is defending one's own innocence, warding off a perceived attack, meeting an attack with a counterattack (a righteous stance of indignation), or whining (an innocent-victim stance). (4)

While this is stating the obvious, if you and your partner are using one or more of these behaviors, I strongly recommend that you evaluate your approach to conflict. Even if you are hurt or upset by your spouse, you can reduce the risk of your relationship ending by eliminating these four behaviors from your relationship.

Perhaps you are asking how to remove the four horsemen from your relationship. If so, Dr. Gottman, in his book "*The Science of Trust,*" suggested the following six steps:

Begin with an attitude and the skill of listening by:

- Awareness of what your partner is saying.

- Turning toward your partner.

- Tolerance—with difficult conversations.

- Non-defensive listening.

- Understanding as a goal.

- Empathy for what your partner is experiencing.

He believes that these skills are the basis for the conversation that can create emotional connection during sliding-door moments. (5) A sliding-door moment is similar to what I have been referring to as critical moments.

In an effort to help you apply these ideas in your relationship, I have identified common statements that reflect the four horsemen in action and alternative responses. My hope is that you and your partner learn to communicate more effectively and implement healthy patterns into your relationship. As you review the unhealthy and healthy responses below, I invite you to consider how you can communicate more effectively with your spouse. Are you using any of the four horsemen Dr. Gottman has outlined? If so, consider the alternative responses I have provided.

Four Horsemen	Unhealthy	Healthy
Criticism	You are never going to get over this problem.	I worry about our relationship. Sometimes I worry that you won't stop.
Contempt	Look at you. Nobody would ever want to be with you. If you leave me, you will spend the rest of your life alone.	I am concerned about you and me if we can't work things out. I know it will be hard for me.
Defensiveness	I wouldn't yell if you would just tell me the truth.	I am upset right now. I need you to know that I am hurting, and I can't be close right now.
Stonewalling	Giving silent treatment to your partner or not giving them feedback.	I am not sure what to say. Would you mind if I take some time to make sure I communicate what I am feeling and thinking in a healthy way?

I believe that we turn to unhealthy forms of communication for the following reasons:

- We saw the four horsemen being used while growing up, and we haven't learned how to communicate more effectively.

- We are experiencing emotional pain.

- We have yet to learn how to effectively communicate.

- We are hurting, and we want our partner to feel our pain.

- Our spouse has hurt us, and we want them to hurt too.

If you are using any of the four horsemen behaviors in your communication, I invite you to step back and evaluate why. Why are you choosing to communicate the way you do? How does this type of communication help you? If you are like most people I have worked with, you haven't learned how to communicate more effectively. For your relationship's sake, I encourage you to review the principles and ideas outlined above.

Before I move on to the next crucial moment, I want to share an approach I created to help couples de-escalate during fights or arguments. It is what I call *"7 Rules for Fighting."*

Here are the 7 Rules for Fighting:

Rule #1: Recognize

The first step you can take to avoid conflict is to know when you have been triggered. You may think to yourself, "I'm feeling triggered or flooded." When you have awareness, you can make a more conscious decision on how to respond.

You are now prepared to move on to Rule #2:

Rule #2: Take a Time-Out

According to researchers, there is an optimal heart rate for solving problems. If your heart rate is over 100 heartbeats per minute, you may be emotionally flooded. "The research of stress physiologist Loring Rowell has shown that when the heart rate exceeds 100 bpm, the body starts secreting adrenaline, and the sympathetic nervous system responses of fight or flight begin to activate." (6,7)

When we are emotionally flooded, our survival brain (fight, flight, or freeze) takes over as it tries to protect us from perceived dangers. Things that aren't normally threatening may feel dangerous and our responses may become more reactive. A helpful tool in regulating ourselves to shift back into our rational mind is taking a break. This is the purpose of a time-out. By stepping away from the threat, you are allowing your mind and body to deactivate the natural fight or flight response.

I recommend that the time-out be communicated as soon as you recognize that you are flooded. The longer you wait, the more difficult it will be to pull away from an argument or fight.

Many people hesitate to take a time-out because they are afraid that they will never come back to the issue. Therefore, when you take a time-out, you should follow these two guidelines: 1) Time-outs should come with a time limit and be specific (e.g., 30 minutes, or let's talk tomorrow morning at 7:30), and 2) When you ask for a time-out, communicate your desire to solve the issue at hand. It could sound like this, "I recognize that I am getting flooded; I need to take a 30-minute break. I do want to resolve this problem with you because our relationship matters to me."

Note: Some people have a hard time with time-outs because it can trigger a feeling of being abandoned or rejected. If you or your partner feel this way, you need to address the fear directly. You can do this by affirming your desire to solve the problem and by sharing your belief that you will work through your differences (e.g., I want to figure this out because our relationship matters).

Rule #3: Self-Evaluation

Your awareness will be key in this step. While all the steps are important, this step will allow you to look inside yourself. You will be more successful in this step if you ask yourself questions like 1) What is happening to me? 2) Why am I getting upset? and 3) Does this issue trigger bigger hurts and pains in me (e.g., past conflicts, core beliefs—I'm not enough, or I'm a failure)? If the conflict triggered an issue from the past, you would want to write it down so you can address it with your partner.

Rule #4: What Is My Partner Experiencing?

In step four, your task is to try and identify what your partner is feeling and thinking. This may be one of the more difficult steps because their actions, choices, or behaviors have hurt you. Here are a few questions that may help you be more effective: 1) What is my partner feeling about what just happened between us? 2) What emotions could my partner be feeling right now? 3) Did our interaction trigger something from our past or their past that is painful to them?

Before you move on to the next step, do a quick body check. Are you feeling less tension than before you began step three? If you are still feeling angry or upset at your partner, spend more time on step four. If you attempt to resolve the issue without being emotionally prepared, you and your partner will likely continue your fight or argument.

This step is hard for many of my clients because they feel that what their partner has done is wrong. They ask me, "Why should I have to think about what my partner is feeling or thinking?" My best answer is that healthy communication requires us to be clear without using the four horsemen. If you learn to communicate your hurt and pain without using criticism, contempt, defensiveness, or stonewalling, you will be communicating more effectively. You can still express your frustration, but it will be communicated in a clear way (e.g., it hurts me when you avoid looking at me).

Finally, I invite you to ask yourself this question, "Am I ready to share what I have experienced in an honest way without blaming my partner?" and "Am I ready to listen to how my companion experienced our conflict?" If you are not ready, you may benefit by asking yourself these questions: 1) Do I want to resolve this issue? 2) What is preventing me from wanting to resolve this conflict? 3) Am I too upset to resolve this issue right now? If so, let your partner know you are not ready. Then focus on how you can communicate your thoughts and feelings without blaming your partner. If you cannot find the desire to resolve this conflict with your partner, I would recommend you journal your thoughts about why you don't want to work through this issue. I suggest you write until you come up with an answer.

When your mind and heart are in the right place, you are prepared to share and listen. It's now time to move on to step five. If you do this prematurely, your attempt at solving the issue at hand will not turn out well and will discourage you and your partner.

Rule #5: Come Together and Discuss Your Responses to Steps #3 and #4

Begin this step by having one partner go first. The person who is sharing what the conflict did to them should avoid blaming.

Here's an example of this process:

Juan: I felt like I didn't know how to get my point across and that made me feel helpless. I have realized the feeling of helplessness triggers a feeling in me of being unlovable. I now understand that when I am feeling helpless, I pull back because I am afraid of being hurt."

The listening partner's job is to listen with an open mind. Once the person sharing is done, the listening partner should thank their partner for sharing.

Below is a healthy response:

Karla: I appreciate you for telling me how you were feeling. I need to listen more intently in that situation. I want you to know that you are important to me, and I don't want you to feel unlovable in our relationship.

Partner one will also share what they felt partner two may have been experiencing.

Juan: As I thought about what you may have been feeling, I realized I don't know. I did wonder if I made you feel like you weren't important to me. Am I close?"

Karla: Thank you for taking time to think about how I was feeling. I also appreciate you for being vulnerable with me. It means a lot to me that you considered what I was feeling.

Next, Karla would share what she was feeling. This transitions the couple to Karla sharing what she was experiencing (i.e., you are right, I felt like I wasn't important to you. I was also scared because we keep having the same argument. I really want to stop fighting.)

Karla would then share what she thought Juan might be feeling or experiencing during the conflict. She may already know since Juan shared what he was feeling at the beginning of this step. Either way, both partners have now shared and listened to each other.

Rule #6: Discuss How Steps #3, #4, and #5 Went

In step six, you step back to evaluate what just happened. This is the evaluation period where both partners share how they feel about their discussion. If step five went well, this should be celebrated.

You could use this question to measure the effectiveness of the exercise you just completed:

Question: On a scale between 0 (very little frustration) and 10 (very high frustration), what is my current level of frustration regarding the issue my partner and I have been trying to discuss?

If step five did not go well and your scores are high, watch out for the Zeigarnik effect. The issue is not yet resolved. My suggestion is to step back and evaluate what is holding you back from resolving the issue at hand.

Rule #7: What Can We Do to Improve?

If you have completed the first six steps, then step seven is a form of celebration and review. First, begin by expressing your appreciation to your partner for going through this process with you. It shows that both of you are committed to improving your communication. Second, review what went well and what you feel your partner did well. This validates their efforts and helps you focus on positive things in your partner.

If you and your partner have enough positive experiences, using the *Seven Rules for Fighting* will help you gain confidence in your ability to discuss and solve problems. If you don't get it right the first few times, keep trying. Eventually, your efforts will pay off and you will discover that you have a tool that you can use anytime you need to. In addition, using this approach will eliminate the chance of doing or saying hurtful things because you are emotionally compromised (flooded).

Note: I suggest that you and your partner spend time discussing your own rules. Your rules can be guided by your personal values and the boundaries you want to have in your new and improved relationship.

I have identified three crucial moments (experiences) in relationships where your responses can make or break your relationship. For a quick review, they are:

- Promote safety through honesty.
- Create an environment where you can address your fears.
- Avoid elevated conflict by implementing the seven rules for fighting.

This chapter concludes with a few additional ideas you can use to improve your mindset as you respond to crucial moments in your relationship.

How to Improve Your Mindset for Crucial Moments

Ideas for Each Partner

- Discuss what happened, and its impact on you.
- Turn toward your partner, not away.
- Address your own issues (i.e., fears, trauma, anxiety).
- Explore how the past is influencing you now instead of influencing present.
- Self-introspection (i.e., what kind of person do I want to be in this relationship?).
- Commit to becoming a person of integrity.
- Practice daily self-care (e.g., relaxing to music that calms you, going for a walk, etc.).

Ideas for Your Relationship

- Engage in daily acts of service.
- Laugh together.
- Schedule time to connect—even briefly.
- Learn together.
- Pray together (spiritual intimacy).
- Attempt to repair when you are feeling disconnected.
- Remember, your partner isn't an enemy.

Key Takeaways from This Chapter

As you change, there are moments that can wake you up. Two stories were shared about how a betraying partner and betrayed partner began their change process. We addressed questions like: 1) What motivates us to change? 2) Can we accelerate the change process? 3) How can we stay motivated to keep changing?

- There are things you can do to improve your success during crucial moments. They are: 1) increase relationship safety through honesty; 2) address your fears by learning to be open and honest with each other; and 3) avoid elevated conflict.

- You can improve your mindset during crucial moments by preparing in advance. Behaviors like self-care, self-introspection, and addressing your own issues can help.

- We also discussed *Seven Rules for Fighting*. As you and your partner implement these guidelines into your relationship, you will discover how to communicate more effectively. Even if you aren't perfect in the beginning, you can learn to address the real issues by using these steps.

Chapter Fifteen

Heal as You Create Healthy Intimacy

"The lives of most people are histories of their search for intimacy, of their attempts to be socially, physically, and emotionally close to others."
-Victor L. Brown, Jr.

What exactly is intimacy? Is intimacy sex? Is it allowing others to get close to us? Can you and your partner be intimate without having sex? If so, what makes your interaction intimate? As we begin this chapter, I invite you to consider how you view intimacy in your relationship.

Far too often, we use words and assume that others understand and agree with our definitions. I hope to avoid making the same mistake by clearly explaining intimacy in this chapter. I also have a goal to help you change your relationship by helping you create true intimacy. I agree with Victor L. Brown's quote at the beginning of this chapter. I believe that our lives revolve around our desire for intimacy. We long for closeness and connection. To help you improve in this area, I will provide some of the most effective strategies I have found that have helped couples rebuild intimacy after sexual betrayal.

Before I get too far down the road, I should define intimacy. However, I want you to go first. What is your definition of intimacy, and how would you describe it to others?

Here is my definition:

Intimacy is the deep connection and understanding shared between individuals, which transcends beyond superficial interactions. (1) This profound bond is built on trust, honesty, commitment, and loyalty. When we experience true intimacy, we allow others to see our genuine selves. We could say that intimacy enables others to see into our world. Intimacy, then, is being seen and seeing others for who they are. Maybe the best description can be found in this explanation:

Intimacy = In-to-me-see

When we create intimacy in our relationships, it is because we allow ourselves to be seen. We do not hold back. We do not hide. If we are going to develop deep intimate relationships, we must be comfortable being seen. Arthur Aron and his colleagues suggest that increased intimacy leads to the psychological inclusion of the other within the self so that the boundaries of the self-extend to include the other's well-being and desirable and undesirable characteristics.(2)

As you read this chapter, I desire to help you and your partner recognize your relationship's potential for intimacy. I will help you accomplish this by exploring how to apply seven types of intimacy in your relationship. If used correctly, each form of intimacy will help you create a better relationship.

Note: I realize that for some of you reading this book the idea of working toward a more intimate relationship may be complicated right now. For example, if either of your commitment levels to your relationship is low, this chapter will be hard for you to read. This chapter may be difficult if one partner wants to reconnect and the other is not yet ready. If the partner who sexually acted outside of the relationship has not stopped their behavior, the ideas and exercises found throughout the chapter will not be effective. Also, if the betrayed partner is still experiencing elevated levels of trauma, I would suggest addressing the traumatic symptoms (e.g., nightmares, avoidance, negative self-beliefs, etc.) before trying to implement the practices found in this chapter.

A quick side Note: I debated whether I should leave this chapter in the book because some couples are not yet ready for a deeper level of intimacy. However, in the end, I decided that it wouldn't be right for me to write a book about rebuilding your relationship and avoid discussing the topic of intimacy. Each chapter in this book was carefully chosen and placed in a specific order. That's why I purposely decided to place the topic of intimacy as the final step in your healing journey. It is my belief that learning how to create an intimate bond after betrayal will be the more important step for your healing. We live far below our potential in our relationships. We can all be better. I promise that if you and your partner apply the principles discussed in this chapter, you will achieve deeper levels of intimacy.

Now, if you are ready to create deeper levels of intimacy, let's get started.

As you practice the intimate interactions described in this chapter, you will realize that you have more opportunities for true intimacy than you have previously considered.

I believe we are the creators of our connections. Every day we make decisions that influence the intimacy we experience. Our partners, our friends, and our family members are not responsible for the intimacy we create, but we are. Nobody can create intimacy for you. Herein lies your opportunity. Once you have established a safe environment, if you apply the principles that create intimacy described below, you can develop a beautiful intimate relationship.

Sadly, most couples live far below their intimacy potential. This does not have to be your relationship. If you have read this far, I know you long for a better relationship with your partner. I also know that you have experienced pain and heartache. Even with all of that, you are here. You are reading to learn more about how to improve your relationship. I hope you and your partner commit to the principles of intimacy discussed in this chapter because they are the engine that drives all human connection.

While I want to dive straight into the seven types of intimacy, it is important that we discuss the essential principles that allow us to create intimacy. If you strive to implement these principles, your potential for creating true intimacy will significantly improve. You will find that these principles listed below will go hand in hand with ideas shared in other chapters of this book.

Principles for Achieving Intimacy

1. Each of us must establish our own identity.

It is difficult to create intimacy when you do not know who you are or who you want to be. Therefore, understanding your identity is a crucial step to creating intimate relationships. At this point, you may be wondering about your identity.

Here are some questions for you to consider:

1. What kind of person do I want to be?
2. When other people think of me, I would like for them to see me as _____ type of person (List as many characteristics as possible).
3. What kind of partner do you want to be in your relationships?
4. If you have children, how would you like your children to describe you?
5. How do you want others to describe you?

6. If spirituality is important to you, how would you like your relationship with your Higher Power to be?

As you ponder these questions, I invite you to give serious consideration to each one. The more time you spend pondering your identity, the person you want to become will come into focus. Throughout my career, I have asked many people these questions. Unfortunately, many have not given them serious consideration. As you reflect on these questions, who will you become? Who will you be today? This week? This month? This year?

2. Becoming intimate with others requires us to develop a repertoire of relationship skills.

Have you ever been with a person who seems to make everyone around them feel good? If so, you have observed someone who has developed their relationship skills. We are not born with an inherent nature to be good in relationships. Learning how to listen, be kind, show compassion, express empathy, comfort others in need, and many other relationship skills are learned.

Consider these questions and reflect if you have learned these skills. Please circle the answer that best represents how you are doing in each area. At the bottom, you can add up your score from each column.

	Strongly Disagree	Disagree	Neither Agree Nor Disagree	Agree	Strongly Agree
A. My partner would say I am good at listening.	0	1	2	3	4
B. People who are close to me have told me that I am kind and caring.	0	1	2	3	4
C. I am comfortable being with others when they are suffering.	0	1	2	3	4

D. When others are having a difficult time, I can feel their pain.	0	1	2	3	4
E. I offer comfort to others when they are in need.	0	1	2	3	4
Total					

Now add up your scores. Lowers scores (0-10) indicate that you need significant improvement in these areas. Scores between (11-15) suggest a need for improvement. Finally, if you scored between (16-20), it will reflect a personal belief that your relationship skills in key areas are solid.

If you would like to improve your relationship skills, please remember that they are learned. What this means is that you can improve relationships with practice. You can increase empathy, you can increase your listening skills, and you can comfort others in need. If you are wondering how, I would suggest that you start by reviewing Chapter 5, which addresses the healing power of empathy and compassion. Then read books that will help you improve your skills in these areas (See recommended readings list in Appendix G).

Finally, if you believe that you do not have the ability to create better relationships, I invite you to have some compassion for yourself. Instead of accepting the internal narrative that you aren't good at relationships, you should determine to practice the skills described throughout this book. As you prepare through study and learning and then implement what you have learned, you will become better in your relationships.

3. Intimacy expands and deepens within marriage more than in any other relationship.

One of the benefits of a committed relationship is the level of intimacy two people can create. There is no other relationship that has the potential for good and bad in our lives. Throughout this book, we have discussed many of the difficulties that come from betrayal, so I won't belabor these challenges. However, if we explore the opportunity you and your partner must expand and deepen your bond, joy, and fulfillment can help your relationship to become strong.

Not long ago, I was pondering why marriage matters. While many today would say that marriage is outdated, I believe the opposite. Never before in the history of civilization has commitment between two people been more important. Our society is only as strong as our relationships. Therefore, when two people commit or recommit to their relationship, the underlying message that it gives becomes important to society. By expressing commitment to each other, couples are saying we matter. We will take care of each other; we will honor and support one another. It is in this context that intimacy expands and deepens.

Here's a short exercise to help you and your partner practice deepening your relationship.

Exercise: Take a few minutes (Up to 3 minutes) to write down your answer to these questions:

1. What was the best thing that happened to you today?

2. What was the hardest thing that happened to you today?

3. What is the most common thought and emotion you have felt today?

Once you and your partner have completed writing your answers, take turns reading your responses to each other. While your partner is reading, take mental notes, listen carefully, and express appreciation to them once they are done. Then switch roles. When you have both shared your answers, discuss with each other what you thought or felt while the other was sharing.

If you would like to deepen your relationship, make a habit of doing this exercise. After a few days and weeks, you will know more about each other than most couples.

Below are additional ways that marriage can deepen your bond unlike any other.

- In your relationship, you can create mutual goals (e.g., having children, traveling, etc.)

- Shared financial goals (e.g., planning for retirement together, purchasing a home)

- You are making a life-long commitment to each other (e.g., till death do us part)

- Shared responsibilities (e.g., sharing household responsibilities, chores, raising children)

- Shared values (e.g., aligning your desires for the future, working together to create something special)

- Deeper levels of intimacy (e.g., emotional, physical, sexual)

4. Enduring relationships are between whole people.

The fourth principle of intimacy is that strong and enduring relationships are between whole people. Generally, the word whole means complete, but in this context, complete means that we are people of integrity. When we are divided, we are not whole. Conversely, when we are whole people, what you see in public is the same behavior that you would see in private. When we become whole people, it doesn't mean we are perfect; instead, it means we do our very best to align our values and actions. My friend Ken Patey described it this way: When our values and actions are in harmony, we are WSIWYGs.

Computer people know the term "what you see is what you get."

One way to improve our ability to achieve deeper forms of intimacy is to become whole people. This is a journey and not an event. We all can make mistakes, but when we consistently choose to act consistent with our values, we become whole people.

If you want to measure your level of being whole, consider these questions:

1. Can I trust myself?

2. Do I do my best to act consistent with my values?

3. Do I do what I tell others I am going to do?

Now that we have discussed the principles that allow us to create intimate relationships, let's explore seven types of intimacies.

7 Types of Intimacy

Before we begin discussing how to implement seven types of intimacy in your relationship, I invite you to take a free relationship intimacy test. The assessment is designed to help you identify how you and your partner are doing in seven types of intimacy. When you complete the assessment, you will be given feedback on your level of intimacy in each of the seven categories of intimacy. You can find the *Relationship Intimacy Test* at https://bit.ly/RYR—Introduction for this book.

Verbal Intimacy

Verbal intimacy is a type of closeness that is based on your communication, including sharing thoughts and ideas with your partner. This type of intimacy is improved when you are honest and open in your communication. Verbal intimacy can be created in many of our relationships, but in intimate relationships, it can ignite deeper conversations that become emotionally intimate.

Verbal intimacy can be described as the practice of openly sharing thoughts and ideas with your partner and others. One-way verbal intimacy improves our relationship is that it helps us to know one another on a more profound level. If your partner knows what you are thinking, they do not need to guess. By improving your verbal intimacy skills, your partner will know more about you and your thoughts.

For example, if you say, "Today I was thinking about the kids and how I can be more involved in their life," your partner would know a few things about you. First, you were thinking about the children. Second, you want to be more involved in their life. This conversation could be enhanced even more if you add this, "I have been thinking I need to find a way to have a better relationship with them." This addition indicates that you want to improve your interactions with the children.

When you share your personal ideas and thoughts, you let your partner know more about you. This form of communication can improve your verbal intimacy and create a better environment in your relationship.

Example of a verbally intimate conversation:

Partner #1: I enjoyed spending time with you this evening.

Partner #2: Thanks! What did you like the most?

Partner #1: Our conversation. I appreciated you sharing what has been on your mind lately.

Partner #2: I also enjoyed hearing about what has been happening in your life. It's been a while since we talked this way.

Note: Notice the question, "What did you like the most?" A well-placed question was an invitation for their partner to share more. While it may seem like a simple question, it expresses an interest in what their partner liked about the evening. Also, Partner #1 gave a great opening, "I enjoyed spending time with you this evening." Again, this may seem simple, but it sends a message of appreciation. After this short conversation, how do you think the couple would feel about their relationship? My guess is both would feel connected.

Below are a few questions from the verbal intimacy section of the Relationship Intimacy Test.

1. My partner and I talk about random things (e.g., politics, world news, upcoming activities, anything).

2. If something good has happened to me, I share my exciting news with my partner.

3. I have a hard time talking with my partner about basic stuff.

4. I don't have much to talk with my partner about.

Since most of our communication in relationships is non-verbal, verbal intimacy has limitations. It may be that verbal intimacy is a building block for achieving a more intimate relationship. Let's explore the next form of intimacy.

Emotional Intimacy

Emotional intimacy is a type of closeness that goes beyond words. It encompasses an emotional connection and usually involves sharing core emotions (e.g., sadness, happiness, fear, anger, disgust, and surprise). When we create emotional intimacy in our relationships, you can expect trust, vulnerability, and safety to be present. Emotional intimacy often arises when two people feel comfortable expressing their deepest feelings or fears and when they openly share their experiences. When two people can genuinely share their joys and sorrows, they experience emotional intimacy. Couples who consistently experience emotional intimacy are more likely to feel a deeper connection with their partner.

If we were to compare verbal intimacy to emotional intimacy, the latter involves much deeper emotional connections. Furthermore, it is possible to have verbal intimacy without having emotional intimacy, but emotional intimacy is essential for building deeper connections in our relationship. If we observe a couple, emotional intimacy might sound like this:

Partner #1: I was feeling anxious today.

Partner #2: Would you like to talk about it?

Partner #1: Sure. On my way to the store today, I realized it has been exactly two years since I discovered your betrayal. Since then, I haven't been able to shake the feeling I felt.

Partner #2: Thanks for sharing what you have been experiencing with me. Do you mind sharing more of what you have been thinking about? I want to be here for you. I realize I made serious mistakes, and I know that these fears are going to come up. I'm here now and want to show you I am committed to you and our relationship.

Note: In this case, it is important to notice that Partner #1, the betrayed partner took a risk. They expressed that they were feeling anxious. This is a bid attempt for connection. Based on my clinical experience, there is a low probability that Partner #2 did well with such statements right after discovery. However, for Partner #1 to show such a vulnerability would be a good indicator that this partnership has grown since discovery. Partner #2's response, "Would you like to talk about it?" is a great response. It allows Partner #1 the opportunity to share and suggests that Partner #2 is open to listening to their partner.

Partner #1 is now feeling safe enough to share what happened. "…I realized it has been two years since I discovered your betrayal. I haven't been able to shake the feeling." Again, this is a vulnerable statement. Partner #2 then expresses appreciation to their partner for opening up and then invites their partner to share even more. However, they don't stop there; they become vulnerable too by saying, "I realize I made serious mistakes, and I know that these fears are going to come up." They conclude the statement by voicing their commitment to their partner.

In this case, both partners are taking risks. As they share their emotions, they will naturally form a deeper emotional bond.

Below are a few questions from the emotional intimacy section of the Relationship Intimacy Test.

1. I can share emotions with my partner without fear of being misunderstood.

2. I feel like I have to withhold my true feelings and emotions from my partner.

3. I struggle to be supportive of my partner when they are showing emotions (i.e., crying, sad)

Since most deep connections involve emotional intimacy, it is imperative that you learn how to express emotions and be present with others who are sharing their emotions. If you want to form a deep bond with your partner, I strongly recommend that you develop your emotional intimacy skills.

Cognitive/Intellectual Intimacy

When couples create cognitive/intellectual intimacy in their relationship, they enjoy sharing their thoughts and ideas with each other. They share what they learn or discover. If they have a problem, they will share their challenge with their partner. Couples who enjoy intellectually intimate conversations have stimulating conversations. As they try to solve a problem or analyze a play, or break down a basketball game, they create intimacy through their conversations. I have observed this form of intimacy stops as soon as the discovery of betrayal occurs. Instead of sharing their stimulating thoughts with each other, both partners become protective and reserved. However, as couples work through betrayal, I have observed that they begin discussing their ideas with one another again. I remember one couple, in particular, made significant progress when they decided to renew sharing their dreams and goals with each other. They reported that it was refreshing to look at their future together.

Here are a few examples of how cognitive/intellectual intimacy can be shared:

- Reading a book together
- Enjoying a TV series together
- Watch a movie and discuss the characters. What did you like or dislike?
- Working on a house project (i.e., painting, improving the backyard)
- Discussing a current-day topic (i.e., politics, the economy)
- Doing research together (i.e., what is the best way to grow a garden)
- Setting financial goals together
- Creating a couple's bucket list of things you would like to do together
- Setting a goal for health and fitness together (i.e., run a 5K together, lift weights)
- Play a challenging game together (i.e., go to an escape room)

Below are a few questions from the cognitive/intellectual intimacy section of the Relationship Intimacy Test.

1. My partner and I can have stimulating conversations with each other.
2. I don't have a lot in common with my partner
3. We share common goals in our relationship

Spiritual Intimacy

Spiritual intimacy refers to the closeness between individuals who share similar beliefs and values related to spirituality, faith, or religion. It is the bond between two people grounded in the recognition of a spiritual presence or values. This sense of shared meaning or purpose may come from organized religion, personal spirituality, or a shared belief system. Spiritual intimacy often involves engaging in activities or practices that foster a connection to a higher power, such as prayer, meditation, or worship services. This type of intimacy can provide a sense of comfort, meaning, and purpose to your relationship.

Here are a few suggestions that you and your partner can use to increase the spiritual intimacy in your relationship:

- Spend time in nature together.

- Pray with each other.

- Pray for each other.

- Attend religious services together and discuss what you have learned and felt.

- Read holy writ with each other.

- Meditate together.

- Ponder on the uniqueness of your partner and who they really are.

Below are a few questions from the spiritual intimacy section of the Relationship Intimacy Test.

1. My partner and I have similar beliefs about how to practice religion.

2. I have had spiritual experiences that I cannot share with my partner because they wouldn't understand.

3. I feel a spiritual connection with my partner.

Creative Intimacy

When couples have creative intimacy in their relationship, they enjoy sharing their dreams and passions with each other. They literally share their creative self with one another and get excited to share a new business idea with their partner. For instance, when they get an idea to remodel a room in the house, they instantly share it with their partner. The power of creative intimacy comes when you allow yourself to dream with your partner. Let's travel the world. Let's build a chicken coop and raise chickens. Or how about we take a dance class together and learn to swing dance? You get the idea? Creative intimacy happens when you feel safe enough to share your creative self with your partner. It is beautiful to watch as couples plan a trip, design a new kitchen, or share a new dish with their partner.

A common sign I look for when I see couples healing is that they resume sharing their passions with each other. If you would like to improve your creative intimacy with your partner, here's a quick exercise to help you get started.

Exercise: Here are a few ways you can improve in the area of creative intimacy:

1. Write down three of your aspirations and share them with your spouse.

2. Create a list of things you would like to do together, and rank order them. Then create a plan for doing each of the things on your list. If you do at least one activity a week, it can improve your relationship.

3. As you participate in an activity together, take time to be creative. For example, if you and your partner choose to visit a flea market together, set a goal about how much money you are going to spend and see if you can barter to get the best deal.

4. Set a goal to do an activity together and work together to support each other in reaching the goal.

Below is a list of ideas that some couples have used to improve the level of creative intimacy in their relationship.

- Do a remodeling project together.
- Share something that you are excited about with your partner.
- Tell your partner about something you want to create.
- Make a list of fun things you would like to do together—let the creative juices flow.
- Learn a new skill together (dancing, pottery, etc.).
- Share something you are creating with your partner (i.e., art, music, talent, or skill).

Below are a few questions from the creative intimacy section of the Relationship Intimacy Test.

1. I am comfortable sharing what I am passionate about with my partner.

2. I can share my dreams with my partner.

3. My partner and I are comfortable working on projects together.

Physical/Sexual Intimacy

I'm not sure if there is another type of intimacy that suffers more after betrayal than physical intimacy. After betrayal, betrayed partners frequently struggle with any form of touch. I have had many people ask their partners to stop touching them. In addition, it is common for betrayed partners to have body image issues. As a result, many have feelings of being sexually inadequate or not enough for their partner. Another common challenge betrayed partners face after discovering betrayal is their thoughts during intimacy. My research shows that betrayed partners often worry about what their partner is thinking while they are being sexual together. Overcoming the consequences after betrayal requires significant effort by both partners and should not be taken lightly.

While some believe that healing from betrayal is an individual journey, reclaiming physical intimacy requires two people committed to finding a connection in this area. The betraying partner plays a significant role in this process. For example, a deeper connection will not be formed if the following actions occur:

- Continued relapses.

- Pre-maturely pushing for physical intimacy before the betrayed partner is ready.

- Blaming your partner for your sexual behaviors outside of the relationship.

- Being insensitive to your partner's sexuality.

- Making physical intimacy about you and your needs.

As you eliminate these issues and strive to improve in the other levels of intimacy described above, you will gradually feel more comfortable with your sexual interactions. I firmly believe that reclaiming your sexual relationship is possible and important. However, at this point, it becomes equally critical to understand physical intimacy in a new way. Let me explain what I mean.

When most people think of relationship intimacy, sex is what comes to their minds. However, I believe that physical intimacy is so much more than just sex. Physical intimacy is an integral part of a healthy relationship. It can create a deep sense of connection, trust, and pleasure between partners. Always remember, physical intimacy is never about satisfying your sexual needs only. There are several ways through which physical intimacy can improve your relationship both emotionally and physically.

Here are a few of the benefits of physical intimacy:

- *Reduces stress and improves overall health*—A hug, a kiss, a hand or foot massage, or even sex can release endorphins, which reduces stress and anxiety levels. In addition, physical intimacy has physical health benefits as well. It can lower blood pressure, increase immunity, and even reduce the risk of heart disease.

- *Builds trust and communication*—When two people are attuned to each other, physical intimacy opens doors to communication. It forces partners to voice their desires and needs, hence creating a space for open and honest communication. By expressing your wants and needs and listening to your partner's desires, you are being vulnerable with each other. This is a form of effective communication.

- *Enhance your emotional connection*—Physical intimacy provides an opportunity to experience pleasure and gives a boost of endorphins. Healthy touch boosts our happy hormones and can help partners feel happier and closer to each other.

- *Creates a bond between partners*—Engaging in physical intimacy often is a great way to reinforce the bond and express your commitment to each other. The act of touching, holding, and cuddling generates non-verbal communication and creates the potential for other forms of intimacy (i.e., verbal, emotional, and intellectual). It is these moments that help couples heal and recommit to each other.

Here are a few suggestions that you and your partner can use to increase the physical intimacy in your relationship:

- Hold hands when you are in public while watching a movie or when you are in close proximity to each other.

- When you have been away from each other for a few hours, give a hug to your partner for at least 12 seconds. Feel the embrace in a non-sexual way. Enjoy your partner's presence during the hug.

- Give each other a foot or hand massage.

- Touch each other in non-sexual ways during the day (i.e., a quick touch on the shoulder, a touch on the arm, a kiss, rubbing your noses together while looking into each other's eyes).

As you intentionally improve the other forms of intimacy, the physical intimacy in your relationship can improve as well. However, you will need to be patient with the process as you rebuild trust in your relationship.

Below are a few questions from the physical intimacy section of the Relationship Intimacy Test.

1. I enjoy holding, cuddling, and kissing my partner.

2. I am satisfied with the level of touch we have in our relationship.

3. In our relationship, my partner takes time to meet my sexual needs.

4. I am able to relax and enjoy sex with my partner.

5. I feel a strong connection with my partner when we are being sexual.

Psychological Intimacy

I will conclude our discussion on this topic by introducing the most important type of intimacy. I have never heard other professionals use the term psychological intimacy. It is a concept that I have created to explain to individuals who are dating, are in a relationship, or couples who are striving to improve their relationship. For many years, I did my best to describe a type of intimacy that was easy to explain but wasn't in any textbooks that I had read. The people I taught understood this concept and it helped them comprehend some of their struggles in their relationships. It also helped single people identify what to look for in healthy relationships.

The concept is this, the deepest forms of intimacy are built upon four parts:

- Trust
- Honesty
- Loyalty
- Commitment.

In our relationships, these four components are developed over time. However, the outcome is always negative when they are missing from our relationships. Conversely, when they are present, our minds relax because we have determined that we are safe. Therefore, if we want to improve in all areas of intimacy outlined above, we should focus on improving psychological intimacy in our interactions. If we do so, we can actively pursue more profound levels of intimacy in the other categories.

Let's explore how each of them can improve your relationship after betrayal.

Trust—Many betrayed partners lose confidence in their partners. In some cases, both partners lose faith in each other. In order to re-establish trust, betraying partners have to become people of integrity. They have to keep their commitments to their partners. Additional ways through which they can increase trust include:

- Preparing and doing a disclosure
- Completing an emotional restitution letter
- Increasing accountability around their sexual acts (some people reach out to a sponsor, religious leader, or group for support)
- Participate in regular emotional check-ins with their spouse (see FANOS discussion from Chapter 14)
- Striving to be emotionally open

Honesty—When couples heal, rigorous honesty is one of the most important practices that re-establishes trust. While we have already discussed the importance of honesty in Chapter Ten, I believe it is important to emphasize the healing power of honesty in the healing process. When couples are completely truthful and transparent in all their interactions and communications, even when it gets uncomfortable, difficult, or inconvenient, they develop trust in each other. Perhaps this is why the disclosure process is so helpful.

When you apply rigorous honesty to your communication, you become a person who is comfortable being completely open regarding your thoughts, feelings, and actions. By doing this, you avoid any form of deception or dishonesty, however minor or well-intentioned it may be. If you are going to develop psychological intimacy, this form of authenticity can heal your relationships. It should also be noted that most recovery programs emphasize the importance of rigorous honesty. Rigorous honesty requires courage, vulnerability, and integrity, which later transforms into a healing relationship.

Loyalty—An oft-overlooked but important element of healthy relationships is loyalty. After going through betrayal, the idea of being loyal to your partner can appear far-fetched. However, I have observed that as trust and honesty increase, so does loyalty. When you think of being loyal to your partner, what comes to your mind?

Here's how I would define loyalty when applied to relationships. Loyalty means being faithful and committed to the relationship and staying true to your agreement to work on and grow the relationship together. In difficult times, being loyal requires actively choosing to stay committed to the relationship and working together as a team to overcome challenges. Overall, loyalty involves being dedicated to the well-being and happiness of your partner and the relationship and always acting in their best interest.

I understand that some of you reading this book may think, "Wait, are you expecting me to stay committed to my partner even though they cheated on me?" My answer is… it depends. Yes, if your partner is doing absolutely everything they can to repair and make amends for their behaviors AND you have the desire to try. No, if there is no commitment to overcoming or stopping their unwanted sexual behaviors.

Please notice key words from the definition above:

- Staying true to your commitment.
- Grow the relationship together.
- Working together as a team to overcome challenges.

- Being dedicated to the well-being and happiness of your partner.

If, moving forward, both you and your partner commit to living by the principle of loyalty in your relationship, healing will surely be accelerated. Imagine committing to your partner by being true, showing through your actions that you want to grow together, working together to overcome obstacles, and focusing on your partner's well-being and happiness. This is how you mend a broken relationship. If you choose to do these things, your relationship will heal. Here's a short exercise to help you improve your dialogue around the topic of loyalty.

Exercise: Begin this exercise by reviewing the four bullet points above (e.g., staying true to your commitment). Take a few minutes to write down how you will show your loyalty by doing each of the four behaviors. Once you have finished writing your response, review your list and ask yourself this question, "Am I ready to commit and do the things I have written down? Give yourself a score between 0 (Not ready) and 7 (I am ready). If your scores are low, something is holding you back and needs to be discussed (remember the Zeigarnik effect). If your scores are high, let's say a six or seven, you are ready to discuss your answers with your partner. If your scores are lower than a six, I would encourage you to pause and reflect on why they are so low. What needs to be resolved for you to show loyalty to your partner?

Note: If you are the betrayed partner, your loyalty has been shaken by your partner's betrayal. Often betrayed partner's loyalty in a relationship is dependent upon their partner showing a commitment to loyalty. Betraying partners, if you expect your partner to be loyal to you before your actions are in alignment with being loyal yourself, be careful, as your expectations are unrealistic. As your demonstration of loyalty increases, your partner's desire to be loyal or stay committed can increase as well.

Finally, if you are the betrayed partner and your desire to repair the relationship is low, you should honestly confess this to your partner. If they are doing everything that they can to repair the relationship, and you reject their attempts, the best thing you can do is let them know that you no longer desire this relationship. In other words, you are no longer committed to the relationship.

Commitment—The fourth element of psychological intimacy is commitment. After sexual betrayal, both partners must re-evaluate their commitment to the relationship. This evaluation should not be taken lightly as it has significant long-term consequences. It is also important to consider how you will show commitment to your relationship.

Besides being faithful, your commitment can be demonstrated in many ways. Here are a few ways to show your commitment to your partner:

- Be present and actively engage in the relationship. This means investing time and effort into the relationship.

- Be dependable, and follow through on your promises, no matter how small they are.

- Be supportive of your partner's goals and dreams, and work together to achieve them.

- Increase your communication with your partner. When you talk about your thoughts and feelings with your partner (e.g., I was thinking or I had an idea), you are letting them into your mind. This allows them to see into your thoughts. Furthermore, it can be a way of showing your commitment to your partner.

- Express your appreciation and gratitude for the good things that your partner does. Acknowledge their efforts and celebrate milestones and accomplishments together. I have observed a couple doing this on their one-year anniversary of the discovery. They decided to focus on what they had learned during that year. Instead of reliving the pain and hurt, they both wrote down what they had learned about themselves and their relationship. Then they read to each other what they had written.

Healing increases as you and your partner apply the four elements of psychological intimacy in your relationship. Conversely, if you cannot incorporate these essential parts into your day-to-day living, the odds of your fighting and arguing are high. Furthermore, it will make healing and recovery almost impossible. If I were to prioritize actions to heal your relationship, I would focus on being rigorously honest, truthful in your interactions, completely loyal, and totally committed. When these four elements are implemented in a relationship, every other form of intimacy described above becomes possible.

Here are three ways to assess and improve your current level of intimacy:

- Go to https://www.bit.ly/RYR (Chapter 15). If you have been following the support material, you may have already completed the *Relationship Intimacy Test (RIT)* and received additional feedback on how to improve your relationship. I would invite you to take it again as you approach the end of this book. If you haven't taken the RIT, I would invite you to do so now.

- Complete the assignment "Evaluate 7 Types of Intimacy in Your Relationship," as found in Chapter 15 support material.

- In an advanced course on Relationship Intimacy, I offer additional support for couples who are seeking extra guidance. The course is titled, 7 Principles to Rebuild Your Relationship after Sexual Betrayal. You can learn more at https://www.humanintimacy.com/course/7-principles-ryr

Intimate Interactions, Intimate Relationships, and Intimate Experiences

Have you ever heard these two words together: Intimate interactions?

In 1981, Robert Hinde wrote an interesting article about intimacy. In the article, he asked if it was possible to measure intimacy. He suggested that one way to explore intimacy in relationships is to evaluate the number of intimate interactions couples share. (3)

Intimate interactions are communicative exchanges between people. In line with the etymological origins of the word *intimacy*, most definitions of intimate interaction converge on a notion of sharing the personal (i.e., innermost, private) aspects of the self. Such interactions can be verbal or non-verbal expressions. Below I provide an example and a suggestion on how you can create an intimate interaction (both verbally and non-verbally):

- Verbal sharing can involve self-disclosure of personal facts, opinions, and beliefs and the verbalization of feelings and emotions.

  ◊ Share personal facts about yourself.

  ◊ Share your opinion.

  ◊ Share one of your beliefs.

  ◊ Share an emotion.

  ◊ Share something you are feeling.

- Nonverbal sharing can include a shared meaningful glance, a smile or wink, affectionate touching, or shared expressions of emotion such as tears or laughter. Creating these interactions means sharing vulnerable aspects of the self with your partner.

  ◊ Smile or wink at your partner.

  ◊ With your partner's consent, embrace or hug for 12 seconds.

  ◊ Listen to something that makes you and your partner laugh.

  ◊ Cuddle without words; just feel your bodies together.

◊   Make and hold eye contact while you smile at each other.

As you and your partner engage in intimate interactions, you naturally develop a more intimate relationship.

- Intimate relationships are built upon intimate interactions.
- Let me say that again.
- Intimate relationships are built upon intimate interactions.
- One more time…
- Intimate relationships are built upon intimate interactions.

10 Additional Ideas for Increasing Intimate Interactions with Your Partner:

- Share personal experiences or feelings you have been having.
- Share ideas or things you hope to accomplish.
- Leave a note for your partner expressing appreciation for them.
- Make eye contact and hold it for an extended period of time.
- Spend quality time with each other in an intimate setting (e.g., looking at a sunset).
- Hold your partner's hand.
- Kiss for more than three seconds.
- Give each other a massage (i.e., foot, hand, or body).
- Unexpectedly give a gift to your partner.
- Display acts of kindness (e.g., do a household chore that your partner normally does).

Additional Strategies You Can Use to Improve Intimacy in Your Relationship

To improve your intimacy, you can:

- Prioritize open and honest communication, ensuring that you listen actively and empathetically to your partner while clearly expressing your needs, desires, and boundaries.

- Cultivate a judgment-free zone, offering support and encouragement for your partner in your unique way.

- Invest time and effort into nurturing the relationship, regularly engage in shared experiences to build memories, and foster a sense of unity.

- Remain open to vulnerability while giving yourself and your partner space for growth and personal development.

- If you have offended your partner, seek forgiveness. Try to understand your partner by acknowledging their struggles. Recognize that we are all imperfect and may hurt or disappoint each other. However, if you desire to repair your relationship, both partners need to express their commitment to healing and moving forward.

Creating intimacy in relationships is a continuous process. We cannot put our relationship connection on autopilot without experiencing problems. If the deepest desire of our hearts is to achieve true human intimacy, we should exert our most exceptional effort.

Love is a choice; make it every day.

Making Love

If there were two words that I had the power to change the meaning of in the English language, they would be "making love." While most people think of making love as sex, I wish we could see these words as how we treat and interact with each other. I like the way Barbara Fredrickson described love in her book, *Love 2.0*, "Love is that micro-moment of warmth and connection that you share with another living being." (4) The idea of love being a creation feels more real to me. If we look at love as something we create, then we can identify times we were being loving and times we were not.

When a person is acting unkind or sexually acting out, they are not making love. In fact, their actions are not loving at all. In contrast, if I have hurt you and I desire to make amends for my actions, I can choose to be with you as you express your hurt and pain. At that moment, when you sit with your partner in their pain and suffering, you are making love.

In this way of looking at love, it would be fair to say that love can be very fleeting. One minute I may be loving, and the next, I may be unloving. Barbara Fredrickson described the up and downs of love this way, "Love, as you'll see, is not lasting. It's actually far more fleeting than most of us would care to acknowledge.

On the upside, though, love is forever renewable. And perhaps most challenging of all, love is not unconditional. It doesn't emerge no matter what, regardless of conditions. On the contrary, you'll see that the love your body craves is exquisitely sensitive to contextual cues. It obeys preconditions. Yet once you understand those preconditions, you can find love countless times each day." (5)

Unfortunately, our society and our families have not been successful at teaching us how to love on a deeper level. As a result, many of us have had to learn how to make true love on our own. Some people have told me they have learned this from their grandparents, neighbors, friends, teachers, and religious leaders. Regardless of where we learn, if we want love in our lives, we have to develop our relationship skills. Only through learning and practicing the art of making love do we reach our potential as loving people.

There are no limits to how loving we can be. We can be loving and still create boundaries with people who hurt us. We can show love for our partners when they are angry. Every day, we choose how loving we will be, especially in difficult moments. You can choose to respond with kindness and compassion. We all have a choice regarding how loving we will be.

On a personal level, I am trying to make love every day because that is the type of person I want to be, and I hope you will join me in my effort to be a loving person each and every day. If you do, together, we will make the world a better place because we are making true love.

Key Takeaways from This Chapter

- Intimacy is when we allow others to see into us. We open up and become vulnerable because we long to be seen, heard, and felt. We all have a natural desire for a deep intimate bond.

- There are four principles that, if applied right, can help us achieve a deeper level of intimacy in our relationship. These four principles are: 1) We need to have our own identity; 2) We need to develop and practice using relationship skills; 3) In our most committed relationship, precisely marriage, our love can expand and deepen in ways that it can't in other relationships; and 4) when we are whole, we are more capable of achieving a deep bond with our partner.

- By implementing seven types of intimacy, our relationships can heal. The foundation of all human intimacy is safety which comes when we create psychological intimacy. Other forms of intimacy (verbal, emotional, intellectual, spiritual, creative, and physical) take their cue from psychological intimacy. Our level of relationship intimacy expands when we strive to improve in each area of intimacy.

- A great way to improve intimacy in our relationships is to increase the number of intimate interactions we have with one another.

- Love is a choice. Make it every day.

Thank You!

As we reach the end, I want you to know that I have thought a lot about you. I have tried to be sensitive to the challenges that betrayal creates. I have also kept in mind what it is like for the betraying partner to stop their sexual behaviors while simultaneously attempting to repair their relationship. Please know that I understand this journey is not easy. In each chapter, I have provided exercises in the form of a writing assignment or assessment. I have created many free resources and supplemental material for this book which can be found at https://www.bit.ly/RYR

In conclusion, I invite you to review the concepts discussed in this book. You may need to read and re-read some chapters until they become a part of the way you think and feel. Change is not easy; it will require significant effort. You may struggle and make mistakes, but please keep trying. It will be worth your time and effort and will turn you into a better person. As you move forward, you will see how this has improved your relationship. I wish you the best in your healing and recovery journey.

Thank you so much for letting me be a part of your experience. May you be blessed as a couple as you strive to rebuild your relationship. As the author of this book, I sincerely hope you have found insight and guidance on building a better, more sustainable relationship.

Remember, you can make love every day! It is a choice.

Best regards
Dr. Kevin Skinner

References

Introduction:

1. Barbara, A. Steffans & Robyn, L. Rennie (2006). *The Traumatic Nature of Disclosure for Wives of Sexual Addicts,* Sexual Addiction & Compulsivity, 13:2-3, 247-267, DOI 10.1080/10720016060870802

2. Skinner, K. B., (2022). Findings from Trauma Inventory for Partner's of Sex Addicts (TIPSA). Unpublished Results (See Chapter One Support Material for Results)

Chapter One:

1. Ogden, P., Pain, C., & Minton, K. (2014). Trauma and the body: A sensorimotor approach to psychotherapy. Nota.

2. Ibid

3. D. J. Siegel, The Mindful Therapist: A Clinician's Guide to Mindsight and Neural Integration (New York: WW Norton, 2010).

4. J. E. LeDoux, "Emotion Circuits in the Brain," Annual Review of Neuroscience 23, no. 1 (2000): 155–84.

5. Kabat-Zinn, J. (2013). Full catastrophe living: Using the wisdom of your body and mind to face stress, pain, and illness. Bantam Books Trade Paperbacks.

6. Skinner, K. B., (2022). Findings from Trauma Inventory for Partner's of Sex Addicts (TIPSA). Unpublished Results (See Chapter One Support Material for Results)

7. Gottman, J. M. (2011). *The Science of Trust: Emotional Attunement for couples.* W.W. Norton.

8. Ibid

9. Zeigarnik, B. (1984). Kurt Lewing and Soviet Psychology. Journal of Social Issues, 40, 181-192)

Chapter Three:

1. Porges, S. W. (2011). Polyvagal theory: Neurophysiological foundations of emotions, attachment, communication, and self-regulation / Stephen W. Porges.

2. Dispenza, J. (2018). Breaking the habit of being yourself: How to lose your mind and create a new one. Hay House.

3. Ibid

4. Retrieved from: https://financialpost.com/entrepreneur/three-techniques-to-manage-40000-negative-thoughts

5. J. C. Coyne and A. DeLongis, "Going Beyond Social Support: The Role of Social Relationships in Adaptation," Journal of Consulting and Clinical Psychology 54, no. 4 (August 1986): 454–60, cited in T. E. Robles and J. K. Kiecolt-Glaser, "The Physiology of Marriage: Pathways to Health," Physiology and Behavior 79, no. 3 (August 2003): 409–16.

6. Skinner, K. B., (2023) Unpublished Data from source Sexual Betrayal and Your Relationship (V.2.4)

7. Skinner, K. B.,(2023) Unpublished Data from Assessing Pornography Addiction.

8. Retrieved from: https://www.tennessean.com/story/money/2015/01/23/buffalo-face-lifes-storms/22187351/

9. Ibid

10. Tangney, J. P., &; Dearing, R. L. (2004). Shame and guilt. Guilford Press.

11. Ibid

12. DeYoung, P. A. (2015). Understanding and treating chronic shame a relational/neurobiological approach. Routledge.

13. Wallace, A. C. (1997). Setting Psychological Boundaries: A Handbook for Women, pg. 6. Bergin & Garvey

14. Skinner, K. B., (2023) Unpublished Data from Sexual Betrayal and Your Relationship (V.2.4)

15. Porges, S. W. (2011). Polyvagal theory: Neurophysiological foundations of emotions, attachment, communication, and self-regulation / Stephen W. Porges.

16. Skinner, K. B., (2023). Unpublished Data from Sexual Betrayal and Your Relationship (V.2.4)

17. Porges, S. W. (2011). Polyvagal theory: Neurophysiological foundations of emotions, attachment, communication, and self-regulation / Stephen W. Porges.

18. Ibid

19. Ibid

20. Porges, S. W. (2021). Polyvagal safety. WW Norton.

21. A., V. der K. B. (2015). The body keeps the score: Mind, brain and body in the transformation of trauma. Penguin Books.

22. Dana, D., & Porges, S. W., (2018). The polyvagal theory in therapy: Engaging the rhythm of regulation. W.W. Norton et Company.

23. Ibid

24. Ibid

25. Retrieved from: https://www.forbes.com/sites/christinecomaford/2012/04/04/got-inner-peace-5-ways-to-get-it-now/?sh=6de4ae166727

26. Neff, K. (2011). Self-compassion: Stop beating yourself up and leave insecurity behind. Hodder & Stoughton.

27. Hill, D. (2015). Affect regulation theory: A clinical model. W.W. Norton et Company.

28. A., V. der K. B. (2015). The body keeps the score: Mind, brain and body in the transformation of trauma. Penguin Books.

29. Ibid

30. Ibid

31. Retrieved from: http://www.metalearn.net/articles/the-question-is-the-answer-part-2-why-we-stop-asking-questions-and-how-to-start-again

32. Wilkes, P. (2012). The Art of Confession: Renewing Yourself through the practice of Honesty. Workman Pub. Co.

33. 33. Retrieved from: https://dearpeggy.com/results.html

34. Ibid

35. Corley, M. D., & Schneider, J. P. (2012). Disclosing secrets: An addicts' guide for when, to whom, and how much to reveal. Tucson, AZ: Recovery Resource Press.

36. Lembke, A. (2021). Dopamine nation: Finding balance in the age of indulgence. Dutton, an imprint of Penguin Random House LLC.

37. Ibid

38. Vaughn, P. (2010). *Help for Therapists (and their clients) in dealing with affairs.* Dialog Press.

Chapter Four:

1. Kaufman, G. (1992). Shame: The power of caring. Schenkman Books, Inc.

2. Barbara A. Steffens & Robyn L. Rennie (2006) The Traumatic Nature of Disclosure for Wives of Sexual Addicts, Sexual Addiction & Compulsivity, 13:2-3, 247-267, DOI: 10.1080/10720160600870802

3. DeYoung, P. A. (2022). Understanding and treating chronic shame: Healing right brain relational trauma. Routledge.

4. Ibid

5. Hawkins, D. R. (2014). Power vs. force: The hidden determinants of human behavior. Hay House.

6. Ibid

7. Hughes, D. A. (2011). Attachment-focused family therapy. W.W. Norton

8. Ibid

9. Hughes, D. A. (2011). Attachment-focused family therapy. W.W. Norton.

10. Tangney, J. P., &; Dearing, R. L. (2004). Shame and guilt. Guilford Press.

11. Statement Wikimedia Foundation Powered by MediaWiki

12. Skinner, K.B., (2023) Sexual Betrayal and Your Relationship (V2.4). Unpublished Data from Survey Monkey

13. Porges, S. W. (2021). *Polyvagal safety.* WW Norton.

14. Tangney, J. P., &; Dearing, R. L. (2004). Shame and guilt. Guilford Press.

15. Skinner, K. B., (2020). Treating sexual addiction: A compassionate approach to recovery. KSkinner Corp.

16. Burns, D. (2020). *Feeling great: The revolutionary new treatment for depression and anxiety.* Pesi Publishing Media.

17. Retrieved from: https://www.merriam-webster.com/dictionary/gaslighting

18. Decety, J., & Ickes, W. J. (Eds.). (2009). The social neuroscience of empathy. Cambridge, MA: MIT Press.

19. Tracy, Jessica; Robins, Richard (2007). "Self-conscious emotions: Where self and emotion meet." In Sedikides, C. (ed.). Frontiers of social psychology. The self. Psychology Press. pp. 187–209.

Chapter Five:

1. The Dalai Lama (1995). The Power of Compassion. London: Thorsons; and The Dalai Lama (2001)

2. An Open Heart: Practising Compassion in Everyday Life (ed. N. Vreeland). London: Hodder & Stoughton. See also Geshe Tashi Tsering (2008)

3. The Awakening Mind: The Foundation of Buddhist Thought: Volume 4. London: Wisdom Press.

4. Germer, C. K. (2014). The mindful path to self-compassion: Freeing yourself from destructive thoughts and emotions. Nota.

5. Porges, S. W. (2021). Polyvagal safety: Attachment, communication, self-regulation. W.W. Norton & Company.

6. Gilbert, P., &; Choden. (2015). Mindful compassion. Robinson.

7. Neff, Kristin D., Self-Compassion: The Proven Power of Being Kind to Yourself. Harper Collins, 2011.

8. Ibid

9. Retrieved from: http://ccare.stanford.cdu/uncatcgorizcd/the-scientific-benefits-of-self-compassion-infographic/

10. Neff, Kristin D., Self-Compassion: Stop Beating Yourself Up and Leave Insecurity Behind. William Morrow

11. Retrieved from: http://ccare.stanford.edu/uncategorized/the-scientific-benefits-of-self-compassion-infographic/

12. Porges, S. W. (2021). Polyvagal safety: Attachment, communication, self-regulation. W.W. Norton & Company.

13. HANH, Thich Nhat, (2023). True love: A practice for awakening the heart. SHAMBHALA.

14. Ibid

15. Salzberg, Sharon (1995). Loving-Kindness: The Revolutionary Art of Happiness. Shambhala Publications. p. 119. ISBN 9781570629037.

16. Retrieved from: https://www.audible.com/pd/Mindfulness-and-the-Brain-Audiobook/B007XVNQ8W?action_code=ASSGB149080119000H&share_location=pdp

Chapter Six:

1. Barbara A. Steffens & Robyn L. Rennie (2006). The Traumatic Nature of Disclosure for Wives of Sexual Addicts, Sexual Addiction & Compulsivity, 13:2-3, 247-267, DOI: 10.1080/10720160600870802

2. Skinner, K.B., (2023). Sexual Betrayal and Your Relationship (V2.4). Unpublished Data from Survey Monkey

3. American Psychiatric Publishing. (2013). Diagnostic and statistical manual of mental disorders.

4. Skinner, K.B., (2023) Sexual Betrayal and Your Relationship (V2.4). Unpublished Data from Survey Monkey

5. Ibid

6. Ibid

7. Baumeister, R. F., &; Tierney, J. (2012). Willpower: Rediscovering the greatest human strength. Penguin Books.

8. Vogeler HA, Fischer L, et al (2020).*Assessing the Validity of the Trauma Inventory for Partners of Sex Addicts (TIPSA)*.Sexual Addiction & Compulsivity.doi.org/10.1080/10720162.2020.1772158

Chapter Seven:

1. Vaughan, P. (2010). Help for Therapists (and their clients) in dealing with affairs. Dialog Press.

2. Collins, J., &; Lazier, W. C. (2020). Be 2.0 turning your business into an enduring Great Company. Penguin/Portfolio.

3. Ibid

4. Ibid

5. Harris, N. B. (2020). The deepest well. Pan Macmillan.

6. A., V. der K. B. (2015). The body keeps the score: Mind, brain and body in the transformation of trauma. Penguin Books.

7. Ratey, J. J. (2008). Spark: The revolutionary new science of exercise and the brain. Little, Brown Spark.

8. Germer, C. K. (2014). *The mindful path to self-compassion: Freeing yourself from destructive thoughts and emotions.* Nota.

9. Vanzant, I. (2015). *Trust: Mastering the 4 essential trusts: Trust in god, trust in yourself, trust in others, trust in life.* Smiley Books.

10. Cloud, H., &; Townsend, D. J. (2000). Boundaries in marriage. Zondervan Pub.

11. Wallace, A. C. (1997). Setting psychological boundaries: A handbook for women. Bergin &; Garvey.

12. Ferrini, P. (1996). The silence of the heart. Heartways Press.

13. Vanzant, I. (2015). *Trust: Mastering the 4 essential trusts: Trust in god, trust in yourself, trust in others, trust in life.* Smiley Books.

14. Goyal M, Singh S, Sibinga EMS, et al. Meditation Programs for Psychological Stress and Well-being: A Systematic Review and Meta-analysis. JAMA Intern Med. 2014;174(3):357–368. doi:10.1001/jamainternmed.2013.13018

15. Slomski A. Mindfulness Noninferior to Medication for Quelling Anxiety. JAMA. 2023;329(1):12. doi:10.1001/jama.2022.23506

16. Polusny MA, Erbes CR, Thuras P, et al. Mindfulness-Based Stress Reduction for Posttraumatic Stress Disorder Among Veterans: A Randomized Clinical Trial. JAMA. 2015;314(5):456–465. doi:10.1001/jama.2015.8361

17. Retrieved from: https://www.hcalth.harvard.edu/staying-healthy/yoga-for-better-mental-health

18. Ibid

19. Siebert, A. (2011). Resiliency advantage: Master change, thrive under pressure, and bounce back from setbacks. Readhowyouwant.com Ltd.

20. Ghodsbin F., Ahmadi Z. S., Jahanbin I., Sharif F. The effects of laughter ther-apy on general health of elderly people referring to jahandidegan community center in Shiraz, Iran, 2014: a randomized controlled trial. International Jour-nal of Community Based Nursing and Midwifery. 2015;3(1):p. 31.

21. Bennett P. N., Parsons T., Ben-Moshe R., et al. Laughter and humor therapy in dialysis. Seminars in Dialysis. 2014;27(5):488–493. doi: 10.1111/sdi.12194.

22. Bennett M. P., Lengacher C. A. Humor and laughter may influence health. I. History and background. Evidence-based Complementary and Alternative Medicine. 2006;3(1):61–63. doi: 10.1093/ecam/nek015

23. Bennett M. P., Lengacher C. Humor and laughter may influence health: II. Complementary therapies and humor in a clinical population. Evidence-Based Complementary and Alternative Medicine. 2006;3(2):187–190. doi: 10.1093/ecam/nel014.

24. Myers's, S. M., & Booth, A. (1999). Marital Strains and Marital Quality: The Role of High and Low Locus of Control. Journal of Marriage and Family Vol. 61, No. 2 (May, 1999), pp. 423-436. DOI: 10.2307/353759

25. Ibid

26. Voss, C. (2016). Never split the difference. Penguin.

27. Retrieved from: https://www.scientificamerican.com/article/proper-breathing-brings-better-health/

28. Retrieved from: https://my.clevelandclinic.org/health/articles/9445-diaphrag-matic-breathing

Chapter Eight:

1. Barkley, R. A., M. Fischer, et al. (2006). "Young adult outcome of hyperactive children: adaptive functioning in major life activities." J Am Acad Child Ado-lesc Psychiatry 45(2): 192-202.

2. Biederman, J., S. V. Faraone, et al. (2006). "Functional impairments in adults with self-reports of diagnosed ADHD: A controlled study of 1001 adults in the community." J Clin Psychiatry 67(4): 524-540.

3. Reid RC, Carpenter BN, Gilliland R, Karim R. Problems of self-concept in a patient sample of hypersexual men with attention–deficit disorder. J. Addict. Med. 5(2), 134–140 (2011).

4. Reid, R. C., Davtian, M., Lenartowicz, A., Torrevillas, R. M., & Fong, T. W. (2013). Perspectives on the assessment and treatment of adult ADHD in hypersexual men. Neuropsychiatry, 3(3), 295–308. https://doi.org/10.2217/npy.13.31

5. Retrieved from: https://www.cdc.gov/violenceprevention/aces/fastfact.html

6. Retrieved from: https://www.ajpmonline.org/article/s0749-3797(98)00017-8/pdf

7. Retrieved from: https://www.sciencedirect.com/science/article/abs/pii/S1555415518308432

8. Retrieved from: https://www.ncbi.nlm.nih.gov/pmc/articles/PMC3696245/#:~:text=Anxiety%20and%20depression%20have%20been,common%20diagnoses%20among%20hypersexual%20individuals.

9. Raymond NC, Coleman E, Miner MH. Psychiatric comorbidity and compulsive/impulsive traits in compulsive sexual behavior. Compr Psychiatry. 2003;44:370–80. [PubMed] [Google Scholar]

10. Black DW, Kehrberg LL, Flumerfelt DL, Schlosser SS. Characteristics of 36 subjects reporting compulsive sexual behavior. Am J Psychiatry. 1997;154:243–9. [PubMed] [Google Scholar]

11. Reid RC, Carpenter BN, Lloyd TQ. Assessing psychological symptoms patterns of patients seeking help for hypersexual behavior. Sex Rel Ther. 2009;24:47–63. [Google Scholar]

12. Butler MH, Pereyra SA, Draper TW, Leonhardt ND, Skinner KB. Pornography Use and Loneliness: A Bidirectional Recursive Model and Pilot Investigation. J Sex Marital Ther. 2018 Feb 17;44(2):127-137. doi: 10.1080/0092623X.2017.1321601. Epub 2017 Jun 8. PMID: 28448246.

13. Retrieved from: https://sexandrelationshiphealing.com/blog/what-is-an-arousal-template/

14. Ibid

15. Mateos-Aparicio P, Rodríguez-Moreno A. The Impact of Studying Brain Plasticity. Front Cell Neurosci. 2019;13:66. [PMC free article] [PubMed] [Reference list]

16. Retrieved from: https://www.gottman.com/blog/an-open-letter-on-porn/

17. Ibid

18. Retrieved from: https://www.commonsensemedia.org/sites/default/files/research/report/2022-teens-and-pornography-final-web.pdf

19. Retrieved from: https://www.commonsensemedia.org/sites/default/files/research/report/2022-teens-and-pornography-final-web.pdf

Chapter Nine:

1. Broadwell, M. M., (1969). *Teaching for learning (XVI) (http:www.wordsfitlyspoken.org/gospel_guardian/v20/v20n41p1-3a.html). Wordsfitlyspken.org. The Gospel Guardian. Retrieved 11 May 2018*

2. Ibid

3. Ibid

4. Ibid

5. Ibid

6. Baumeister, R. F., & Tierney, J. (2012). Willpower: Rediscovering the greatest human strength. Penguin Books.

7. Ibid

Chapter Ten:

1. Retrieved from: https://dictionary.cambridge.org/dictionary/english/principle

2. Retrieved from: https://www.merriam-webster.com/dictionary/integrity

3. Viscott, D. S. (1997).*Emotional resilience: Simple truths for dealing with the unfinished business of your past.* Crown Trade Paperbacks.

4. Lembke, A. (2021). Dopamine nation finding balance in the age of indulgence. Penguin Random House

5. Ibid

6. Retrieved from: https://pubmed.ncbi.nlm.nih.gov/28396395/

7. Lembke, A. (2021). Dopamine nation finding balance in the age of indulgence. Penguin Random House

8. Pennebaker, J. W. (1997). Opening up: The healing power of expressing emotions. Guilford Press.

9. Ibid

10. Derlega VJ, Metts S, Petronio S, Margulis ST. Self-disclosure. Sage Publications; Thousand Oaks, CA: 1993.

11. Corley, M. D., & Schneider, J. P. (2012). Disclosing secrets: An addicts' guide for when, to whom, and how much to reveal. Tucson, AZ: Recovery Resource Press.

12. Ibid

13. Ibid

14. Vaughn, P., (2010). Help for Therapists (and their clients) in dealing with affairs. Dialog Press, San Diego, CA.

15. Lembke, A. (2021). Dopamine nation finding balance in the age of indulgence. Penguin Random House

16. Neff, K. (2021). Self-compassion: The proven power of being kind to yourself. Yellow Kite, an imprint of Hodder & Stoughton.

17. Ibid

18. Vaughn, P., (2010). Help for Therapists (and their clients) in dealing with affairs. Dialog Press, San Diego, CA.

19. Retrieved from: https://www.verywellmind.com/instinct-theory-of-motivation-2795383

20. Davidson, R. J., &; Begley, S. (2013). The emotional life of your brain. Hodder and Stoughton.

Chapter Eleven:

1. Festinger, L. (2009).*A theory of cognitive dissonance*. Stanford University Press.

2. Seligman, M. E., & Maier, S. F. (1967). Failure to escape traumatic shock. Journal of Experimental Psychology, 74(1), 1-9.

3. Coyne, J. C., & Racioppo, M. W. (2000). Learned helplessness: A review of the research and implications for family therapy. Family Process, 39(3), 275-292.

4. Maier, S. F., & Seligman, M. E. (1976). Learned helplessness: Theory and evidence. Journal of Experimental Psychology: General, 105(1), 3-46.

5. Wallace, A. C. (1997). Setting psychological boundaries: A handbook for women. Bergin & Garvey.

6. Palmer, V. T. (2016). Moving beyond betrayal: The 5-step boundary solution for partners of sex addicts. Central Recovery Press.

7. Ibid

8. Ibid

9. Cloud, H., &; Townsend, D. J. (2000). Boundaries in marriage. Zondervan Pub.

   Ibid

10. Gottman, J. M. (2011). *The Science of Trust: Emotional Attunement for couples*. W.W. Norton.

Chapter Twelve:

1. Howes, M., (2022). Good apology: Four steps to make things right. Grand Central Pub.

2. Ibid

3. Retrieved from: https://www.merriam-webster.com/dictionary/expiation

4. Dispenza, J. (2014). *You are the placebo*. Encephalon.

5. Ibid

6. Howes, M., (2022). Good apology: Four steps to make things right. Grand Central Pub.

7. McFarlane, J., et al. (2020). Polyvagal Theory: A Framework for Understanding Neurophysiology and Emotion Regulation. Psychotherapy Theory Research Practice, Training, 57(1), 5-17. doi:10.1037/pth0000267

Chapter Thirteen:

1. Gottman, J. M. (2011). *The Science of Trust: Emotional Attunement for couples*. W.W. Norton.

2. Siegel, D. J. (2017). *Mind: A journey to the heart of being human*. W.W. Norton & Company.

Chapter Fourteen:

1. Viscott, D. S. (1997). *Emotional resilience: Simple truths for dealing with the unfinished business of your past*. Crown Trade Paperbacks.

2. Gottman, J. M. (2011). *The Science of Trust: Emotional Attunement for couples.* W.W. Norton.

3. Ibid

4. Gottman, J. M., & Silver, N., (1999). *The seven principles for making marriage work: A practical guide from the country's foremost relationship expert.* Random House.

5. Gottman, J. M. (2011). *The Science of Trust: Emotional Attunement for couples.* W.W. Norton.

6. Rowell, L. B. (1993). Human cardiovascular control. New York: Oxford University Press.

7. Gottman, J. M. (2011). *The Science of Trust: Emotional Attunement for couples.* W.W. Norton.

Chapter Fifteen:

1. https://www.encyclopedia.com/social-sciences-and-law/sociology-and-social-reform/sociology-general-terms-and-concepts/intimacy

2. Aron, A.; Aron, E. N.; Tudor, M.; & Nelson, G., (1991)."Close relationships as including the other in the self." Journal of Personality and Social Psychology 60:241–253.

3. Hinde, R. A., (1981). "The Bases of a Science of Interpersonal Relationships." In Personal Relationships, ed. S. W. Duck and R. Gilmour. London: Academic Press.

4. Fredrickson, B. (2014). *Love 2.0: How our supreme emotion affects everything we feel, think, do, and become.* Plume.

5. Ibid

Appendix A

Relationship History Timeline

The relationship history time line is designed to help you explore all of the important relationships you have had throughout your life. This exercise will help you see patterns and identify specific time frames when your relationships were good or not so good. The time line is divided into different periods of time. You may have close relationships in one time frame and limited interactions with others. As you go through each time frame, please be as specific as possible about your age, what the relationships were like, and how close you felt to others during the specific time frame (i.e., birth to age five).

To get the most out of this exercise, you may want to print out the Relationship History Time line so you can write about your experiences.

Example:

Age: Five-Seven

Relationship experience: My parents separated. They were fighting a lot.

Thoughts you felt at that time: Nobody really cares about me.

Emotions you felt at that time: I felt alone and sad.

Age:

Birth	Age 5	Seven (7)

|▬ ▬ ▬ ▬ ▬ ▬ ▬ ▬ ▬ ▬ ▬ ▬|▬ ▬ ▬ ▬ ▬|

Parents' conflict/separation ending in divorce

Other significant relationship experiences from this time frame:

_____
_____
_____
_____

Age:

Relationship Experience:

Thoughts you felt at that time:

Emotions you felt at that time:

Age:

Birth   **Five (5)**

| ┠━ ━━ ━━ ━━ ━━ ━━ ━━ ━━ ━━ ━━ ━┨

Other significant relationship experiences from this time frame:

_____
_____
_____
_____

Age:

Relationship Experience:

Thoughts you felt at that time:

Emotions you felt at that time:

Age:

Six (6)   **Eleven (11)**

| ┠━ ━━ ━━ ━━ ━━ ━━ ━━ ━━ ━━ ━━ ━┨

Other significant relationship experiences from this time frame:

_____

_____

_____

_____

Age:

Relationship Experience:

Thoughts you felt at that time:

Emotions you felt at that time:

Age:

Twelve (12)   **Seventeen (17)**

|— — — — — — — — — — — — —|

Other significant relationship experiences from this time frame:

_____

_____

_____

_____

Age:

Relationship Experience:

Thoughts you felt at that time:

Emotions you felt at that time:

Age:

Eighteen (18)   **Twenty-Five (25)**

|— — — — — — — — — — — — —|

Other significant relationship experiences from this time frame:

_____

_____

_____

_____

Age:

Relationship Experience:

Thoughts you felt at that time:

Emotions you felt at that time:

Age:

Twenty-Six (26)   **Present**

|——— —— —— —— —— —— —— —— ——|

Other significant relationship experiences from this time frame:

_____

_____

_____

_____

Note: It is common to have multiple relationship experiences during the same range of time. Please take the time to identify all key relationships from each time period.

Things you may want to identify:

- Themes from your relationships (i.e., I am the one who ends relationships, everyone cheats on me).

- Is there an event/s from my past that still bother me today? If so, how?

Appendix B

Sexual History Time line

The sexual history time line is designed to help you explore all of the sexual experiences you have had throughout your life. This exercise will help you see patterns, and identify specific time frames when your sexual behaviors began, increased in intensity, and changed. The time line is broken up into different periods of time. You may have little to know sexual experiences in one time frame and a lot in other time frames. Be as specific as possible about your age, what the sexual experience was, and how many times it happened during that specific time frame.

Example:

Age: Five

Sexual experience: My friend introduced me to pornography, and we started touching each other.

Frequency: It only happened one time.

Age:

Birth   **Five (5)**

Age:

Sexual Experience:

Frequency (amount of times it happened):

Six (6)   **Eleven (11)**

Age:

Sexual Experience:

Frequency (amount of times it happened):

Twelve (12)   **Seventeen (17)**

Age:

Sexual Experience:

Frequency (amount of times it happened):

Eighteen (18)   **Twenty-Five (25)**

Age:

Sexual Experience:

Frequency (amount of times it happened):

Twenty-Six (26)   **Present**

Note: It is common to have multiple sexual experiences during the same range of time (e.g., masturbation begins, exposed to pornography, first sexual experience, etc.). If this is the case, you can find a downloadable copy of this exercise in the free support content area.

Appendix C

Key Life Inventory

All of us have key life events that alter our lives for good or bad. In this assignment, your task is to identify the significant events that have changed your life. Take into account big events, from the death of a loved one to moving to your first sexual experiences. Other things you might include: moving out, parents fighting, a parent with mental health challenges or substance abuse problems, or being bullied on a playground. Write down as many experiences as you can think of for the next few minutes. Once you are done, place your experience on the time line.

Event: **Age:**

_____

_____

_____

_____

_____

_____

_____

_____

_____

_____

_____

_____

_____

_____

_____

_____

_____

_____

_____

_____

Now place each of the events above on the time line below:

Time line:

_____

Review: Please respond to the following questions in your journal:

Now that you have identified key life events you have experienced, what sticks out to you the most? Identify any common themes between the events, and then identify the events that had the biggest impact on your life.

Appendix D

Sexual Experiences and Our Thoughts, Feelings, Behaviors, and Beliefs

Excercise: Take a few minutes and identify a sexual experience you have had that you are not proud of. Then place the thoughts, feelings, behaviors, and beliefs you formed about yourself due to your identified sexual behavior.

Experience	Influence on Thoughts	Influence on Feelings	Influence on Behaviors	Influence On Beliefs
Example: My parents caught me viewing pornography on the family computer. My mom told me it would ruin my relationships.	I was confused. I felt like I had done something wrong. I thought that there must be something wrong with me. At the time, I also felt curious and wanted to see more of it. These conflicting thoughts made me think that I was different than everyone else.	I was embarrassed. My whole family knew what I had done. I was ashamed. I felt like a liar when I got older and began hiding my porn.	I didn't want to keep looking, but I was a curious teenage boy, so I learned how to cover my tracks. I hid my behavior and learned to lie.	I'm a fraud. If others knew what I was doing, they wouldn't want to be with me.

Appendix E

Patterns of Conflict and the Karpman Triangle

Below is an example of both partners who are caught in the Karpman Triangle (aka the Drama Triangle). Think about your most recent conflict and try to identify what role or roles you have taken during the disagreement with your partner.

3 Roles We Take on During Conflict Betraying Partner	Things I Have Said or Done
Victim	
Persecutor	
Rescuer	

3 Roles We Take on During Conflict Betrayed Partner	Things I Have Said or Done
Victim	
Persecutor	
Rescuer	

Appendix F

A Model for Healing from Betrayal Trauma

In Chapter Seven, we discussed a model for healing for betrayed partners. Below is a short evaluation you can take to assess your progress toward healing based on the items discussed in the Model for Healing from Sexual Betrayal.

A Model to Address Sexual Betrayal: The Essential Tools for Healing

	Core Treatment Solution #1: Seek Genuine Understanding and Create a Safe and Trusting Environment	Core Treatment Solution #2: Internal Exploration: Resolve Difficult Emotions and Hurtful Beliefs	Core Treatment Solution #3: Creating a Positive Support Network While Reducing Negative Interactions	Core Treatment Solution #4: Strengthening Your Inner Self
Component #1	Model compassion	Explore new and old wounds (Key Life Events Inventory)	Boundaries	Self-trust

Component #2	Understand clients/ help them feel felt	Identify triggers	Establish close connections	Self-care
Component #3	Provide education and clear guidance	Find core beliefs about self and others	Build a support team	Mindfulness/ Yoga
Component #4	Help clients listen to their inner voice	Process painful memories and difficult emotions	Inner circle (identify who's where)	Resiliency
Component #5	Establish working goals to help the client feel hope	Treat PTSD symptoms	Understand spiritual connections	Create genuine happiness

Please take a few minutes and give yourself a score between 0 (zero) healing and 10 (a lot) of healing on each of the 20 items below.

Model for Healing	I Am Feeling, Doing, or Experiencing This 0 (Not At All) - 10 (A Lot)
1. How much self-compassion have I been giving myself?	
2. I have someone who helps me "feel felt."	
3. I have a healing plan in place.	
4. I am learning to listen and trust my inner voice.	
5. I have clear goals I am working on to help me heal.	
6. I am addressing past issues that may be holding me back from healing.	

7. I can recognize my triggers, and I am learning to respond to them.	
8. I am working to address any negative core beliefs I have about myself and others.	
9. I am learning how to process (work through) difficult and painful memories.	
10. I am doing my best to resolve my PTSD symptoms.	
11. I have created boundaries with my partner and others and am good at maintaining them.	
12. I have people close to me who I feel close to.	
13. I have created a support team for times when I need support.	
14. I am intentional about who I let close to me and who I keep at a distance.	
15. I feel a connection with my higher power.	
16. I trust myself and the decisions I am making.	
17. I practice self-care.	
18. I participate in mindfulness and/or yoga practices.	
19. Even through my difficult experiences, I feel I am resilient.	
20. I am choosing to be happy and find joy in my life.	

Appendix G

Healing and Recovery Resources

Resources for Betrayed Partner

Online Support:

Class:

- Treating Trauma from Sexual Betrayal: The Essential Tools for Healing (Online Course for Healing) as found at https://www.humanintimacy.com/course/treating-trauma-from-sexual-betrayal

Websites:

- www.bloomforwomen.com (Online programs and expert help for healing from crisis and trauma.)
- www.addorecovery.com (Outpatient clinics for treating sexual compulsivity and sexual betrayal)

Books:

- Back from Betrayal (by Jennifer P. Schneider, M.D.)
- Disclosing Secrets (by M Deborah Corley, Ph.D. and Jennifer P Schneider, M.D.)
- Facing Heartbreak (by Stefanie Carnes, Ph.D., and Mari A. Lee).
- Mending a Shattered Heart (by Stefanie Carnes, Ph.D.)
- Treating Trauma from Sexual Betrayal: The Essential Tools for Healing (by Kevin Skinner, Ph.D.)
- Your Sexually Addicted Spouse: How Partners Can Cope and Heal (by Barbara Steffens and Marsha Means)

Support groups for betrayed partners whose lives have been changed by sexual compulsivity:

- www.cosa-recovery.org (COSA) COSA is a Twelve Step recovery program for men and women whose lives have been affected by compulsive sexual behavior.

- http://www.sanon.org (S-Anon) S-Anon is a program of recovery for those who have been affected by someone else's sexual behavior.

Support for Domestic Violence or Self-Harm:

Domestic Violence:

- http://www.thehotline.org (1-800-799-7233)

Suicide Hotline:

- Suicide Hotline: http://suicidepreventionlifeline.org (1-800-273-8255)
  - http://www.spsamerica.org
  - 988 (in the United States)

Resources for Betraying Partner

Sexual Addiction:

- Treating Sexual Addiction: A Compassionate Approach to Recovery (By Dr. Kevin Skinner)

- Facing the Shadow (By Dr. Patrick Carnes)

- Out of the Shadows (By Dr. Patrick Carnes)

- Sex Addiction 101: A Basic Guide to Healing from Sex, Porn, and Love Addiction (By Robert Weiss)

- Always Turned On: Sexual Addiction in the Digital Age (By Robert Weiss and Jennifer Schneider)

- Letting Go: The Path of Surrender (By David R. Hawkins)

Website for Online Support:

100-Day Support Class:

- https://www.humanintimacy.com/course/treating-sexual-addiction

Resources for Couples

- 7 Principles to Rebuild Your Relationship after Sexual Betrayal

  https://www.humanintimacy.com/course/7-principles-ryr

Relationship Skill Building:

- The Seven Principles for Making Marriage Work: A Practical Guide from the Country's Foremost Relationship Expert (By John Gottman and Nan Silver)

- The Relationship Cure: A 5-Step Guide to Strengthening Your Marriage, Family, and Friendships (By John Gottman)

- Love 2.0: Finding Happiness and Health in Moments of Connection (By Barbara Fredrickson)

- Hold Me Tight: Seven Conversations for a Lifetime of Love (By Susan Johnson)

- Love Sense (By Susan Johnson)

General Trauma:

- Getting Past Your Past (by Francine Shapiro)

- The Body Keeps the Score (by Bessel van der Kolk)

- Trauma and Memory: Brain and Body in a Search for the Living Past: A Practical Guide for Understanding and Working with Traumatic Memory (By Peter Levine)

General Resources

Family History (Book on how your past influences your present behaviors):

- It Didn't Start with You (By Mark Wolynn)

- The Deepest Well (By Nadine Burke Harris)

Emotional Regulation (How to address stress and stay connected with others):

- Emotional Intelligence (By Daniel Goleman)

- True Love (By Thich Nhat Hanh)

- The Mindfulness Workbook for Addiction: A Guide to Coping with the Grief, Stress, and Anger that Trigger Addictive Behaviors) (By Rebecca Williams and Julie Kraft)

Additional Website Support:

- www.sexhelp.com (Find a certified sexual addiction therapist)
- www.iitap.com (An organization that trains sex addiction therapists)
- www.self-compassion.org (Self-Compassion)
- www.brenebrown.com (Vulnerability)
- www.tarabrach.com (Powerful meditation)

My Favorite Books:

- The Power of Moments: Why Certain Experiences Have Extraordinary Impact (By Chip and Dan Heath)
- The Seven Decisions: Understanding the Keys to Personal Success (By Andy Andrew)
- Grit: The Power of Passion and Purpose (By Angela Duckworth)
- Spark: The Revolutionary New Science of Exercise and the Brain (By John Ratey)
- Never Split the Difference (By Chris Voss)
- The Body Keeps the Score (Bessel van der Kolk)

Appendix H

Change: The What and Why Exercise

Instructions: Make a list of things that you want to change. Take 3 minutes to write down everything that comes to your mind. Once you are done, rank order each item from most important = 1 to least important.

Example:

What I Want to Change	Rank of Importance

In an effort to reinforce David's reason for listing "being faithful to Julie" as number one, I gave him this Exercise:

Now that you have identified the most important thing you want to change, please write for two minutes why you want to change that specific thing in your life.

Why (_____):

Example: I love Julie. I know that my actions have not shown it, but I do. Even though she makes me mad sometimes, I can't imagine life without her. She has a fun personality. She is beautiful. She is a good mom. She is creative.

I want to show her that I can be faithful. I am choosing her, and I hope she will choose me again.

_____

_____

_____

_____

_____

Now review your list and rank order your "whys" from the most important to the least important.

Why I Want to Change	Rank of Importance

Finally, take a few minutes and write about your top three 'whys.' Why did you choose these three?

Appendix I

Commitment Exercise

The following exercise is designed to help you consider what you are willing to commit to in your relationship if you choose to move forward.

Take twenty minutes each day for one week to write down thoughts that you have about recommitting to your relationship. It is important to take the time to write your thoughts, ideas, and impressions down. Each day begins with a blank piece of paper. On the sixth day, review the previous five days' notes and answer these questions:

1. What is the main theme of my five days of writing?

2. Is there information that I still need before I can make my commitment?

3. What am I committing to do in my relationship?

4. Do I believe I can keep my commitments? If yes, what gives you that confidence? If not, what do you need to resolve before you can make a commitment?

5. What am I committing to?

Appendix J

Gaslighting Inventory

Introduction

In working with couples attempting to rebuild trust after sexual betrayal, one of the greatest challenges the betrayed partner faces is developing trust again. In many instances, they have been lied to, deceived, and made to feel that something is wrong with them. These actions in relationships are defined as gaslighting behaviors.

Based on new research findings, as gaslighting increases, so do PTSD symptoms in betrayed partners. As a result, we believe that by addressing the specific gaslighting behaviors, relationship healing can begin. As the betrayer gains awareness of how they lied and manipulated their partner, they can begin to take genuine steps towards healing the hearts of those whom they have hurt. The betrayed is able to witness a more open and honest partner.

If these issues are not addressed, relationship healing will be more challenging and difficult. In contrast, by openly discussing the gaslighting behaviors in an open and honest way, couple healing can be real.

Instructions: This assignment is for both partners. The first section is for the betraying partner. Your task is to reflect on each question below and write down whether you engaged in the behavior or not. If you did engage in the behavior, your task is to write down an amends for each behavior you did while acting out.

Section #1 for the Betraying Partner

Denial:

1. How often did you deny your involvement in pornography or other sexual behaviors? Please give an example. How do you think this influenced your partner?

2. In your relationship, how often were you open and honest about your struggle with pornography or other sexual behaviors?

3. How have you looked your partner straight in the eyes and denied that you were viewing pornography or sexually acting out?

4. Even when your partner had evidence regarding your sexual behaviors, how often did you lie to cover up your behavior?

5. If you disclosed your sexual behaviors, did you only share half the story with your partner?

6. To what extent did you claim to have stopped sexually acting out, but later did you reveal that you hadn't stopped at all?

7. Have you told your partner that they were crazy to cover up your behaviors?

8. Did you lie about the money you spent while sexually acting out?

Blame (Gaslighting)

1. Have you blamed your partner for your sexual conduct?

2. Have you told your partner that your relationship problems were because of their personal issues?

3. Have you taken responsibility for your sexual behaviors rather than making your partner feel your problems were their fault? If so, how has this helped your relationship?

4. Did your partner express their concerns because they "felt like something wasn't quite right," but you told your partner it was because of their insecurities?

5. Did you tell your partner if they were more sexual, you would not have viewed pornography or acted out in other ways?

Section #2 for the Betrayed Partner

This section is for the betrayed partner. Please read each of the 13 questions above (8 in Denial and 5 in Blame) and identify if that specific behavior happened in your relationship. Next, if that behavior (e.g., looked you in the eye and lied to you) occurred, how did it influence in the following areas: 1) how you feel about yourself; 2) how you feel about your partner; and 3) your approach to your relationship. Please be as specific as possible.

Appendix K

Resources for Emotional Regulation

- Deep breathing — https://youtu.be/F28MGLlpP90
- Regular relaxation — https://youtu.be/ClqPtWzozXs
- Guided meditations — https://www.tarabrach.com
- Humming — The Humming Effect (book by Jonathan and Andi Goldman)
- The basic exercise — https://youtu.be/rbowIy6kONY

Books by
Dr. Kevin Skinner

TREATING SEXUAL ADDICTION
A COMPASSIONATE APPROACH TO RECOVERY

Dr. Kevin B. Skinner, LMFT, CSAT-S

TREATING TRAUMA FROM SEXUAL BETRAYAL
THE ESSENTIAL TOOLS FOR HEALING

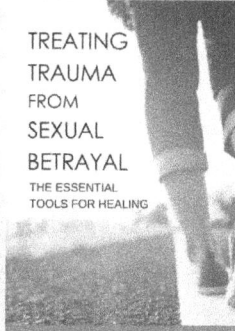

Dr. Kevin B. Skinner, LMFT, CSAT-S

REBUILD YOUR RELATIONSHIP AFTER SEXUAL BETRAYAL
A COUPLES GUIDE TO HEALING AND RECOVERY

Dr. Kevin B. Skinner, LMFT, CSAT-S

Even more content:

HUMAN INTIMACY
FROM CRADLE TO GRAVE

humanintimacy.com

Content on Human Intimacy:

- Treating Sexual Addiction 100 Day Course
- Test your relationship assessment
- Book clubs
- And much more!

www.ingramcontent.com/pod-product-compliance
Lightning Source LLC
Chambersburg PA
CBHW031458270326
41930CB00006B/147